Data Infrastructure Management

Insights and Strategies

Data Infrastructure Management
Insights and Strategies

Greg Schulz

CRC Press
Taylor & Francis Group
Boca Raton London New York

CRC Press is an imprint of the
Taylor & Francis Group, an **informa** business

AN AUERBACH BOOK

CRC Press
Taylor & Francis Group
6000 Broken Sound Parkway NW, Suite 300
Boca Raton, FL 33487-2742

© 2019 by Greg Schulz
CRC Press is an imprint of Taylor & Francis Group, an Informa business

No claim to original U.S. Government works

Printed on acid-free paper

International Standard Book Number-13: 978-1-138-48642-3 (Hardback)

Visit the Taylor & Francis Web site at
http://www.taylorandfrancis.com

and the CRC Press Web site at
http://www.crcpress.com

Contents

Preface

This book follows from my previous books, *Software-Defined Data Infrastructure Essentials: Cloud, Converged, and Virtual Fundamental Server Storage I/O Tradecraft** (aka "The Blue Book"), *Resilient Storage Networks: Designing Flexible Scalable Data Infrastructures*† (aka "The Red Book"), *The Green and Virtual Data Center*‡ (aka "The Green Book"), and *Cloud and Virtual Data Storage Networking*§ (aka "The Yellow, or Gold, Book").

Data Infrastructure Management: Insights and Strategies provides fundamental coverage of physical, cloud, converged, and virtual server storage I/O networking technologies, trends, tools, techniques, and tradecraft skills. Software-defined data centers (SDDC), software data infrastructures (SDI), software-defined data infrastructures (SDDI, and traditional data infrastructures support business applications including components such as a server, storage, I/O networking, hardware, software, services, and best practices, among other management tools. Spanning cloud, virtual, container, converged (and hyper-converged), as well as legacy and hybrid systems, data infrastructures exist to protect, preserve, and serve data and information.

Although there are plenty of new things, sometimes those new things get used in old ways, and sometimes old things can get used in new ways. As you have probably heard before, the one thing that is constant is change, yet something else that occurs is that as things or technologies change, they get used or remain the same. A not-so-bold prophecy would be to say that next year will see even more new things, not to mention old things being used in new ways.

For example, many technology changes or enhancements have occurred from the time I started writing this book until its completion. There will be more from the time this goes to the publisher for production, then until its release and you read it in print or electronically. That

---

* Schulz, G. (2017). *Software-Defined Data Infrastructure Essentials: Cloud, Converged, and Virtual Fundamental Server Storage I/O Tradecraft*. 1st Edition. Taylor & Francis Group/CRC Press.

† Schulz, G. (2004). *Resilient Storage Networks: Designing Flexible Scalable Data Infrastructures*. 1st Edition. Elsevier/Digital Press.

‡ Schulz, G. (2009). *The Green and Virtual Data Center*. 1st Edition. Taylor & Francis Group/CRC Press.

§ Schulz, G. (2011). *Cloud and Virtual Data Storage Networking*. 1st Edition. Taylor & Francis Group/ CRC Press.

is where my companion website, www.storageio.com, along with my blog, www.storageioblog.com, and Twitter @StorageIO come into play. There you can further expand your tradecraft, seeing what's current, new, and emerging, along with related companion content to this book.

Who Should Read This Book

Data Infrastructure Management is for people who are currently involved with or looking to expand their knowledge and tradecraft skills (experience) of data infrastructures, along with associated topics. Software-defined data centers (SDDC), software data infrastructures (SDI), software-defined data infrastructures (SDDI), and traditional data infrastructures are made up of software, hardware, services, and best practices and tools spanning servers, I/O networking, and storage from physical to software-defined virtual, container, and clouds. The role of data infrastructures is to enable and support information technology (IT) and organizational information applications.

If you are looking to expand your knowledge into an adjacent area or to understand what's "under the hood," from converged, hyper-converged, to traditional data infrastructures topics, this book is for you. For experienced storage, server, and networking professionals, this book connects the dots and provides coverage of virtualization, cloud, and other convergence themes and topics.

This book is also for those who are new or need to learn more about data infrastructure, server, storage, I/O networking, hardware, software, and services. Another audience for this book is experienced IT professionals who are now responsible for or working with data infrastructure components, technologies, tools, and techniques.

How This Book Is Organized

There are three parts in addition to the front and back matter (including Appendix A and a robust Glossary). The front matter consists of Acknowledgments and About the Author sections; a Preface, including Who Should Read This Book and How This Book Is Organized; and a Table of Contents. The back matter indicates where to learn more, along with my companion sites (www.storageio.com, www.storageioblog.com, and @StorageIO). The back matter also includes the Index.

In each chapter, you will learn—as part of developing and expanding (or refreshing) your data infrastructures tradecraft—hardware, software, services, and technique skills. There are various tables, figures, screenshots, and command examples, along with who's doing what. You will also find tradecraft tips, context matters, and tools for your toolbox, along with common questions as well as learning experiences.

Feel free to jump around as you need to. While the book is laid out in a sequential hierarchy "stack and layer" fashion, it is also designed for random jumping around. This enables you to adapt the book's content to your needs and preferences, which may be lots of small, quick reads or longer, sustained, deep reading.

Acknowledgments

Thanks and appreciation to all of the vendors, vars, service providers, press and media, freelance writers as well as reporters, investors and venture capitalists, bloggers, and consultants, as well as fellow Microsoft MVPs and VMware vExperts. Also, thanks to all Twitter tweeps and IT professionals around the world that I have been fortunate enough to talk with while putting this book together.

I would also like to thank all of my support network as well as others who were directly or indirectly involved with this project.

Special thanks to Tom Becchetti and Greg Brunton. Thanks to John Wyzalek, my publisher, along with everyone else at CRC/Taylor & Francis/Auerbach, as well as a big thank you to Theron Shreve at DerryField Publishing Services and his associates, Marje Pollack, Susan Culligan, and Lynne Lackenbach, for working their magic.

Finally, thanks to my wife Karen (www.karenofarcola.com) for having the patience to support me and take care of "Little Buddy Bjorn" while I worked on this project.

To all of the above and, to you the reader, thank you very much.

About the Author

Greg Schulz is Founder and Senior Analyst of the independent IT advisory and consultancy firm Server StorageIO (www.storageio.com). He has worked in IT at an electrical utility and at financial services and transportation firms in roles ranging from business applications development to systems management and architecture planning.

Greg is the author of the SNIA Emerald Endorsed reading book *Software-Defined Data Infrastructure Essentials* (CRC Press, 2017), as well as the Intel Recommended Reading List books *Cloud and Virtual Data Storage Networking* (CRC Press, 2011) and *The Green and Virtual Data Center* (CRC Press, 2009) as well as *Resilient Storage Networks* (Elsevier, 2004), among other works. He is a multi-year VMware vExpert as well as a Microsoft MVP (Cloud Data Center Management) and has been an advisor to various organizations including CompTIA Storage+ among others.

In addition to holding frequent webinars, on-line, and live in-person speaking events and publishing articles and other content, Greg is regularly quoted and interviewed as one of the most sought-after independent IT advisors providing perspectives, commentary, and opinion on industry activity. Greg is also a licensed FAA commercial drone pilot who generates GBytes of big data every few minutes of flight time. You can view some of his video and other digital works at www.picturesoverstillwater.com.

Greg has a B.A. in computer science and a M.Sc. in software engineering from the University of St. Thomas. You can find him on Twitter @StorageIO; his blog is at www.storageioblog.com, and his main website is www.storageio.com.

Part One

Applications, Data, and IT Data Infrastructures

Part One comprises Chapters 1 and 2, and provides an overview of the book as well as key concepts including industry trends, different environments, and applications that rely on IT data infrastructures. Data infrastructures are what are inside data centers including software defined data centers (SDDC), legacy, software defined virtual, cloud, serverless, hybrid among others.

Buzzword terms, trends, technologies, and techniques include applications and landscapes, AI, analytics, automation, big data, blockchain, bitcoin, backup, cloud, converged, container, landscapes, IoT, storage class memory (SCM), persistent memory (PMEM), data protection, performance, availability, capacity, and economics (PACE), serverless, server storage I/O networking, software-defined, structured and unstructured, among others.

Chapter 1

IT Data Infrastructure Fundamentals

What You Will Learn in This Chapter

- How/why everything is not the same in most IT environments
- What are data infrastructures and their fundamental components
- IT data infrastructure terminology
- IT industry trends and server storage I/O demand drivers
- How to articulate the role and importance of data infrastructures
- Data infrastructure management, strategy, and insight

This opening chapter kicks off our discussion of IT data infrastructure management, strategy, and insights. Key themes, buzzwords, and trends addressed in this chapter include server storage I/O resources, application and data demand drivers, fundamental needs and uses of data infrastructures, and associated technologies.

Our conversation is going to span hardware, software, services, tools, techniques, cloud, serverless, container, SDDI, SDDC, SDC, and industry trends along with associated applications across different environments. Depending on when you read this, some of the things discussed will be more mature and mainstream, while others will be nearing or have reached the end of their usefulness.

Key themes in this book include:

- Data is finding new value, meaning that it is living longer.
- Everything is not the same across different data centers, though there are similarities.
- Hardware needs software; software needs hardware.
- Role and importance of data infrastructures.
- Servers and storage get defined and consumed in various ways.

- Clouds, public, private, virtual private and hybrid servers, services and storage.
- Context matters regarding server, storage I/O, and associated topics.
- The best server, storage, I/O technology depends on what are your needs.

1.1. Getting Started

Data infrastructure fundamentals include hardware systems and components as well as software that, along with management tools, are core building blocks for converged and nonconverged environments.

When I am asked to sum up, or describe IT data infrastructures in one paragraph, it is this: Data infrastructures are defined by combining hardware, software, as well as services into a platform to protect, preserve, secure, and serve information via applications and their data. Likewise, servers, including so-called serverless, need memory and storage to store data. Data storage is accessed via I/O networks by servers whose applications manage and process data. The fundamental role of a computer server is to process data into information; it does this by running algorithms (programs or applications) that must be able to have data to process. The sum of those parts is the data infrastructure (legacy or software defined) enabled by hardware, software, and other services.

Although some people may tell you that they are dead, data centers are very much alive, particularly in clouds, where they are called *availability zones* (AZs) among other terms, as shown in Figure 1.1. Some context is that *data center* is used as a generic term to refer to the physical facility as well as what's inside of it and, in some cases, even the applications that are deployed there.

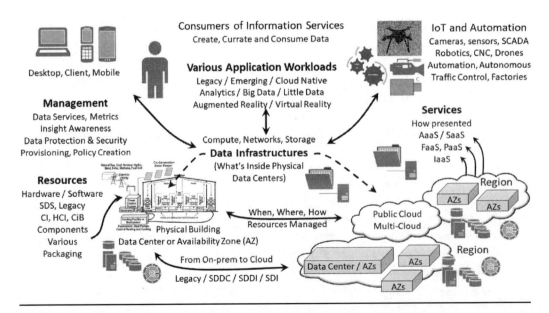

Figure 1.1   Users, Application Landscapes, Data Infrastructures, and Data Centers

When you hear the term *software-defined data center* (SDDC), *software-defined infrastructure* (SDI), along with *software-defined data infrastructure* (SDDI), among other variations, these are referring to what's inside the data center or AZ. Data infrastructure resources, including hardware, software, and service resources, are defined to support applications, along with their workload needs, to provide information services to users, clients, and customers of those capabilities (across the top of Figure 1.1).

Figure 1.1 shows how data infrastructures are what is inside physical data centers supporting various application landscapes to provide information services to users, customers, consumers, or devices. Data centers—also known as *habitats for technology*—are where the servers, storage, I/O network hardware, along with power, cooling, and other equipment exist, all of which are defined by software to provide platforms for various applications.

Application landscapes are the various workloads that are deployed upon and use data infrastructure resources. Different application landscapes range from traditional operational and transaction-oriented database systems to email and messaging, business intelligence (BI), and analytics, along with enterprise resource planning (ERP), such as those from SAP, among others.

Other application landscapes include development environments, workspace, and virtual desktop infrastructures (VDI), as well as big data, batch, and real-time analytics; augmented reality (AR), virtual reality (VR), gaming, and other immersive workloads. Some different landscapes include artificial intelligence (AI), machine learning (ML), deep learning (DL), and cognitive, along with the Internet of Things (IoT) and Internet of Devices, among others.

Keep in mind that all applications have some software code along with data and data structures that define how information gets created, transformed, and stored. Some data infrastructure decisions include where applications code and data get deployed, as well as what granularity of resources is needed.

For example, does a given application landscape, such as SAP, need a cluster of servers deployed as bare metal (BM) or Metal as a Service (MaaS), or as software-defined virtual machines (VM), docker (or windows) containers managed by Kubernetes (K8s), mesos, Openshift, or OpenStack, among others? Perhaps the application can be deployed into a serverless or Function as a Service (FaaS) deployment model, among others.

Data infrastructure management insight and strategy topics include decision making, along with making sure that applications, along with their data, configuration settings, and resources, are protected, secured, preserved, and served as needed.

Data infrastructure decision making includes whether to do it yourself (DiY), buy, rent, or subscribe to a license from the software vendor, as well as from a services and hardware perspective. Decision making also includes what resources are needed, as well as where to place different workloads to meet their service-level objective (SLOs) and other service criteria.

Additional data infrastructure management tasks include maintaining insight, situational awareness, proactive monitoring, problem resolution and remediation, ongoing maintenance, policy management, data protection including backup, business continuance (BC), business resiliency (BR), high availability (HA), disaster recovery (DR), and security, among others discussed later.

Likewise, the fundamental role of data storage ("storage") is to provide persistent memory for servers to place data to be protected, preserved, and served. Connectivity for moving data between servers and storage, from servers to servers, or from storage to storage is handled via

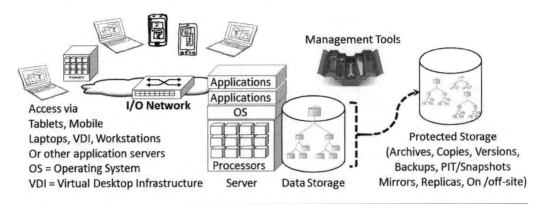

Figure 1.2   IT data infrastructure fundamentals: the "big picture."

I/O networks (internal and external). There are different types of servers, storage, and I/O networks for various environments, functionalities, as well as application or budget needs.

Figure 1.2 shows a very simplistic, scaled-down view of data infrastructure resources, including servers, storage, and I/O components supporting applications being accessed via tablets, mobile devices, laptops, virtual desktop infrastructure (VDI), workstations, IoT/IoD Supervisory Control and Data Acquisition (SCADA), sensors, computer numerical control (CNC), cameras, autonomous vehicles, robotics, and other servers. Also shown in Figure 1.2 is storage (internal or external, dedicated and shared) being protected by some other storage system (or service).

Keeping in mind that Figure 1.2 is the data infrastructure resouces "big picture" (e.g., what's inside data centers) and a simple one at that means we could scale it down even further to a laptop or tablet, or, in the opposite direction, to a large web-scale or cloud environment of tens of thousands of servers, storage, and I/O components, hardware, and software.

A fundamental theme is that servers process data using various applications programs to create information; I/O networks provide connectivity to access servers and storage; storage is where data gets stored, protected, preserved, and served from; and all of this needs to be managed. There are also many technologies involved, including hardware, software, and services as well as various techniques that make up a server, storage, and I/O enabled data infrastructure.

Data infrastructure fundamental focus areas include:

- Organizations—Markets and industry focus, organizational size
- Applications—What's using, creating, and resulting in server storage I/O demands
- Technologies—Tools and hard products (hardware, software, services, packaging)
- Tradecraft—Techniques, skills, best practices, how managed, decision making
- Management—Configuration, monitoring, reporting, troubleshooting, performance, availability, data protection and security, access, and analytics, capacity planning, automation, resource lifecycle, policy definition along with orchestration

Applications are what transform data into information. Figure 1.3 shows how applications, which are software defined by people and software, consist of algorithms, policies, procedures,

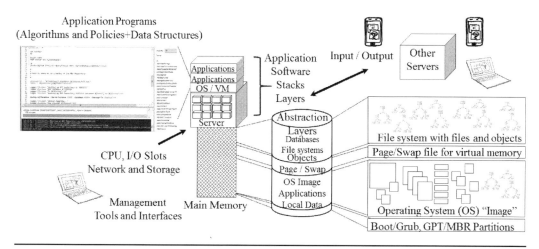

Figure 1.3 How data infrastructure resources transform data into information.

and rules that are put into some code to tell the server processor (central processing unit [CPU]) what to do. Note that CPUs can include one or more cores per socket, with one or more sockets per server. Also note that there can be one or more threads of execution per core. There are also physical CPUs as well as virtual CPUs (vCPUs) provided via software-defined virtual and cloud environments, as well as logical processors (LPs), which refer to core threads.

Application programs include data structures (not to be confused with infrastructures) that define what data looks like and how to organize and access it using the "rules of the road" (the algorithms). The program algorithms along with data structures are stored in memory, together with some of the data being worked on (i.e., the active working set).

Persistent data is stored in some form of extended memory—storage devices such as non-volatile memory (NVM), also known as storage class memory (SCM), as well as persistent memory (PMEM). Other storage includes solid-state devices (SSD), hard disk drives (HDD), or tape, among others, either locally (also known as on-prem, on-premises, or on-site) or remotely. Also shown in Figure 1.3 are various devices that perform input/output (I/O) with the applications and server, including mobile devices as well as other application servers. In Chapter 2 we take a closer look at various applications, programs, and related topics.

1.2. What's the Buzz in and around IT Data Infrastructures?

There is a lot going on, in and around data infrastructure server, storage, and I/O networking connectivity from a hardware, software, and services perceptive. From consumer to small/medium business (SMB), enterprise to web-scale and cloud-managed service providers, physical to virtual, spanning structured database (aka "little data") to unstructured big data and very big fast data, a lot is happening today. Some industry as well as customer data infrastructure buzz includes newer, faster physical servers with more cores, memory, and I/O bandwidth, along with expansion capabilities. These new servers also have new storage and I/O networking capabilities that are available in various packaging, from hyper-converged infrastructure (HCI) aggregated to converged infrastructure (CI), cluster and cloud in a box (CiB), as well as individual systems and components for legacy and software-defined deployments.

Serverless is another favorite buzz topic that some marketers use to define software that is independent of hardware or that uses fewer servers. However, discussions center around data infrastructures (cloud-based or otherwise) that remove the concept of using and managing a server—merely push your code and it runs. Serverless, also known as *Function as a Service* (FaaS), is also referred to as *containers* including *Docker, Windows,* and *Kubernetes,* among other names.

Figure 1.3 takes a slightly closer look at the server storage I/O data infrastructure, revealing different components and focus areas that will be expanded on throughout this book.

Some buzz and popular trending topics, themes, and technologies include, among others:

- NVM, NVM Express (NVMe), SCM, PMEM, including NAND flash SSD
- Software defined data centers (SDDC), networks (SDN), and storage (SDS)
- Converged infrastructure (CI), hyper-converged infrastructure (HCI)
- Serverless, Function as a Service (FaaS), blockchain, distributed ledgers
- Scale-out, scale-up, and scale-down resources, functional and solutions
- Virtualization, containers, cloud, and operating systems (OS)
- NVM express (NVMe), NVMe over Fabric (NVMeoF), GPU, PCIe, IP, and Gen-Z accessible storage
- Block, file, object, and application program interface (API) accessed storage
- Data protection, business resiliency (BR), archiving, and disaster recovery (DR)

In Figure 1.4 there are several different focus topics that enable access to server and storage resources and services from various client or portable devices. These include access via server I/O networks, including:

- Direct attached dedicated and shared
- Local area networks (LAN)

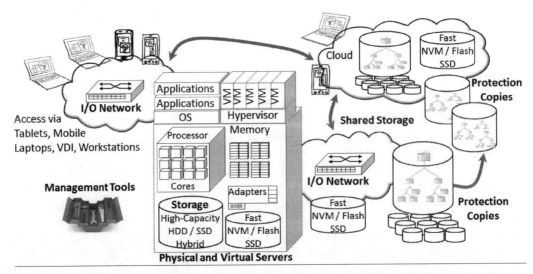

Figure 1.4 Data infrastructure server, storage, and I/O network resources.

- Storage area networks (SAN)
- Metropolitan area networks (MAN), and wide area networks (WAN)

Besides technologies, tools, and trends, another topic is where to place resources: on-prem, off-site in a cloud, co-location (co-lo), or managed service provider, and at what granularity. Granularities can include serverless, FaaS, SaaS, AaaS, PaaS, container, VM or cloud instance, dedicated instance, physical machine, BM or MaaS, among others.

Also, keep in mind that hardware needs software and software needs hardware, including:

- Container management (Docker, Mesos, K8, Openshift, Windows)
- Operating systems (OS), Docker, Kubernetes, Linux, and Windows containers
- Hypervisors (Xen and KVM, Microsoft Hyper-V, VMware vSphere/ESXi)
- Data protection and management tools
- Monitoring, reporting, and analytics
- File systems, databases, and key-value repositories

All of these are critical to consider, along with other applications that all rely on some underlying hardware (bare metal, virtual, or cloud abstracted). There are various types of servers, storage, and I/O networking hardware as well as software that have various focus areas or specialties, which we will go deeper into in later chapters.

There is a lot of diversity across the different types, sizes, focus, and scope of organizations. However, it's not just about size or scale; it's also about the business or organizational focus, applications, needs (and wants), as well as other requirements and constraints, including a budget. Even in a specific industry sector such as financial services, healthcare or life science, media and entertainment, or energy, among others, there are similarities but also differences. While everything that comes to server storage I/O is not the same, there are some commonalities and similarities that appear widely.

Figure 1.5 shows examples of various types of environments where servers, storage, and I/O have an impact on the consumer, from small office/home office (SOHO) to SMB (large and small), workgroup, remote office/branch office (ROBO), or departmental, to small/medium enterprise (SME) to large web-scale cloud and service providers across private, public, and government sectors.

In Figure 1.5 across the top, going from left to right, are various categories of environments also known as market segments, price bands, and focus areas. These environments span different industries or organizational focus from academic and education to healthcare and life sciences, engineering and manufacturing to aerospace and security, from media and entertainment to financial servers, among many others.

Also shown in Figure 1.5 are some common functions and roles that servers, storage, and I/O resources are used for, including network routing and access and content distribution networks (CDN). Other examples include supercomputing, high-performance computing (HPC), and high-productivity computing. Some other applications and workloads shown in Figure 1.5 include general file sharing and home directories, little data databases along with big data analytics, email and messaging, among many others discussed further in Chapter 2.

Figure 1.5 also shows that the role of servers (processors [sockets, cores, threads, ASIC, FPGA, GPU], memory, and I/O connectivity) combined with some storage can be deployed in

Different Industries, Database, Web, Application Development/DevOpp, Big Data and Analytics, Networking and CDN. Research, Medical/Life Science, Financial Video, VDI, High Performance Compute (HPC), General Purpose, Public and Private Clouds, Data Protection, Rich Content, File and Data Serving

Various Environments

Consumer, SOHO, ROBO

Workgroup, Departmental, SMB

SME, Enterprise and Cloud Scale

Different Attributes

Local and Remote

Scale-up, Scale-down, Scale-out

Physical, Virtual, Cloud

Software and Hardware Defined

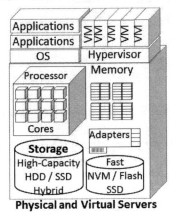

Management Tools

Management Functions

Data Protection

Provision and Repair

Analyze and Remediate

Monitor and Report

Figure 1.5 Different environments with applications using data infrastructure resources.

various ways from preconfigured engineered packaged solutions to build your own leveraging open source and available (aka commodity or white box) hardware.

Besides different applications, industry, and market sectors concerned with server, storage, and I/O topics, there are also various technology and industry trends. These include, among others, analytics, application-aware, automation, cloud (public, private, community, virtual private, and hybrid) CiB, HCI, CI, containers, and serverless.

Other data infrastructure and applications include data center infrastructure management (DCIM), data lakes, data ponds, data pools and data streams, data protection and security, HCI, insight and reporting, little data, big data, big fast data, very big data, management, orchestration, policies, software defined, structured data and unstructured data, templates, virtual server infrastructures (VSI), and VDI, among others.

Additional fundamental buzz and focus from a technology perspective include:

- Server-side memory and storage (storage in, adjacent to, or very close to the server)
- NVM including 3D NAND flash, 3D XPoint, and others such as phase change memory (PCM), DRAM, and various emerging persistent and nonpersistent memory technologies
- SCM, which have the persistence of NVM storage and the performance as well as durability of traditional server DRAM
- I/O connectivity including IoT (Hubs, gateways, edge, and management interfaces), PCIe, Gen-Z (emerging compute I/O interface), NVMe including NVMeoF, along with its variations, SAS/SATA, InfiniBand, Converged Ethernet, RDMA over Converged Ethernet (RoCE), block, file, object, and API-accessed storage
- Data analytics including batch and real-time analytics, Lambda architectures, Hadoop, Splunk, SAS, Snowflake, AI/ML/DL along with other cogantive workloads, Hortonworks, Cloudera, and Pivotal, among others
- Databases and key-value repositories including blockchain distributed ledgers, SQL (AWS RDS including Auroa, IBM DB2, Microsoft SQL Server and Azure Cosmos,

MariaDB, MemSQL, MySQL, Oracle, PostgresSQL, ClearDB, TokuDB) and NoSQL (Aerospike, Cassandra, CouchDB, Kafka, HBASE, MongoDB, Neo4j, Riak, Redis, TokuDB) as well as big data or data warehouse (HDFS based, Pivotal Greenplum, SAP HANA, and Teradata), among others

1.2.1. Data Infrastructures—How Server Storage I/O Resources Are Used

Depending on your role or focus, you may have a different view than somebody else of what is infrastructure, or what an infrastructure is. Generally speaking, people tend to refer to infrastructure as those things that support what they are doing at work, at home, or in other aspects of their lives. For example, the roads and bridges that carry you over rivers or valleys when traveling in a vehicle are referred to as infrastructure.

Similarly, the system of pipes, valves, meters, lifts, and pumps that bring fresh water to you, and the sewer system that takes away waste water, are called infrastructure. The telecommunications network—both wired and wireless, such as cell phone networks—along with electrical generating and transmission networks are considered infrastructure. Even the planes, trains, boats, and buses that transport us locally or globally are considered part of the transportation infrastructure. Anything that is below what you do, or that supports what you do, is considered infrastructure.

This is also the situation with IT systems and services where, depending on where you sit or use various services, anything below what you do may be considered infrastructure. However, that also causes a context issue in that infrastructure can mean different things. For example in Figure 1.6 the user, customer, client, or consumer who is accessing some service or application may view IT in general as infrastructure, or perhaps as business infrastructure.

Those who develop, service, and support the business infrastructure and its users or clients may view anything below them as infrastructure, from desktop to database, servers to storage,

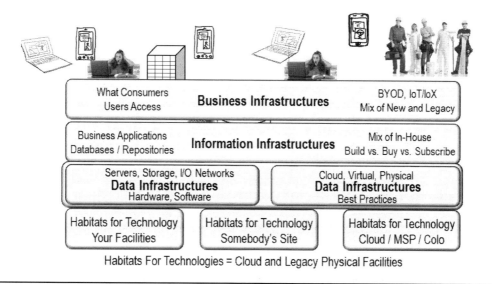

Figure 1.6 IT Information and data infrastructure.

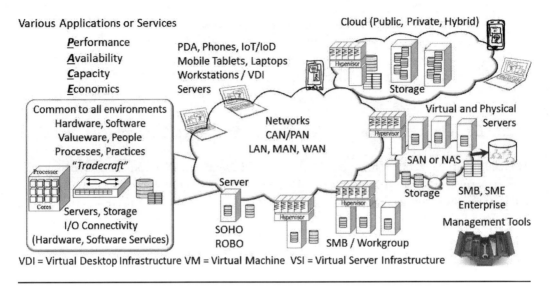

Figure 1.7   Data infrastructures: server storage I/O hardware and software.

network to security, data protection to physical facilities. Moving down a layer in Figure 1.6 is the information infrastructure which, depending on your view, may also include servers, storage, and I/O hardware and software.

For our discussion, to help make a point, let's think of the information infrastructure as the collection of databases, key-value stores, repositories, and applications along with development tools that support the business infrastructure. This is where you may find developers who maintain and create actual business applications for the business infrastructure. Those in the information infrastructure usually refer to what's below them as infrastructure. Meanwhile, those lower in the stack shown in Figure 1.5 may refer to what's above them as the customer, user, or application, even if the actual user is up another layer or two.

Context matters in the discussion of infrastructure. Data infrastructures support the databases and applications developers as well as things above, while existing above the physical facilities infrastructure, leveraging power, cooling, and communication network infrastructures below.

Figure 1.7 shows a deeper look into the data infrastructure shown at a high level in Figure 1.6. The lower left of Figure 1.7 shows the common-to-all-environments hardware, software, people, processes, and practices that comprise tradecraft (experiences, skills, techniques) and "valueware." Valueware is how you define the hardware and software along with any customization to create a resulting service that adds value to what you are doing or supporting. Also shown in Figure 1.7 are common application and services attributes including performance, availability, capacity, and economics (PACE), which vary with different applications or usage scenarios.

Common data infrastructure I/O fundamentals across organizations and environments include:

- While everything is not the same, there are similarities.
- One size, technology, or approach does not apply to all scenarios.

- Some things scale up, others scale down; some can't scale up, or scale down.
- Data protection includes security, protection copies, and availability.
- The amount (velocity), as well as size (volume) of data continues to grow.

Figure 1.8 shows the fundamental pillars or building blocks for a data infrastructure, including servers for computer processing, I/O networks for connectivity, and storage for storing data. These resources including both hardware and software as well as services and tools. The size of the environment, organization, or application needs will determine how large or small the data infrastructure is or can be.

For example, at one extreme you can have a single high-performance laptop with a hypervisor running OpenStack and various operating systems, along with their applications, leveraging flash SSD and high-performance wired or wireless networks powering a home lab or test environment.

Another example can be SDDC software such as VMware running on Amazon Web Services (AWS) dedicated aka bare metal MaaS systems, or Microsoft Azure Stack with Azure software running on an on-prem appliance. On the other hand, you can have a scenario with tens of thousands (or more) servers, networking devices, and hundreds of petabytes (PBs), exabytes (EB), or zettabytes (ZB) of storage (or more).

A reminder that a gigabyte is 1,000 megabytes (e.g., million bytes), a terabyte is 1,000 gigabytes, and a PB is 1,000 terabytes. Also, keep in mind that bytes are referred to in base 2 (e.g., 1024) or decimal base 10 (e.g., 1000). Keep context as to whether 1024 or 1000 are referring to a thousand, as well as bits, which are little b (e.g., Kb [thousand bits]) or bytes, which are big B (e.g., KB [thousand bytes]).

In Figure 1.8 the primary data infrastructure components or pillar (server, storage, and I/O) hardware and software resources are packaged and defined to meet various needs. Data infrastructure storage management includes configuring the server, storage, and I/O hardware and software as well as services for use, implementing data protection and security, provisioning, diagnostics, troubleshooting, performance analysis, and other activities. Server storage and I/O hardware and software can be individual components, prepackaged as bundles or

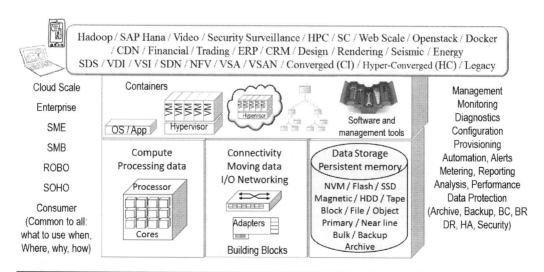

Figure 1.8   Data infrastructure building blocks (hardware, software, services).

application suites and converged, among other options. Note that data infrastructure resources can be deployed at the edge for traditional as well as emerging "fog" computing scenarios, as wll as at data centers and clouds as core sites.

1.2.1.1. Compute Server and Memory

Fast applications need faster software (databases, file systems, repositories, operating systems, hypervisors), servers (physical, virtual, cloud, container, serverless, converged, and hyper-converged), and storage and I/O networks. Servers provide the compute or computational capabilities to run application and other data infrastructure software. Data infrastructure software includes lower-level drivers, operating systems, hypervisors, containers, storage, networking, file systems, and databases, along with other management tools. Servers and their applications software manage and process data into information by leveraging local as well as remote storage accessed via I/O networks. Server compute processing consists of one or more sockets (which compute processor chips plug into). Processor chips include one or more cores that can run one or more threads (workload code). In addition to the compute capabilities, there are also memory management and access, as well as I/O interconnects. Server compute sockets and support chips are arranged on a mother or main board that may also have optional daughter or mezzanine boards for extra resources. Server compute resources also include offload processors such as graphical processing units (GPUs) that handle compute-intensive operations for graphics, video, image processing, and AI/ML/DL analytics, among other workloads. Other processing resources include custom application-specific integrated circuit (ASIC) and field programmable gate arrays (FPGA).

   Application and computer server software is installed, configured, and stored on storage. That storage may be local or external dedicated, or shared. Servers leverage different tiers of memory from local processor cache to primary main dynamic random access memory (DRAM). Memory is storage, and storage is a persistent memory. Note that there are also SCMs (storage class memories) that are also referred to as *persistent memory* (PMEM), meaning they are not volatile as is DRAM. SCM and PMEM are packaged as DIMM (e.g., NVDIMM) as well as PCIe *add-in card* (AiC) and *drive form factors,* among others.

   Memory is used for holding both applications and data, along with operating systems, hypervisors, device drivers, as well as cache buffers. Memory is staged or read and written to data storage that is a form of persistent memory ranging from NVM NAND flash SSD to HDD and magnetic tape, among others.

   Server compute and memory, along with associated I/O network and storage, are packaged as well as deployed in various ways, along with granularity. Some packaging and granularity examples include standalone systems (rack or tower), scale out clusters, appliances, physical and virtual machine (software defined), cloud instance (form of VM), containers, serverless, composable, CI, HCI, and CiB, among others.

1.2.1.2. Data

Servers or other computers need storage, storage needs servers, and I/O networks tie the two together. The I/O network may be an internal PCIe or memory bus, or an external Wi-Fi network for IP connection, or use some other interface and protocol. Data and storage may be coupled directly to servers or accessed via a networked connection to meet different application needs. Also, data may be dedicated (affinity) to a server or shared across servers, depending on deployment or application requirements.

While data storage media are usually persistent or non-volatile, they can be configured and used for ephemeral (temporary) data or for longer-term retention. For example, a policy might specify that data stored in a certain class or type of storage does not get backed up, is not replicated or have high-availability (HA) or other basic protection, and will be deleted or purged periodically. Storage is used and consumed in various ways. Persistent storage includes NVM such as flash and NVM, PMEM, and SCM-based SSD, magnetic disk, tape, and optical, among other forms. Data storage can be accessed as a service including tables (databases), message queues, objects and blobs, files, and blocks using various protocols and interfaces.

1.2.1.3. Networking Connectivity

Servers network and access storage devices and systems via various I/O connectivity options or data highways. Some of these are local or internal to the server, while others can be external over a short distance (such as in the cabinet or rack), across the data center, or campus, or metropolitan and wide area, spanning countries and continents. Once networks are set up, they typically are used for moving or accessing devices and data with their configurations stored in some form of storage, usually non-volatile memory or flash-based. Networks can be wired using copper electrical cabling or fiber optic, as well as wireless using various radio frequency (RF) and other technologies locally, or over long distances.

1.2.1.4. Data Infrastructure Resource Packaging

There are also various levels of abstraction, management, and access, such as via block, file, object, or API. Shared data vs. data sharing can be internal dedicated, external dedicated, external shared and networked. In addition to various ways of consuming, storage can also be packaged in different ways such as legacy storage systems or appliances, or software combined with hardware ("tin wrapped").

Other packaging variations include virtual storage appliance (VSA), as a cloud instance or service, as well as via "shrink wrap" or open-source software deployed on your servers. Servers and storage hardware and software can also be bundled into containers (Docker, Windows, Kubernetes, Openshift), CI, HCI, and CiB, similar to an all-in-one printer, fax, copier, and scanner that provide converged functionality.

1.2.1.5. Data Infrastructure Management Tools

Various software tools (along with some physical hardware tools) are used for managing data infrastructures along with their resources. Some of these tools are used for defining, coordinating, orchestrating (or choreographing) various resources to the requirements of services and applications that need them. Other tools are used for monitoring, reporting, gaining insight, situational awareness of how services are being delivered, customer satisfaction, responsiveness, availability, cost, and security. Other management tools are used for defining how, when, and where data protection—including BC, BR, DR, HA, and backups—is done, along with implementing security.

1.2.2. Why Data Infrastructures Are Important (Demand Drivers)

There is no information recession; more and more data being generated and processed that needs to be protected, preserved, as well as served. With increasing volumes of data of various sizes (big and little), if you simply do what you have been doing in the past, you better have a big budget or go on a rapid data diet.

On the other hand, if you start using those new and old tools in your toolbox, from disk to flash and even tape along with cloud, leveraging data footprint reduction (DFR) from the application source to targets including archiving as well as deduplication, you can get ahead of the challenge.

Figure 1.9 shows data being generated, moved, processed, stored, and accessed as information from a variety of sources, in different locations. For example, video, audio, and still image data are captured from various devices or sensors including IoT based, copied to local tablets or workstations, and uploaded to servers for additional processing.

Besides primary data, additional telemetry, log, and metadata are also collected for processing.

As an example, when I fly one of my drones that records video at 4K (4096 × 2160 or Ultra HD 3840 × 2160 resolution), 60 frames per second (60fps), primary video data is about 1GB every two minutes. This means a 22-minute flight produces about 11GB of video, plus any lower-resolution thumbnails for preview, along with telemetry.

The telemetry data includes time, altitude, attitude, location coordinates, battery status, camera and another sensor status, which for a 22-minute flight can be a couple of MBs. Other

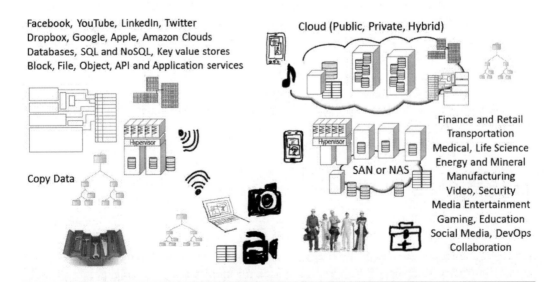

Figure 1.9   Examples of data infrastructure demand drivers and influences.

telemetry and metadata include event as well as error logs among additional information. While the primary data (e.g., video) is a few large files that can be stored as objects or blobs, the metadata can be many small files or stream logs.

Data is also captured from various devices in medical facilities such as doctors' offices, clinics, labs, and hospitals, and information on patient electronic medical records (EMR) is accessed. Digital evidence management (DEM) systems provide similar functionalities, supporting devices such as police body cameras, among other assets. Uploaded videos, images, and photos are processed using AI, ML, DL, and other cognitive services in real time or batch. The upload is indexed, classified, checked for copyright violations using waveform analysis or other software, among other tasks, with metadata stored in a database or key-value repository.

The resulting content can then be accessed via other applications and various devices. These are very simple examples that will be explored further in later chapters, along with associated tools, technologies, and techniques to protect, preserve, and serve information.

Figure 1.9 shows many different applications and uses of data. Just as everything is not the same across different environments or even applications, data is also not the same. There is "little data" such as traditional databases, files, or objects in home directories or shares along with fast "big data." Some data is structured in databases, while other data is unstructured in file directories.

1.2.3. Data Value

Data also may have different values at different times. Very often, context is needed: Data can represent a value or a piece of information, but one must also consider the value or worth of that data item to the organization. The basic three types of data value are no value, has value, or has an unknown value.

Data that has unknown value may eventually have some value or no value. Likewise, data that currently has some form of value may eventually have no value and be discarded, or may be put into a pool or parking place for data with known value until its new value is determined or the time has come to delete the data. In addition to the three basic types of data value, there can be different varieties of data with a value, such as high-value or low-value.

Besides the value of data, access is also part of its life cycle, which means the data may be initially stored and updated, but later becomes static, to be read but not modified. We will spend more time in Chapter 2 looking at different types of applications in terms of data values, life cycles, and access patterns.

General demand drivers of data value include:

- Creation—The Internet of Things (IoT) and the Internet of Devices (IoD), such as sensors and other devices including camera, phones, tablets, drones, satellites, imagery, telemetry, and log detail data, legacy creation, and machine-to-machine (M2M), along with AI, ML, DL, and other cognitive, batch, and real-time analytics in support of digital transformation.
- Curation, Transformation—Transformation, analytics, and general processing, across different sectors, industries, organizations, and focus areas. Also tagging and adding metadata to data where applicable to add value and context.

- Consumption—Content distribution, cache, collaboration, downloads, various consumers.
- Preservation—With more data being stored for longer periods of time, combined with other factors mentioned above, simply preserving data is in itself a large demand driver.

Additional demand drivers include:

- Increased number of devices creating and consuming data
- More volumes of data being created, processed, and stored, faster
- Telemetry and log data (call detail, transactions, cookies, and tracking)
- Larger data items (files, images, videos, audio)
- More copies of items being kept for longer periods of time
- Data finding new value now, or in the future
- Mobile and consumerized access of information services
- IoT-generated data including telemetry as well as rich content
- Virtual machines and virtual disks creating virtual data sprawl

In addition to the above drivers, there are also various industry- or organization-focused applications including government, police and military, healthcare and life sciences, security and surveillance video, media and entertainment, education, research, manufacturing, energy exploration, transportation, finance, and many others.

1.3. Data Infrastructures Past, Present, and Future

There is always something new and emerging, including the next shiny new thing (SNT) or shiny new technology. Likewise, there are new applications and ways of using the SNT as well as legacy technologies and tools.

If you are like most people, your environment consists of a mix of legacy applications (and technology) as well as new ones (e.g., "brownfield"); or perhaps everything is new, and you are starting from scratch or "greenfield" (i.e., all new). On the other hand, you might also be in a situation in which everything is old or legacy and is simply in a sustaining mode. Likewise, your environment may span from onsite, also known as on-prem (on premises or at the premise customer site), as well as cloud, managed service, or co-lo based.

In addition to new technology, some existing technology may support both new and old or legacy applications. Some of these applications may have been re-hosted or moved from one operating hardware and operating system environment to another, or at least upgraded. Others may have been migrated from physical to software-defined virtual, cloud, container, or serverless environments, while still others may have been rewritten to take advantage of new or emerging technologies and techniques.

1.3.1. Where Are We Today? (Balancing Legacy with Emerging)

A trend has been a move from centralized computer server and storage to distributed and edge, then to centralized via consolidation (or aggregation), then back to distributed over different generations from mainframe to time-sharing to minicomputers to PCs and client servers, to the web and virtualized to the cloud. This also includes going from dedicated direct attached storage to clustered and shared storage area networks (SAN) or network attached storage (NAS) to direct attached storage (DAS), to blob and object storage, virtual and cloud storage, and back to direct attached storage, among other options.

What this all means is that from a server storage I/O hardware, software, and services perspective, consideration is needed for what is currently legacy, how to keep it running or improve it, as well as what might be a shiny new thing today but legacy tomorrow, while also keeping an eye on the future.

This ties into the theme of keeping your head in the clouds (looking out toward the future) but your feet on the ground (rooted in the reality of today), and finding a balance between what needs to be done and what you want to do. Figure 1.10 shows, for example, how enterprise and other storage options are evolving, taking on new or different roles while also being enhanced.

Some of the changes that are occurring include traditional enterprise-class storage systems being used for secondary roles or combined with software-defined storage management tools, virtualization, cloud, and other technologies. Also shown in Figure 1.10 from a high level are how traditional lower-end or open technologies are handling more enterprise workloads.

Common to what is shown in Figure 1.10 as well as in other scenarios is that the trend of using commercial off-the-shelf (COTS) servers continues to evolve. COTS are also known as commodity, industry standard, and white box products, with motherboards, processors, and memory. This means that servers are defined to be data and storage systems or appliances, as well as being application servers with different hardware configurations to support those needs. Besides physical servers, many cloud providers also offer cloud machines (instances) with various standard configurations ranging from high-performance computing to memory- or I/O-intensive, among other options.

Another trend centers around convergence (all-in-ones and others), where server, storage, and I/O hardware is designed with software to support applications as well as storage and management functions as turnkey solutions. We shall have more to say about these and other trends later.

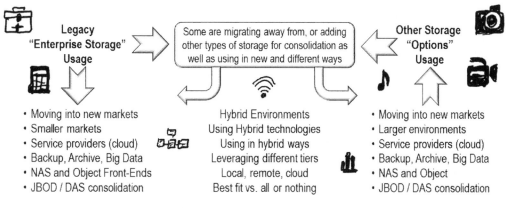

Return On Innovation (ROI) = Using "things" in hybrid ways = Use new and old things in new ways

Figure 1.10   Server and storage yesterday and today.

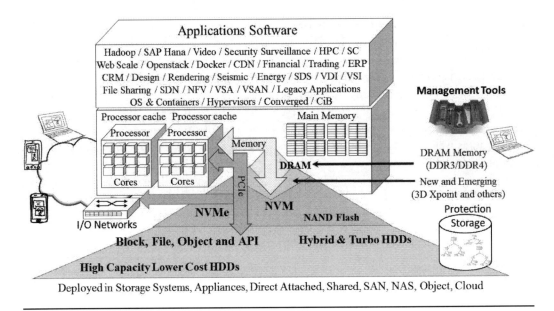

Figure 1.11   Evolving server and storage I/O leveraging new technologies.

1.3.2. Where Are We Going? (Planning, Lessons Learned)

To see and understand where we are going will help us to see where we have been and where we are currently. At first glance, Figure 1.11 may look similar to what you have seen in the past, but what's different and will be covered in more depth in subsequent chapters is the role of servers being defined as storage. In addition to being defined as media content servers for video, audio, or other streaming applications, as a database, email, the web, or other servers, servers are also increasingly being leveraged as the hardware platform for data and storage applications.

A closer look at Figure 1.11 will also reveal new and emerging non-volatile memory that can be used in hybrid ways, for example, as an alternative to DRAM or NVRAM for main memory and cache in storage systems or networking devices, as well as as a data storage medium. Also shown in Figure 1.11 are new access methods such as emerging Gen-z, along with NVMe as well as 100 GbE (and faster) to reduce the latency for performing reads and writes to fast NVM memory and storage. NVMe, while initially focused for inside the server or storage system, will also be available for external access to storage systems over low-latency networks.

Building off of what is shown in Figure 1.11, Figure 1.12 provides another variation of how servers will be defined to be used for deployments as well as how servers provide the processing capability for running storage application software. In Figure 1.12 the top center is a shrunk-down version of Figure 1.11, along with servers defined to be storage systems or appliances for block SAN, NAS file, and Object, Blob, or table (database), or other endpoint API including converted, nonconverged, and virtual and cloud-based applications.

Figure 1.12 shows how the primary data infrastructure building block resources, including server, storage, I/O networking hardware, software, and services, combine to support various

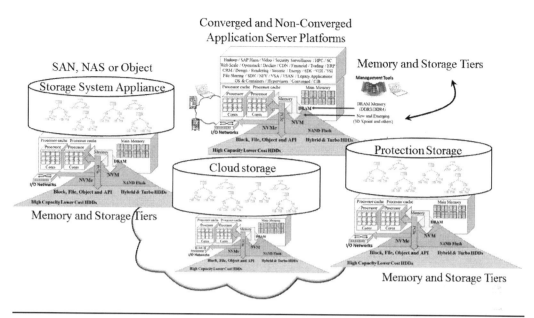

Figure 1.12   Servers as storage and storage as servers, converged and nonconverged.

needs. Not shown in detail is the trend toward protecting data at ingest vs. the past trend of protecting after the fact. This also means collecting telemetry, metadata, and other information about data when it is being stored, to reduce the overhead complexity of searching or scanning data after the fact for management and protection purposes.

Figure 1.12 also illustrates that fundamentals for server, storage, and I/O networking need to have a focus spanning hardware, software, services, tools, processes, procedures, techniques, and tradecraft, even if the resulting solutions are cloud, converged, virtual, or nonconverged. Remember, the primary role of data infrastructures and servers, storage, and I/O resources is to protect, preserve, and serve existing as well as new applications and their data in a cost-effective, agile, flexible, and resilient way.

Some additional considerations about data infrastructure management insight and strategy on a go-forward basis include where applications will best be deployed. This also means where the data is generated or primarily accessed from, along with how it is used and shared by other applications across different locations.

With the increased deployment of mobile users and consumers of information services, data infrastructures will also need to support a traditional browser or virtual terminal–based access, as well as smart device apps using iOS-, Android-, and Windows-based platforms, among others.

Likewise, continued deployment of IoT devices will place additional demands on remote and edge-based infrastructures, as well as central and core, including on-prem as well as cloud-based, data infrastructures. Then there are the new technology trends to factor in, from AI to blockchain distributed ledgers; compute offload including GPU, FPGA, and ASIC; to data ponds, data lakes, and oceans of information to be considered in subsequent chapters.

1.4. Data Infrastructure Management Tradecraft

There are many different tasks, activities, and functions concerned with servers, storage, and I/O hardware, software, and services, depending on your environment. Likewise, depending on your focus area or job responsibility, you might be focused on lower-level detailed tasks, or higher-level vision, strategy, architecture, design, and planning, or some combination of these tasks.

In general, common management tasks and activities include, among others:

- Vision, strategy, architecture design, project planning, and management
- Configuration of hardware and software; change management
- Troubleshooting, diagnostics, and resolution
- Remediation; applying hardware or software updates
- Maintaining inventory of hardware and software resources
- Disposition of old items, resources, life-cycle management
- Migrations, conversions, movement, media maintenance
- What to buy, lease, rent, subscribe, or download for acquisition
- Data protection (archiving, backup, HA, BR, BC, DR, and security)
- Reporting, analysis, forecasting, chargeback or show-back
- Service-level agreements (SLA), service-level objective (SLO) management

Trends involving data infrastructure management tradecraft (skills) include capturing existing experiences and skills from those who are about to retire or simply move on to something else, as well as learning for those new to IT or servers, storage, I/O, and data infrastructure hardware, software, and services. This means being able to find a balance of old and new tools, techniques, and technologies, including using things in new ways for different situations.

Part of expanding your tradecraft skillset is knowing when to use different tools, techniques, and technologies from proprietary and closed to open solutions, from tightly integrated to loosely integrated, to bundled and converged, or to a la carte or unbundled components, with do-it-yourself (DIY) integration. Tradecraft also means being able to balance when to make a change of technology, tool, or technique for the sake of change vs. clinging to something comfortable or known, vs. leveraging old and new in new ways while enabling change without disrupting the data infrastructure environment or users of its services.

Additional trends include the convergence of people along with their roles within organizations and data infrastructures. For some environments, there is a focus on specialization, such as hardware or software focus, server, storage, I/O networking, operating system or hypervisor-centric (e.g., VMware vs. Hyper-V, KVM, Xen), and Docker, Kubernetes, and Windows containers.

Other focus areas include data protection, such as backup, BC, BR, DR, as well as security and audit, in addition to performance, capacity planning, forecast, and modeling. In other environments, there is a trend of having cross-functional teams that have a specialist who is also a generalist in other areas, as well as a generalist who has one or more specialties. The idea is to remove barriers to productivity that often are tied to products, technology, platforms, or organizational political turf wars, among others.

Another trend is around the *Development Operations* (DevOps) movement, with variations of No Operations (NoOp) among variations for both legacy and new startup environments. Some context is needed around DevOps, in that it means different things for various situations. For example, in some settings—notably, smaller, new, startup-type organizations—as its name implies, the people who develop, test, and maintain application code also deploy, manage, and support their code. This approach of DevOps is different from some traditional environments in which application code development, testing, and maintaining is done in an organization separate from technical infrastructure (e.g., data infrastructure and operations).

There are also hybrid variations—for example, some will see DevOps as new and different, while others will have déjà vu from how they used to develop application code, push it into production, and provide some level of support. Another variation of DevOps is *development for operations,* or *development for data infrastructure,* or *development areas* (take care of the tools and development platforms) or what some may remember as system programmers (e.g., sys progs). For those not familiar, sys progs were a variation or companion to system admins who deployed, patched, and maintained operating systems and wrote specialized drivers and other specials tools—not so different from those who support hypervisors, containers, private cloud, and other software-defined data infrastructure topics.

Put another way, in addition to learning server storage I/O hardware and software tradecraft, also learn the basic tradecraft of the business your information systems are supporting. After all, the fundamental role of IT is to protect, preserve, and serve information that enables the business or organization; no business exists just to support IT.

1.5. Data Infrastructure Terminology (Context Matters)

For some of you this will be a refresher; for others, an introduction of server and storage I/O talk (terms and expressions). There are many different terms, buzzwords, and acronyms about IT and particularly server storage I/O–related themes, some of which have more than one meaning.

This is where context matters; look for context clarification in the various chapters. For example, SAS can mean serial attached SCSI in the context of physical cabling, or the protocol command set, as a disk or SSD device, as a server to storage, or storage system to storage device connectivity interface. SAS can also mean statistical analysis software for number crunching, statistics, analysis, big data, and related processing. Yet another use of SAS is for shared access signature as part of securing resources in Microsoft Azure cloud environments.

Context also matters in terms that are used generically, similar to how some people refer to making a copy as making a Xerox, or getting a Kleenex vs. a tissue. Thus, a "mainframe" could be legacy IBM "big iron" hardware and software or a minicomputer or large server running Windows, Unix, Linux, or something other than a small system; others might simply refer to that as a server or a server as the mainframe, as the cloud, and vice versa (Hollywood and some news venues tend to do this).

The following is not an exhaustive list nor a dictionary, rather some common terms and themes that are covered in this book and thus provide some examples (among others). As examples, the following also include terms for which context is important: a bucket may mean one thing in the context of cloud and object storage and something else in other situations.

Likewise, a container can mean one thing for Docker and micro-services and another with reference to cloud and object storage or archives.

ARM	Can mean Microsoft public cloud Azure Resource Manager as well as a type of compute processor.
BaaS	Back-end as a Service, Backup as a Service, among others.
Buckets	Data structures or ways of organizing memory and storage, because object storage buckets (also known as containers) contain objects (or blobs) or items being stored. There are also non-object or cloud storage buckets, including database and file system buckets for storing data.
Containers	Can refer to database or application containers, data structures such as archiving and backup "logical" containers, folders in file systems, as well as shipping containers in addition to Windows, Linus, Docker, or compute micro-services.
Convergence	Can mean packaging such as CI and HCI, as well as hardware and software, server, storage, and networks bundled with management tools. Convergence can occur at different layers for various benefits.
CSV	Comma Separated Variables is a format for exporting, importing, and interchange of data such as with spreadsheets. Cluster Shared Volumes for Microsoft Windows Server and Hyper-V environments are examples.
DevOp	Can refer to development for data infrastructure or technical operations, as well as environments in which developers create, maintain, deploy, and support code, once in production.
Flash	Can refer to NAND flash solid-state persistent memory packaged in various formats using different interfaces. Flash can also refer to Adobe Flash for video and other multimedia viewing and playback, including websites.
Objects	There are many different types of server and storage I/O objects, so context is important. When it comes to server, storage, and I/O hardware and software, objects do not always refer to object (or blob) storage, as objects can refer to many different things.
Orchestration	Can occur at different levels or layers and mean various things.
Partitions	Hard disk drive (HDD), solid-state device (SSD), or other storage device and aggregate subdividing (i.e., storage sharing), database instance, files or table partitioned, file system partition, logical partition or server compute and memory tenancy.
PCI	Payment Card Industry and PCIe (Peripheral Computer Interconnect Express)
PM	Physical machine, physical memory, paged memory, persistent memory (aka PMEM), program manager or product manager, among others.
RAID	Can be hardware or software, system, array, appliance, software defined, mirror and replication, parity and erasure code based.
Serverless	Can refer to micro-services including cloud based, such as AWS Lambda, Function as a Service (FaaS). Context is also used to describe software that is available, sold, or not dependent on a particular brand of server. Keep in mind that software still requires a physical server to exist somewhere—granted, it can be masked and software defined.

SMB	Small/Medium Business, refers to the size or type of an organization or target market for a solution (or services). SMB is also the name for Server Message Block protocols for file and data sharing, also known as CIFS (Common Internet File System) aka Windows file sharing.
SME	Small/Medium Enterprise, a type or size of organization; also refers to a Subject Matter Expert skilled in a given subject area.
Virtual disk	Abstracted disks such as from a RAID controller, software-defined storage such as Microsoft Storage Spaces, as well as virtual machine including Hyper-V VHD/VHDX, VMware VMDK, and qcow, among others.
VM	Virtual Memory (Operating System Virtual Memory, Hypervisor Virtual Memory, Virtual Machine Memory), Virtual Machine, Video Monitor.

You can find a more comprehensive glossary at the end of this book.

Tip: Knowing about the tool is important; however, so too is knowing how to use a tool and when along with where or for what. This means knowing the tools in your toolbox, but also knowing when, where, why, and how to use a given tool (or technology), along with techniques to use that tool by itself or in conjunction with multiple other tools.

Part of server storage I/O data infrastructure tradecraft is understanding what tools to use when, where, and why, not to mention knowing how to improvise with those tools, find new ones, or create your own.

Remember, if all you have is a hammer, everything starts to look like a nail. On the other hand, if you have more tools than you know what to do with, or how to use them, perhaps fewer tools are needed along with learning how to use them by enhancing your skillset and tradecraft.

1.6. Common Questions and Tips

A common question I get asked is *"Why can't we just have one type of data storage such as NAND flash SSD, or put everything in the cloud?"* My usual answer is that if you can afford to buy, rent, or subscribe to a cloud or managed service provider (MSP) all-flash array (AFA) solution, then do so.

While some organizations are going the all-flash storage approach, most cannot afford to do so yet, instead adopting a hybrid approach. The cloud is similar: Some have gone or will be going all-cloud, others are leveraging a hybrid approach at least near-term. What about virtual storage and storage virtualization for the software-defined data center? Sure, some environments are doing more with software-defined storage (depending on what your definition is) vs. others.

What is the best storage? That depends on how you will be using the storage and with what applications. Will the storage be shared across multiple servers or hypervisors? Do you need to share files and data? What are the Performance, Availability, Capacity, and Economic (PACE) requirements? With what does the storage need to coexist within your environment?

Do cloud and virtual servers need the cloud and virtual storage? If your cloud or virtual server is running at or on a public cloud, such as Amazon or rack space, you may want to access their cloud and virtual storage. If your virtual server is running on one of your own servers, you may be fine using traditional shared storage.

Are clouds safe? They can be if you use and configure them in safe ways, as well as do your due diligence to assess the security, availability, as well as the privacy of a particular cloud provider. Keep in mind that cloud data protection and security are a shared responsibility between you and your service provider. There are things that both parties need to do to prevent cloud data loss.

Why not move everything to the cloud? The short answer is data locality, meaning you will need and want some amount of storage close to where you are using the data or applications—that might mean a small amount of flash or RAM cache, or HDD, Hybrid, or similar. Another consideration is available and effective network bandwidth or access.

With serverless so popular, why discuss legacy, on-prem, bare metal, virtual, or even cloud IaaS? Good question, and one that for some environments, specific application landscapes, or pieces of their workloads can make perfect sense.

On the other hand, even though there is strong industry adoption (e.g., what the industry likes to talk about) along with some good initial customer adoption (what customers are doing), serverless on a bigger, broader basis is still new and not for everybody, at least not yet. Given the diversity of various applications and environment needs, data infrastructures that provide flexibility of different deployment models enable inclusiveness to align appropriate resources to multiple needs.

What is the best data infrastructure? The best data infrastructure is the one that adapts to your organization's needs and is flexible, scalable, resilient, and efficient, as well as being effective to enable productivity. That means the best data infrastructure may be a mix of legacy, existing, and emerging software-defined technologies and tools, where new and old things are used in new ways. This also means leveraging public cloud, containers, and serverless, among other approaches where needed. On the other hand, depending on your needs, wants, or preferences, the best data infrastructure may be highly distributed from edge to core, data center to the cloud, or all existing only within a public cloud.

1.7. Strategies

Throughout this book, there are various tips, frequently asked questions (along with answers), examples, and strategy discussions. All too often the simple question of what is the best is asked, looking for a simple answer to what are usually complex topics. Thus, when somebody asks me what is the best or what to use, I ask some questions to try and provide a more informed recommendation. On the other hand, if somebody demands a simple answer to a complicated subject, they may not get the answer, product, technology, tool, or solution they wanted to hear about. In other words, the response to many data infrastructure and related tools, technology, trends, and techniques questions is often, "It depends."

Should your environment be software defined, public cloud, cloud native, or lift and shift (e.g., migrate what you have to cloud or another environment)? What about converged infrastructure vs. hyper-converged infrastructure (aggregated) vs. cluster or cloud in a box vs.

serverless or legacy? Take a step back: What services and resources are needed, and what modes and models of service delivery? Perhaps yours is a one-size solution approach fits-all-needs environment; however, look at how different technologies and trends fit as well as adapt to your environment needs vs. you having to work for the technology.

What data infrastructure resources do your applications and associated workloads need regarding performance, availability (including data protection and security), capacity, and economic considerations? This includes server compute (primary general purpose, GPU, ASIC, FPGA, along with other offloads and specialized processors), memory (DRAM or SCM and PMEM), I/O (local and wide area), storage (performance and capacity), along with management tools.

Another consideration is what your service-level objectives (SLOs) and service-level agreements (SLAs) are for different services provided as part of your data infrastructure. What metrics, report, and management insight are available for chargeback billing, invoice reconciliation and audits, show back for information along with "scare back." Note that "scare back" is a form of show back in which information is provided on local on-prem or public cloud resource usage along with costs that can cause alarm—as well as awareness—about actual spending.

For example, some of your data infrastructure customers decide to deploy their applications in a public cloud, then bring the invoice to you to pay, as well as support. In other words, somebody brings you the bill to pay for their cloud resources, and they want you to take care of it. Some additional considerations include: do they know how much more or less the public cloud costs are compared to the on-prem services costs? Likewise, how can you make informed decisions about costs regarding public vs. private vs. legacy if you do not know what those fees are?

In other words, part of a strategy is to avoid flying blind and have insight and awareness into your application landscape, workload characteristics along with resource usage, and cost to deliver or provide various services.

1.8. Chapter Summary

There is no such thing as an information recession—quite the opposite, in fact, with new as well as existing applications creating, processing, moving, and storing data being kept long-term. The result is that data infrastructures are evolving to meet the various application landscape and workload demands, deployment locations (edge, on-prem, cloud), and models (BM, VM, cloud instance, container, serverless, CI, HCI, CiB, among others).

Keep in mind that data infrastructures—including legacy, SDDC, SDI, and SDDI—are what exist inside physical data centers. Not only are data infrastructures composed of hardware (servers, storage, I/O networks, and related equipment) along with software, management tools, and services, but they are also defined by policies, procedures, templates, and best practices established by people. The fundamental role of data infrastructures is to provide an infrastructure environment platform on which applications transform data into information services for users of those services.

Just as everything is not the same across different environments of various size, scope, or type of business and industry, there are also multiple types of data infrastructures spanning legacy to software defined, on-site and on-prem to off-site, co-lo, MSP, and across one or more public cloud services. Likewise, there are many different application landscapes, from legacy to emerging, with diverse workloads characteristics. The different application workloads require various data infrastructure resources (server compute, memory, I/O, storage space, software licenses) along with performance, availability, capacity, and economic (PACE) considerations.

Also, keep in mind that data centers are still alive. However, their role and function are changing from traditional on-prem to cloud, where they are referred to as AZs. Likewise, data infrastructures—in addition to existing on-prem in legacy data centers to in clouds that define and support AZs—also live at the edge for traditional ROBO and for emerging fog computing (e.g., think small cloud-like functionality at or near the edge).

What this all means is that there is not a one-size-fits-all environment; application workload scenarios and data infrastructures need to be resilient, flexible, and scalable. This also means that there are different strategies to leverage and insight to gain for effective data infrastructure decision making.

General action items include:

- Avoid treating all data and applications the same.
- Know your applications PACE criteria and requirements as well as needs vs. wants.
- Don't be afraid of cloud and virtualization.

Bottom line: The fundamental role of IT data infrastructures including server, storage I/O connectivity hardware, and software and management tools is to support protecting, preserving, and serving data and information across various types of organizations.

Chapter 2

Application and IT Environments

Algorithms + Data Structures = Programs

– Niklaus Wirth (Prentice-Hall, 1976)

What You Will Learn in This Chapter

- Application PACE characteristics, attributes, and landscapes
- Different types of data and characteristics
- Structured and unstructured data, little data, and big data
- Why everything is not the same across data infrastructures
- Data infrastructure deployment models
- Habitats for technology (data centers and AZs)
- How applications are supported by data infrastructures

In this chapter, we build on the fundamentals that were laid down as a foundation in Chapter 1, expanding the focus to various applications and environments. Keep in mind that everything is not the same when it comes to data infrastructures, along with resources including server, storage, I/O hardware, software, cloud, and managed services tools and technology. Likewise, there are different types of environments and applications that we will now take a closer look at in this chapter. Key themes, buzzwords, and trends in this chapter include little data, big data, data value, data volume, data velocity, AI, ML, serverless, structured and unstructured data, application performance, availability, capacity, and economics where applications and data get processed.

2.1. Getting Started

Many storage discussions focus on just the data. However, we are going to expand the discussion since we are covering data infrastructures including servers, storage, and I/O networking hardware as well as software tools. We will extend the theme that applications (programs) that run on servers have algorithms and data structures that reside in memory and data storage. Where we are going with this discussion and why it is important is that different applications rely on servers and storage in various ways; however, storage systems are storage applications deployed on some server platform. Data infrastructure components are converging, as are applications, people, processes, techniques, services, and technologies.

2.1.1. Context for the Chapter

Understanding the interrelationships of various applications and their data dependencies (or vice versa), along with corresponding resource characteristics is important to know. This means learning about the business and organizations that IT systems and applications support, beyond just the basic characteristics of associated technologies. These characteristics include Performance, Availability, Capacity, and Economics (PACE), which are common to all applications and which we will be discussing in greater detail later in this chapter.

Often when it comes to data infrastructures, in particular, server, storage, and I/O networking, the focus is mostly on data or how it is accessed or organized (e.g., structured database, unstructured files, objects, and blobs). This makes sense because the fundamental role of data infrastructure and storage is to protect, preserve, and serve data so that applications can access or transform it into useful information. However, when it comes to servers, storage I/O networking hardware, software, and services, it is also about the applications that handle the processing of data.

Keep in mind that application landscapes include multiple programs or subapplications that comprise a solution, service, or functionality. Likewise, an application consists of one or more programs on one or more servers (or computers) that interact with data. Also, keep in mind that programs are the algorithms, logic, rules, and policies that determine what to do with data, when, where, why, and how. In addition to algorithms, programs also rely on some data that is defined as data structures and stored in memory or persistent storage.

Hence the theme at the top of this chapter: *Algorithms + Data Structures = Programs,* which is not coincidentally the title of a book by Niklaus Wirth that I highly recommend reading (see Appendix for more information). Even if you are not planning on ever doing any programming or system design, simply reading it will give you some different perspectives and appreciation for the relationship between software that are algorithms and their associated data structures.

The importance is understanding what data is being stored and why, how it is used by programs that run on processors (computers or servers), interacting with storage devices via I/O paths. Thus the essence of server storage and I/O convergence relates back to the fundamental premise that applications algorithms require computer processors and storage, including memory for storing data structures.

2.2. Everything Is Not the Same with Data Infrastructures

Just as there are many different types of environments, from small to large web-scale and cloud or managed service providers, along with various types of organization and focus, there are also diverse applications and data needs. Keep in mind that a fundamental role of data infrastructures, and IT in general, is to protect, preserve, and serve information when and where it is needed. What this means is that while everything is not the same, from types and sizes of organization to business and services functionality focus or application needs, there are some common similarities or generalities.

Some of these commonalities come from an organizational or business industry focus, such as defense and security, e-commerce and retail, education, energy, finance, government, legal and law enforcement, healthcare and life sciences, manufacturing, media and entertainment, scientific research, social media and networking, and transportation, among many others. Other commonalities found across different organizations include CRM and sales, marketing and public relations, accounting and payroll, human resources, back-office functions and file sharing, among others.

2.2.1. Various Types of Environments (Big and Small)

There are broad generalities—for example, types of applications, business focus or industry sector, small, medium, large—but there are differences. Likewise, there are technology products, tools, and services that can fit different needs; they may also be optimized for certain things. Some environments are more complex due to their size, others may be small but also complex.

Everything is not the same, although there are similarities and generalities:

- Different environments (industry focus and size)
- Applications and how they are used, together with their characteristics
- Various workloads and size or amount of data
- Requirements and constraints to support information needs

There are various sizes, types, and focuses for environments:

- Uber-large web-scale, cloud, and managed service providers
- Ultra-large enterprise, government, or other organizations and small service providers
- Large enterprise, government, education, and other organizations
- Small/medium enterprise (SME) and other organizations
- Small/medium business (SMB) enterprises, from small office/home office (SOHO) to SME
- Workgroup, departmental, remote office/branch office (ROBO)
- Prosumer (e.g., power user) and consumer

Note that technology solutions and services are also often aligned, positioned, or targeted toward the above general categories by vendors, as well as for consumption by those using the services. What defines the size or category of an organization varies. Organization size can be defined by the number of employees, revenue, business ranking, the number of offices or locations, the number of servers, desktops, or amount of storage or budget spent on hardware and software, among other considerations.

Do you treat everything the same?

- From a performance perspective?
- In terms of availability, including data protection?
- About efficiency (usage) and effectiveness (productivity)?
- Regarding space capacity or type of storage?
- Do you know your costs for servers, storage, I/O, and relates services?
- How you align applicable technology to your business or organization needs?

Understanding the organization and its focus as well as its information needs helps to know the characteristics of the applications and data that is needed. This knowledge is useful for making decisions about configuration, upgrades, performance, availability, capacity, or other changes as well as troubleshooting data infrastructure on a cloud, virtual, or physical basis.

2.2.2. Gaining Data and Application Insight

Gathering insight and awareness into your applications, along with their associated data and characteristics, involves a mix of technology tools, reading what is available in any internal knowledge base as well as external general available information.

Note that while expanding your awareness of new technologies along with how they work is important, so too is understanding application and organization needs. Expanding your tradecraft means balancing the focus on new and old technologies, tools, and techniques with business or organizational application functionality.

This is where using various tools that themselves are applications to gain insight into how your data infrastructure is configured and being used, along with the applications they support, is important.

Some of these tools may be application-specific, while others look at data stored and correlate back to applications, and still others may be performance- or availability-centric.

Which tool is best for your needs will depend on what you need it to do, as well as the budget, size, and scope of the environment. After all, everything is not the same, and what is good for you or me may be different for somebody else.

In addition to using various tools including those that you can install on your server and storage systems (cloud, container, virtual, or legacy), there are also cloud services that can collect information and then analyze and provide reports and insights back to you. Besides cloud-based tools and those you can install and use yourself, there are also service providers, vendors, value-added resellers (VARs), and consultants that can also help with assessing your environment.

These services range from high-level, showing you what and how to collect the information yourself, to turnkey, in-depth data and application discovery, assessment, analytics, automation, event, and resource correlation for recurring or one-off project engagements. What is going to be best for you and your environment will depend on your needs. When in doubt, ask your peers in other organizations or those you know via various venues, user groups, and sites.

There are many different layers, from low to high level, with data infrastructures and the various applications they support and the information services provided. The various layers

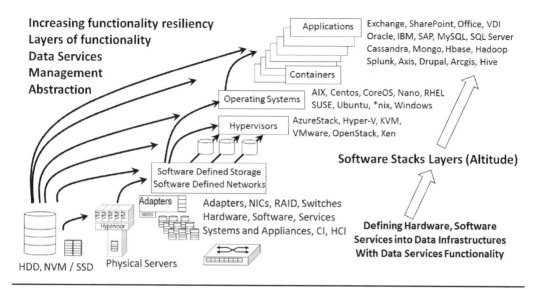

Increasing functionality resiliency
Layers of functionality
Data Services
Management
Abstraction

Figure 2.1   IT and Data Infrastructure Stack Levels, Layers, and Altitude

represent different levels in the IT and data infrastructure stack, which can also be referred to as *stack location* or *altitude*.

For example, at the top of Figure 2.1, upper-level, higher-in-altitude layers include various business applications and workloads, while at the bottom are lower-level components and services. The lower-level resource components, solutions, and services comprising hardware, software, and external services are defined to create data infrastructures and their corresponding upper-level services.

Note that higher-level, upper-altitude layers have more functionality than do the lower-level resources from which they are composed and orchestrated. The importance of Figure 2.1 is both to understand the context and significance of the different layers and levels and how they need to be managed and to gain insight into decision making.

2.2.3. Various Types of Applications

Recall from Chapter 1 that there are different layers of infrastructure depending on where you sit (or stand) when accessing and using information services. Each of the different layers of infrastructure and information services is built on and deployed via underlying layers of applications also known as infrastructure. Some of these applications are also known as tools, utilities, plug-ins, agents, drivers, middleware, or valueware, among other terms, and they may be internal to your organization or delivered via a cloud or managed services provider.

In general, software applications include, among others:

- Frameworks and application suites such as Microsoft Office or Office 365
- Cloud-based Software as a Service (SaaS) and Application as a Service (AaaS)

- Serverless, Function as a Service (Faas)
- Development environment and runtime tools
- Plug-ins, apps, or applets for mobile devices and web browsers
- Agents, drivers, tools, and utilities for workstations and servers
- Application development and business logic tools
- Middleware, productivity, and development platforms
- Databases, file systems, data repositories, and utilities
- Operating systems, hypervisors, and associated management tools
- Server, storage, and I/O networking hardware or appliance firmware

All of these applications can be packaged, delivered, and consumed in various ways.

Depending on your focus, you might be the consumer of some information services for work or entertainment. Shown in Figure 2.2 are examples such as if you are a systems or applications developer, traditional or DevOps-focused, you may be using platform as a service (PaaS) for development along with databases, tools, containers, code management, testing, and middleware, either on-site or via the cloud.

If you are using a traditional desktop environment installed on a workstation, laptop, or tablet, you are using a collection of applications including an operating system, office, and other tools. On the other hand, if you are using a VDI, you are using another collection of applications.

The important takeaway is that there are various layers of infrastructure and applications that in turn support upper- or higher-level applications and functionalities. These applications extend to those that define hardware to be a web server, compute server, storage system, data or database server, content server, or a network router, switch, or cache appliance, to a virtual data center or simply a virtual server among other functions.

What this means is that storage and data management software are installed on a cloud, virtual, or physical server and that storage system can also host different applications—hence the importance of understanding various applications along with their characteristics and data activity.

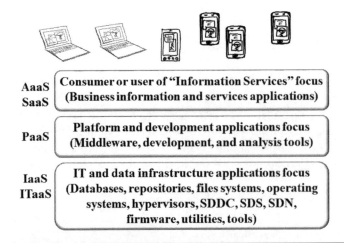

Figure 2.2 Stacking and application layers.

2.2.3.1. Common Application Characteristics

Data infrastructures need to be resilient, flexible, scalable, efficient, and effective to support the diverse application workload productivity needs. Keep in mind that all application workloads have some type of Performance, Availability, Capacity, and Economic (PACE) resource needs.

For some applications, there may be the need for more performance and less capacity; higher availability, including HA, BC, BR, DR, and security; or more space capacity at lower economic cost. Various PACE attributes also vary across different environments and applications—for example, performance (high, medium, or low)—and there are additional dimensions, such as latency response time, queues, usage vs. effectiveness, activity rates vs. data movement, bandwidth or throughput, among others.

Some other application characteristics to consider are that they, or parts of their sub-components, can be stateless or stateful. *Stateful* means that the applications maintain and store data with their persistent storage. *Stateless* means that the application does not maintain its persistent storage or state, instead relying on external stateful persistent storage including file systems, databases, table services, or other repositories. Examples of stateless applications are those that spin up, deploying quickly, such as serverless, FaaS based in support of IoT, or an event that triggers to data being stored in a tablespace, database, blob, object, or file store. A database server is an example of a stateful application.

Popular industry buzz terms, trends, technologies, and topics include digital transformation; cognitive and inferencing, including AI, ML, and DL; and analytics. Analytics include traditional business intelligence (BI), data warehouse in-depth queries of historical data, fast real-time clickstream analytics, big data, and other batch or related analytics.

Analytics, along with cognitive processing, occurs both at the core in cloud and traditional on-prem, as well as software-defined data centers. And analytics and cognitive processing also occur at the edge or on remote sites closer to where data is generated, accessed, processed, and leveraged. What this means is that some data is acted upon quickly at the edge using cloud-like processing, aka fog, for quick turnaround, while more in-depth analytics and processing are done at the core over more massive amounts of data that take more time.

Digital transformation is a popular industry and customer theme, which encompasses many topics from leveraging new, emerging, and existing technology being used in new ways, to how organizations conduct their operations. Digital transformation is more than just an IT industry marketing buzzword. Moving beyond buzzword, digital transformation involves business and organizations continue their journey from traditional applications and access, to modern, fast-based, mobile information services. Besides being generated and processed faster, applications are using and transforming data into diverse information services in more dynamic ways.

This means leveraging new digital mediums from photos, images, videos, audio, ultra-high definition 4K, mobility, and social media, etc. Another aspect is that most organizations continue to evolve with their digital transformations not just to keep up with trends or what somebody else is doing or to get more Facebook likes, but instead to unlock and find new value in their applications and data portfolio to adapt to changing business dynamics and opportunities.

Some will say that data is the key; however, while important, data is just data until it is transformed into information by applications that run on and are supported by data infrastructures located on-prem, in the cloud, across multiple clouds, or at the edge. To enable digital transformation, there needs to be business transformation, IT transformation, along with data infrastructure transformation and modernizing.

However, modernization and transformation mean more than merely replacing old technology with new items, then using them in old ways. Transformation also means leveraging new *and* old things and using them in new ways, while also leveraging lessons of the past to prevent problems in the future.

2.2.3.2. Business Information and Services Applications

There are many different types of "information services" focused applications ranging from consumer entertainment to social media/networking (YouTube, Facebook, Pinterest, LinkedIn, Instagram, Twitter, Yammer, and many others), education, e-commerce, information sites as well as organizational and business-related sites, among others.

Examples include emerging applications that support or enable the Internet of Things (IoT), Internet of Devices (IoD), the web, cloud- and mobile-to-legacy human resources, content management systems (CMS) including Drupal, Axis video, digital asset management (DAM), and digital evidence managers (DEMS) used for managing police body cameras. Others include content delivery networks (CDN) and web cache, as well as customer relationship management (CRM) and sales/marketing-focused applications such as Salesforce.com or Office 365, ArcGIS, Hive data warehouse, Nifi for distributed data distribution, spark and Splunk, among others.

There are also computer-assisted design (CAD) applications and applications for controlling manufacturing devices, enterprise resource planning (ERP) systems such as M1, Epicor, Oracle, and SAP, financial accounting, payroll, banking, insurance, investments, and trading, medical and healthcare, life sciences including pharmaceuticals, as well as research.

More examples include video and entertainment, gaming, security and surveillance, photo sharing such as Shutterfly and Shutterstock, and other content services. Other applications and functionalities include electronic data interchange (EDI), payments and supply-chain management to support manufacturing and other activity, as well as messaging such as email, texting, workflow routing, and approvals.

Content solutions span from video (emerging 8K, 4K, Ultra HD, 2.7K, HD, SD resolution, and legacy streaming video, pre/post-production, and editing), audio, imaging (photo, seismic, energy, healthcare, etc.) to security surveillance (including intelligent video surveillance [ISV] as well as intelligence surveillance and reconnaissance [ISR]).

These and other applications are packaged, delivered, and consumed in various ways from "shrink-wrapped," where the software is bought or leased installed on your data infrastructure servers, storage, I/O networks, and associated software, or provided as a service accessible via a cloud, managed service provider, or other web means. The software may also be made available on a services basis, that is, SaaS or AaaS, among other variations and pricing models.

2.2.3.3. Platform and Development Applications (Tools)

Other applications include those used for creating the previous (among others) applications by traditional developers or DevOps. These tools sit on and rely on the services and capabilities provided by underlying data infrastructures that are also made up of various applications, software tools, and utilities. Platform and development applications, tools, utilities, API and libraries such as TensorFlow, repositories (repos) such as Github and Gitlab, plug-ins, frameworks, middleware, and servers have various functionalities, from code creation to debugging, management libraries, and release coordination tracking, to testing tools.

Other platform and development applications tools include scripts, application program interface (API) extensions or customization capabilities, languages, and automation and code generators. Environments may consist of Java, .Net, Pivotal, and Cloud Foundry, among others, as well as leveraging and building on applications such as statistical analysis software (SAS), Hadoop and its variations including Cloudera, Oracle ERP, SAP, and a long list of others.

Additional tools, sites, and services to add to your vocabulary, some of which will be discussed later in addition to those already mentioned, include Ansible Openshift, Mesos, Kubernetes, Chef, Docker, GitHub, Puppet, Salt, object-oriented framework tools such as those from Pivotal, Microsoft Visual Studio, and Xamarin, Hibernate, JBoss, JRE, Tomcat, and WildFly for Java, and databases, along with AI/ML/DL cognitive and inference, IoT, among others.

There are even some legacy tools supporting decades-old applications based on Basic, COBOL, and C+, Java, Python, Ruby, among others. The above and others can be delivered via platform as a service (PaaS), serverless Function as a Service (FaaS), service and cloud providers, or on-premises and include proprietary as well as open-source-based tools.

2.2.3.4. IT and Data Infrastructure Applications (Tools)

In addition to business information and services applications, along with platform and development applications tools and utilities, there are also IT and data infrastructure applications including tools, utilities, SQL and NoSQL databases, repositories, volume managers and file systems, operating systems, containers, hypervisors, and device drivers.

There is also other software-defined data center (SDDC), software-defined network (SDN), and network function virtualization (NFV), along with software-defined storage (SDS) software tools or applications. Additional data infrastructure applications include cloud platforms such as OpenStack, database tools, monitoring and management, help desk and IT service management (ITSM), analytics, inventory and asset tracking, data center infrastructure management (DCIM), performance management database (PMDB), configuration management database (CMDB), data protection including security, backup/restore, disaster recovery (DR) and high-availability (HA), key management, along with data discovery and search.

Additional data infrastructure applications, management tools, and software include assessment, log analytics and correlation, dashboards with key performance indicators (KPIs), orchestration and resource provisioning, and portals. Automation and policy management tools are also part of the data infrastructure management toolbox, as are troubleshooting, modeling and forecasting, remediation, and lifecycle management. Operating systems, hypervisors, containers along with device drivers and their associated tools are also part of data infrastructure software and applications.

Others include workstation and desktop (physical and virtual desktop infrastructure), file and services such as SharePoint, email and messaging, to name a few. Note that hardware is further defined as firmware, microcode, and basic input/output system (BIOS and UEFI) software, and many storage and I/O networking systems or appliances are in fact servers with storage software installed on a basic operating system.

2.2.4. Various Types of Data

There are many different types of applications to meet various business, organization, or functional needs. Keep in mind that applications are based on programs which consist of algorithms and data structures that define the data, how to use it, as well as how and when to store it. Those data structures define data that will get transformed into information by programs while also being stored in memory and on data storage in various formats.

Just as various applications have different algorithms, they also have different types of data. Even though everything is not the same in all environments, or even how the same applications get used across various organizations, there are some similarities. Likewise, even though there are different types of applications and data, there are also some similarities and general characteristics. Keep in mind that information is the result of programs (applications and their algorithms) that process data into something useful or of value.

Data typically has a basic life cycle of:

- Creation and some activity, including being protected
- Dormant, followed by either continued activity or going inactive
- Disposition (delete or remove)

The above is a simple life cycle, and given that everything is not the same, for some environments there may be additional activities beyond the three mentioned.

In general, data can be

- Temporary, ephemeral or transient
- Dynamic or changing ("hot data")
- Active static on-line, near-line, or off-line ("warm data")
- In-active static on-line or off-line ("cold data")
- Primary or metadata, programs, and templates

General data characteristics include:

- Value—From no value to unknown to some or high value
- Volume—Amount of data, files, objects of a given size
- Variety—Various types of data (small, big, fast, structured, unstructured)
- Velocity—Data streams, flows, rates, load, process, access, active or static

Figure 2.3 shows how different data has various values over time. Data that has no value today or in the future can be deleted, while data with unknown value can be retained.

General characteristics include the value of the data which in turn determines its performance, availability, capacity, and economic considerations. Also, data can be ephemeral

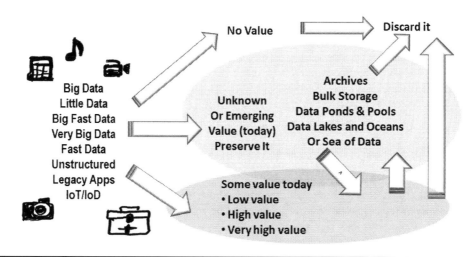

Figure 2.3   Different data with various values over time.

(temporary) or kept for longer periods of time on persistent, non-volatile storage (you do not lose the data when power is turned off). Examples of temporary include work and scratch areas such as where data gets imported into, or exported out of, an application or database.

Data can also be little, big, or big and fast, terms which describe in part the size as well as volume along with the speed or velocity of being created, accessed, and processed. The importance of understanding characteristics of data and how their associated applications use them is to enable effective decision making about performance, availability, capacity, and economics of data infrastructure resources.

2.2.4.1. Data Value

There is more to data storage than how much space capacity per cost. All data has one of three basic values:

- No value = ephemeral/temp/scratch = Why keep?
- Some value = current or emerging future value, which can be low or high
- Unknown value = protect until value is unlocked

In addition to the above basic three, data with some value can also be further subdivided into little value, some value, or high value. Of course, you can keep subdividing into as many more or different categories as needed—after all, everything is not always the same across environments.

NAND Flash, 3D Xpoint-based Intel Optane, among other NVM, along with other emerging storage-class memory (SCM) and persistent memory (PMEM), also known generically as solid-state devices (SSDs), are in your future. Granted, some of you already have various types of SSDs ranging from small MicroSD cards for your smartphones, cameras, drones, security or other video and IoT devices, as well as USB thumb drives, Thunderbolt, SATA, SAS, NVMe storage devices to all-flash arrays (AFA), etc.

While SSDs collectively, including NAND flash–based and emerging SCM and PMEM devices, continue to be popular, they also continue to be used in both on-prem and cloud service provider environments, along with traditional HDD and tape. What is different and changing is how those technologies are being used in new ways, complementing each other as tiered, different classes and categories of storage (déjà vu for some, new for others). Something that is changing and evolving is using various forms of SSDs—notably lower-cost, higher-capacity, less durable (for writes), read-optimized NAND flash—to support tasks previously done by HDD.

An example would be storing bulk data and data protection copies (archives, backups, BC, DR, snapshots, mirrors) while HDDs are being used in roles for which tape has previously been optimal. Tape, meanwhile, is being used where its strengths exist, which is for storing large amounts of data that can be streamed (read or write) at high speeds.

Note that there is a myth that tape is slow, which it is for random access, but the sequential read or write speed of the tape is optimal for massive bulk storing or retrieval of data—in other words, front-end tape with SSD and HDD as a cache buffer for quick, small, random restores, but leverage tape for high-speed bulk storage of large-capacity, infrequently accessed data, just like what the cloud vendors are doing.

Another area where SSD is traditionally not thought of as a cost-effective deployment is for use besides backups for temporary data, scratch, ephemeral, work areas, bust buffers, and other places where speeding up data access can boost productivity. Speaking of which, the best way to measure SSD-based technologies is not in quantity of IOPs, bandwidth, transactions per second, or response time latency, but instead, how much productivity it enables.

Besides boosting productivity—increasing performance of applications—SSDs, in general, can also help get more value out of your servers and software licenses. For example, not only can newer SSD access protocols such as NVMe boost performance, they can also do more I/O work with fewer CPU resources (i.e., they are efficient and useful). What this means is that not only are I/O bottlenecks removed, more work is getting done, and there is also more CPU for doing actual application processing.

With the extra available CPU cycles, more productive work can be done, which also unlocks more value from your existing software licenses. Instead of having to buy more servers and software licenses, those acquisitions can be delayed. This means you get more value out of what you already have, something the database and other software vendors may not like to hear; however, the smart ones will bring this to your attention so that they can keep you as a happy customer.

What this all means is: Leverage the appropriate data infrastructure resources to meet application workload PACE requirements, making sure that there are enough, without overwhelming or starving user productivity. Likewise, look beyond simple cost per capacity; also consider performance, availability, and business outcome enablement. Oh, and start using new and old technology in new ways.

Besides data having some value, that value can also change by increasing or decreasing in value over time, or even going from unknown to known value, known to unknown, or to no value. Data with no value can be discarded, if in doubt, make and keep a copy of that data somewhere safe until its value (or lack of value) is fully known and understood.

The importance of understanding the value of data is to enable effective decision making on where and how to protect, preserve, and store the data in a cost-effective way. Note that cost-effective does not necessarily mean the cheapest or lowest-cost approach, rather it means the way that aligns with the value and importance of the data at a given point in time.

2.2.4.2. Volume of Data

Data is generated or created from many sources, including mobile devices, social networks, web-connected systems or machines, and sensors including IoT and IoD. There is more data growing at a faster rate every day, and that data is being retained for longer periods. Some data being retained has known value, while a growing amount of data has unknown value.

Unknown-value data may eventually have value in the future, when somebody realizes that they can do something with it, or a technology tool or application becomes available to transform the data with unknown value into valuable information.

Some data gets retained in its native or raw form, while other data get processed by application program algorithms into summary data, or is curated and aggregated with other data to be transformed into new useful data. Figure 2.4 shows, from left to right and front to back, more data being created, and that data also getting larger over time. For example, on the left are two data items—objects, files, or blocks representing some information.

In the center of Figure 2.4 are more columns and rows of data, with each of those data items also becoming larger. Moving farther to the right, there are yet more data items stacked up higher, as well as across and farther back, with those items also being larger. Figure 2.4 could represent blocks of storage, files in a file system, rows and columns in a database or key-value repository, or objects in a cloud or object storage system.

In addition to more data being created, some of that data is relatively small in terms of the records or data structure entities being stored. However, there can be a large quantity of those smaller data items. In addition to the amount of data, as well as the size of the data, protection or overhead copies of data are also kept. Another dimension is that data is also getting larger where the data structures describing a piece of data for an application have increased in size.

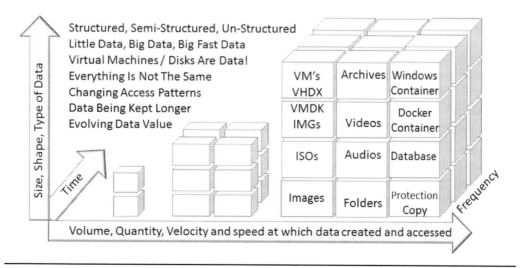

Figure 2.4   Increasing data velocity and volume, more data, and data getting larger.

For example, a still photograph taken with a digital camera, cell phone, or other mobile hand-held device, drone, or other IoT device, increases in size with each new generation of cameras as there are more megapixels.

The by-product of generating, processing, storing, and protecting more data is an expanding data footprint. Data footprint is the combination of actual data (primary and metadata) with protection copies, support, training, testing, development, and other copies. Protection copies including backups, archives, mirrors, and replicas, as well as an underlying Redundant Array of Independent Disks (RAID) (mirror, parity, erasure codes).

What this means is that to store more data longer, tiering it (promote to demote) to appropriate type or class of storage service is essential. This also means that as data value changes, it also must be stored where applicable, along with applying data footprint reduction (DFR) technologies and techniques, which include archiving, backup modernization and bandwidth optimization, data deletion and dedupe, cleanup, compression, consolidation, space-saving snapshots, storage tiering, thin provisioning, etc. The idea with DFR is to support more data growth and longer data retention in a cost-efficient, productive (effective) manner while removing complexity.

Note, however, that not all copies of data are bad overhead, as they can also be productive. For example, having multiple copies of data in different places can boost performance and productivity while reducing network traffic. Likewise, having multiple copies of data can assist with supporting parallel applications that leverage Lambda-type architecture that performs hybrid processing (both quick rapid analysis on one stream), while while a different parallel processing path performs aggregation of new and old data. The longer-running data aggregation path supports more in-depth analytics and other applications.

Other examples include having data copies in different repositories from file systems, bulk storage, data pools, data ponds, data lakes, or oceans of data for cognitive AI, ML, DL training and learning, along with other analytics. Even data centers themselves can serve as big cache copies hosting data locally or applications whose authoritative copy is kept in a cloud.

2.2.4.3. Variety of Data

In addition to having value and volume, there are also different varieties of data, including ephemeral (temporary), persistent, primary, metadata, structured, semistructured, unstructured, little, and big data. Keep in mind that programs, applications, tools, and utilities get stored as data, while they also use, create, access, and manage data.

There is also primary data and metadata, or data about data, as well as system data that is also sometimes referred to as metadata. Here is where context comes into play as part of trade-craft, as there can be metadata describing data being used by programs, as well as metadata about systems, applications, file systems, databases, and storage systems, among other things, including little and big data.

Context also matters regarding big data, as there are applications such as statistical analysis software, Splunk and Hadoop, among others, for processing (analyzing) large amounts of data. The data being processed may not be big in terms of the records or data entity items, but there may be a large volume such as with telemetry. In addition to big data analytics, data, and applications, there is also other data that is very big (as well as large volumes or collections of data sets).

For example video and audio, among others, may also be referred to as big fast data, or very big data. A challenge with larger data items is the complexity in moving over the distance

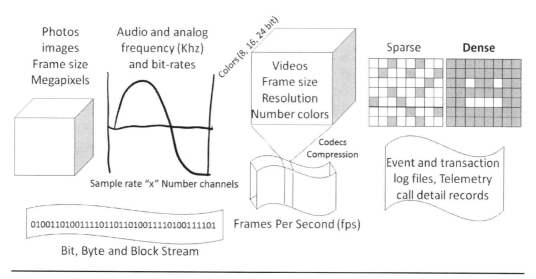

Figure 2.5   Varieties of data (bits, bytes, blocks, blobs, and bitstreams).

promptly, as well as processing requiring new approaches, algorithms, data structures, and storage management techniques.

Likewise, the challenges with large volumes of smaller data are similar in that data needs to be moved, protected, preserved, and served in a cost-effective manner for long periods of time. Both large and small data are stored (in memory or storage) in various types of data repositories.

In general, data in repositories is accessed locally, remotely, or via a cloud using:

- Application services and table spaces
- Object and Application Programming Interface (API)
- File-based using local or networked file systems
- Block-based access of disk partitions, LUNs (logical unit numbers), or volumes

Figure 2.5 shows varieties of data including (left) photos or images, audio, videos, and various log, event, and telemetry data, as well as (right) sparse and dense data.

2.2.4.4. Velocity of Data

Data, in addition to having value (known, unknown, or none), volume (size and quantity), and variety (structured, unstructured, semistructured, primary, metadata, small, big), also has velocity. Velocity refers to how fast (or slowly) data is accessed, including being stored, retrieved, updated, scanned, or if it is active (updated, or fixed static) or dormant and inactive. In addition to data access and life cycle, velocity also refers to how data is used, such as random or sequential or some combination. Think of data velocity as how data, or streams of data, flow in various ways.

Velocity also describes how data is used and accessed, including:

- Active (hot), static (warm and WORM), or dormant (cold)
- Random or sequential, read or write-accessed
- Real-time (on-line, synchronous) or time-delayed

Why this matters is that by understanding and knowing how applications use data, or how data is accessed via applications, you can make informed decisions as to how to design, configure, and manage servers, storage, and I/O resources (hardware, software, services) to meet various needs. Understanding the velocity of the data both for when it is created as well as when used is important for aligning the applicable performance techniques and technologies.

2.2.4.5. Active (Hot), Static (Warm and WORM), or Dormant (Cold)

In general, the data life cycle (called by some cradle to grave, birth or creation to disposition) is create, save and store, perhaps update and read with changing access patterns over time, along with value. During that time, the data (which includes applications and their settings) will be protected with copies or some other technique, and perhaps eventually disposed of.

Between the time when data is created and when it is disposed of, there are many variations of what gets done and needs to be done. Considering static data for a moment, some applications and their data, or data and their applications, create data which is active for a short period, then goes dormant, then is active again briefly before going cold (see the left side of Figure 2.6). This is a classic application, data, and information life-cycle model (ILM), and tiering or data movement and migration that still applies for some scenarios.

However, a newer scenario over the past several years that continues to increase is shown on the right side of Figure 2.6. In this scenario, data is initially active for updates, then goes

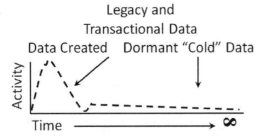

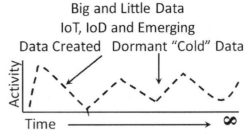

Profile: Data is created, worked with, and then goes dormant after some period of time with a probability of little to no future access or use. Data is updated, read and write vs. write once read many or append. Block and File.
Examples: Databases, general file serving, email, transactional, project-oriented data among others

Profile: Data is created, worked with, and then may go idle briefly, then accessed, then idle, then active, then idle, then active, then idle, then active, many reads, new writes or appends, more meta data.
Examples: EMR, PACs, energy, exploration, Web, reference and lookup, meta data, fixed content, CDN, Big Data, Social Media, Video, Security, DEMs, research, media, entertainment, analytics, seasonal applications. Block, File, Object, API, and Bulk.

Figure 2.6   Changing data access patterns for different applications.

cold or WORM (Write Once Read Many); however, it warms back up as a static reference, on the web, as big data, and for other uses where it is used to create new data and information.

Data, in addition to its other attributes already mentioned, can be active (hot), residing in a memory cache, buffers inside a server, or on a fast storage appliance or caching appliance. Hot data means that it is actively being used for reads or writes: This is what the term *heat map* pertains to in the context of the server, storage data, and applications. The heat map shows where the hot or active data is along with its other characteristics.

Context is important here, as there are also IT facilities heat maps, which refer to physical facilities including what servers are consuming power and generating heat. Note that some current and emerging data center infrastructure management (DCIM) tools can correlate the physical facilities power, cooling, and heat to actual work being done from an applications perspective. This correlated or converged management view enables more granular analysis and effective decision making on how to best utilize data infrastructure resources.

In addition to being hot or active, data can be warm (not as heavily accessed) or cold (rarely if ever accessed), as well as on-line, near-line, or off-line. As their names imply, warm data may occasionally be used, either updated and written, or static and just being read. Some data also gets protected as WORM data using hardware or software technologies. WORM data, not to be confused with warm data, is fixed or immutable: To preserve its context for legal or other reasons, it cannot be modified.

Also, note that some WORM data can also be warm data in that it is read-only, yet read frequently, perhaps residing in a read cache for fast lookup or access.

When looking at data (or storage), it is important to see when the data was created as well as when it was modified. However, you should avoid the mistake of looking only at when it was created or modified: Instead, also look to see when it was last read, as well as how often it is read. You might find that some data has not been updated for several years, but it is still accessed several times an hour or minute. Also, keep in mind that the metadata about the actual data may be being updated, even while the data itself is static.

Also, look at your applications characteristics as well as how data gets used, to see if it is conducive to caching or automated tiering based on activity, events, or time. For example, there is a large amount of data for an energy or oil exploration project that normally sits on slower lower-cost storage, but that now and then some analysis needs to run on.

Using data and storage management tools, given notice or based on activity, which large or big data could be promoted to faster storage, or applications migrated to be closer to the data to speed up processing. Another example is weekly, monthly, quarterly, or year-end processing of financial, accounting, payroll, inventory, or enterprise resource planning (ERP) schedules. Knowing how and when the applications use the data, which is also understanding the data, automated tools, and policies, can be used to tier or cache data to speed up processing and thereby boost productivity.

2.2.4.6. Random or Sequential (Stream), Read or Write Accessed

One aspect of data velocity is order access, including random, sequential, as well as reads and writes that can be large, small, or mixed. Sequential refers to contiguous (adjacent) data accessed, such as on the left side of Figure 2.7, while random access is shown on the right in the figure. Also, note the flat address space shown in Figure 2.7. In addition to random I/O,

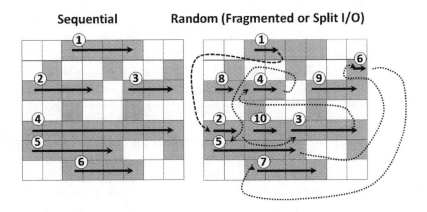

Figure 2.7   Sequential (stream) and random access, large and small I/O.

the right side of Figure 2.7 also represents fragmented, split, or noncontiguous I/O and data placement.

Note that object and blob data tends to be sequential or stream written and read; however, there are some services or API calls that can support random access. Likewise, NAS file processing tends to be sequential stream; however, there are implementations that support random or direct read/write access. Another consideration beyond block, file, or object I/O access is API calls for data, as well as status, metadata, or other information, along with their impact (they cost money with public clouds).

In Figure 2.7 (left), sequential, also known as streaming I/O operations, are shown in order of access (the numbers), with the dark squares representing the size of or how much data is being read or written. For example, (1) shows four data blocks being read or written, then four more (2), followed by three more (3), then eight more (4) in a large (or long) access, then five in (5), finally four in (6). In Figure 2.7 (right), random access is shown by jumping around with a mix of small and large operations.

Note that often data gets described as being active, inactive, read, write, random, or sequential, which it can be. However, as a reminder, it is the applications that are using the data that determine if it is random, sequential stream, large or small I/O, block, file, object, API, or database table accessed. What this means is that focusing on just the data as opposed to also looking at how different application workloads PACE characteristics use data can result in surprises, bottlenecks, or other problems.

In other words, applications = programs, which are made up of both algorithms implemented in code and data structures that define how data is organized. While it may seem like common sense, keep in perspective that it is what the application code is defined to do that determines how the information is used, resulting in various I/O or other resource calls and subsequent data infrastructure impact.

Note that random and sequential can both have large or small access that are reads, writes, or a mix. However, often sequential access is associated with large reads or writes, while random access can be smaller—although note that this is not a hard-and-fast rule, as I/O sizes are getting larger. Likewise, applications may access data using both random and sequential access, for example, randomly accessing some data and then sequentially streaming other data.

Why this matters is that knowing data access patterns of how applications use data, as well as insight into data value, velocity, and other attributes, are important for managing servers, storage, and I/O resources for performance and other activities.

2.2.4.7. Real-Time (On-Line, Synchronous) or Time-Delayed

Real-time and time-delayed refer generally to how data is accessed and used by applications. Some data may be accessed in real time, on-line with no delays, including reads and updates or writes locally. That same data may be accessed in a time-delayed mode remotely, perhaps by accessing a read or buffered cache for collaboration or sharing purposes. Likewise, data written or updated from one location to another might be done asynchronously, in which case the application keeps running while data is written in the background, with eventual consistency (e.g., write behind).

The benefit is that applications can keep running without causing delays to users while data is written at a slower pace. The caveat is that data integrity means that either the application or data infrastructure needs to provide consistency safeguards to protect against data loss. With synchronous access, applications wait for notification that data has been safely written to ensure strong consistency and protect against data loss.

Note that for reads, instead of waiting for data to be retrieved, it can be cached in a local buffer to speed up access. However, cache consistency and coherency needs to exist to prevent stale reads, which mean that if the underlying data changes, the cache or buffers need to be upgraded to avoid using old data.

2.2.4.8. Habitats for Data Infrastructures, Applications, and Data

Not to be confused with habitats for technology, such as physical data centers and cloud AZs, habitats for data are where data is stored. Another aspect of data (along with applications) is where they exist and reside. Data repositories are habitats for where data lives and is stored. These repositories exist in physical facilities either on your own site, colocated (colo), or on shared hosting or cloud managed services. Repositories can be as simple as a file system dedicated to a standalone device, external and shared via portable media, network, or cloud services, among other variations. Other data repositories include structured and unstructured databases and data warehouses for little and big data, both temporary and permanent, near- or long-term.

Data repositories or habitats for data ranging from file systems, databases, and table services to data lakes and ponds, along with data warehouses, can be located at or near the edge where they are used as well as at the core, including legacy data centers and cloud. The repositories may have a main authoritative copy at a given location, with other copies distributed as cached copies for faster access.

Another variation is that quick analysis activity can be done at the edge where data is generated for fast results, while data is sent back to a central or core repository. Once at the core, deeper, more extended running analytics can be run on more substantial historical data to support different types of information insight. Likewise, cognitive AI, ML, and DL models can be trained or tested at the core before deployment at the edge.

Unstructured data repositories include object and file systems, solutions, or services that may also have marketing or functional names such as data ponds, data pools, data lakes, data reservoirs, or data hotels, among others. Different data types may have different velocity, but, in general, as it flows downstream from its source to other destinations, data also gets larger, just like water in a river.

Similarly, data repositories can also overflow, resulting in a flood and causing disruptions if not properly managed—prompting the question of whether it is easier and more cost-effective to take a proactive stand to find and fix problems at the source, or to have insurance to clean them up after the fact. Keep that thought in mind as we go further along our journey in this book.

Some applications store and access data in highly structured databases, such as Intersystem's Caché, Microsoft SQL Server, IBM DB2, MySQL, Microsoft Azure Cosmos, AWS Aurora, or variations including ClearDB, TokuDB, and Aerospike, as well as in memory-based solutions such as MemSQL, Oracle, SAP, HANA, and Sybase, among others. In addition to SQL databases, there are also NoSQL databases and repositories, including Cassandra, Mongo, HBase, CouchDB, Kudo, and Riak, among others.

In additional to traditional databases, there are also repositories optimized for data warehouse and big data analytics, including Teradata, IBM Netezza, Oracle ERP, Pivotal Greenplum, Hadoop, and HDFS, among others. In the case of block-based access, the application, database, or file system works with applications to know what files to access.

In other scenarios, applications access a file by name in a folder or directory that is part of a mount point or share in a file system, either locally or on a remote file server or NAS device. Another means of data access is via an object API, whereby a client requests information from a server via a defined mechanism.

In the case of a database, applications only need to know the schema or how the database is organized to make queries with tools such as Structured Query Language (SQL); the database handles read or writing of data either in a block or file system mode. For block mode, the database is assigned LUNs or storage space where it creates its files or data sets that it manages. If a file system is being used, the database leverages the underlying file system to handle some of the storage management tasks.

Structured data has defined attributes, making searching or other functions relatively easy. This structure, however, can make adding or changing the organization more complex or costly. As a result, there is the growing category of unstructured data, also known as file accessed data. The value proposition of unstructured data is that there is no formal organization other than files stored in a folder or directory in a file system.

2.2.4.9. Metadata Matters

Some file systems and files can support additional metadata or properties. The flexibility of unstructured data causes challenges, however, when it comes to being able to search or determine what the files contain. With a database, the schema or organization makes it relatively easy to search and determine what is stored. With unstructured data, additional metadata needs to be discovered via tools, including search and classification tools.

2.2.4.10. Meta Data Matters, Manifests, and Configuration Settings

Volume managers, file systems, object storage repositories, and databases exist to manage data. However, part of management is knowing what you have. Organizations use IT applications to keep track of things—to know what they have, where it is, and how it is being used, consumed, or produced, among other things. IT, on the other hand, and specifically data infrastructures, rely on metadata for maneuvering resources and for managing data to be protected, preserved, and served.

Metadata is data about the data, which can mean attributes of a volume, file, file system, or object. Also, metadata also exists to keep track of how data infrastructure resources are configured and used, from clustered storage and file systems to hypervisors and other software-defined items. In simple terms, metadata describes the actual data—when it was created, accessed, and updated; by whom; associated applications; and other optional information.

All data has some type of metadata, from a simple create and modified date, size, location or endpoint, security, and ownership, to more advanced information. More advanced metadata includes activity tracking by user or applications, snippets and thumbnail previews that can range from hundreds of bytes to several Mbytes, kept either in a file or object header, file system, database, or another repository.

Metadata exists for:

- Data center infrastructure management (DCIM), from facilities to software
- Application, database, repository, file system, and other settings
- Events, errors, activity, transaction, data protection, and other logs
- Files and objects describing their primary attributes or data being stored

Metadata matters include:

- File size and extents, create, modified, and accessed dates
- Application name or type, access control lists (ACLs)
- WORM and immutable attributes, policy and retention attributes
- Permissions (owner, group, world, read, write, execute, delete)
- Search and discovery for lookup or finding a document
- Policy and automated management including retention or disposition

Another variation of data besides application code (source, binaries, libraries, executables), the data they process, and metadata are templates, manifest (build instructions), scripts, and configuration settings. Both metadata and configurations, templates, manifests, provisioning, and build script data can be raw text, XML, or JSON, among other formats.

2.3. Common Applications Characteristics

Different applications will have various attributes, in general, as well as how they are used, for example, database transaction activity vs. reporting or analytics, logs and journals vs. redo logs, indices, tables, indices, import/export, scratch and temp space. Performance, availability,

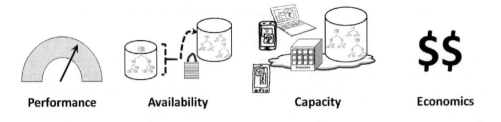

Figure 2.8   Application PACE attributes.

capacity, and economics (PACE) describes the applications and data characters and needs (Figure 2.8).

All applications have PACE attributes, however:

- PACE attributes vary by application and usage
- Some applications and their data are more active than others
- Some applications generate, whereas others consume, data
- Some are compute, memory, I/O, or storage capacity centric
- Some are mission critical; others are not
- PACE characteristics may vary within different parts of an application

Think of applications along with associated data PACE as its personality or how it behaves, what it does, how it does it, and when, along with value, benefit, or cost as well as quality-of-service (QoS) attributes. Understanding applications in different environments, including data values and associated PACE attributes, is essential for making informed server, storage, and I/O decisions from configuration to acquisitions or upgrades—when, where, why, and how to protect, and how to optimize performance including capacity planning, reporting, and troubleshooting, not to mention addressing budget concerns.

Primary PACE attributes for active and inactive applications and data are:

P—Performance and activity (how things get used)
A—Availability and durability (resiliency and protection)
C—Capacity and space (what things use or occupy)
E— Economics and Energy (people, budgets, and other barriers)

Some applications need more performance (server computer, or storage and network I/O), while others need space capacity (storage, memory, network, or I/O connectivity). Likewise, some applications have different availability needs (data protection, durability, security, resiliency, backup, business continuity, disaster recovery) that determine the tools, technologies, and techniques to use.

Budgets are also nearly always a concern, which for some applications means enabling more performance per cost while others are focused on maximizing space capacity and protection level per cost. PACE attributes also define or influence policies for QoS (performance, availability, capacity), as well as thresholds, limits, quotas, retention, and disposition, among others.

2.3.1. Performance and Activity (How Resources Get Used)

Some applications or components that comprise a larger solution will have more performance demands than others. Likewise, the performance characteristics of applications along with their associated data will also vary. Performance applies to the server, storage, and I/O networking hardware along with associated software and applications.

For servers, performance is focused on how much CPU or processor time is used, along with memory and I/O operations. I/O operations to create, read, update, and delete (CRUD) data include activity rate (frequency or data velocity) of I/O operations (IOPs), the volume or amount of data being moved (bandwidth, throughput, transfer), response time or latency, along with queue depths. Activity is the amount of work to do or being done in a given amount of time (seconds, minutes, hours, days, weeks), which can be transactions, rates, IOPs, latency, bandwidth, throughput, response time, queues, reads or writes, gets or puts, updates, lists, directories, searches, pages views, files opened, videos viewed, or downloads.

Server, storage, and I/O network performance include:

- Processor CPU usage time and queues (user and system overhead)
- Memory usage effectiveness including page and swap
- I/O activity including between servers and storage
- Dropped sessions, packets, and timeouts
- Errors, retransmissions, retries, and rebuilds

Figure 2.9 shows a generic performance example of data being accessed (mixed reads, writes, random, sequential, big, small, low- and high-latency) on a local and a remote basis. The example shows how for a given time interval (see lower right), applications are accessing and working with data via different data streams in the larger image left center. Also shown are queues and I/O handling along with end-to-end (E2E) response time.

Also shown on the left in Figure 2.9 is an example of E2E response time from the application through the various data infrastructure layers, as well as, lower center, the response time from the server to the memory or storage devices. Various queues are shown in the middle of Figure 2.9 which are indicators of how much work is occurring, if the processing is keeping up with the work or causing backlogs. Context is needed for queues, as they exist in the server, I/O networking devices, and software drivers, as well as in storage among other locations.

Some basic server, storage, I/O metrics that matter include:

- Queue depth of I/Os waiting to be processed and concurrency
- CPU and memory usage to process I/Os
- I/O size, or how much data can be moved in a given operation
- I/O activity rate or IOPs = amount of data moved/I/O size per unit of time
- Bandwidth = data moved per unit of time = I/O size × I/O rate
- Latency usually increases with larger I/O sizes, decreases with smaller requests

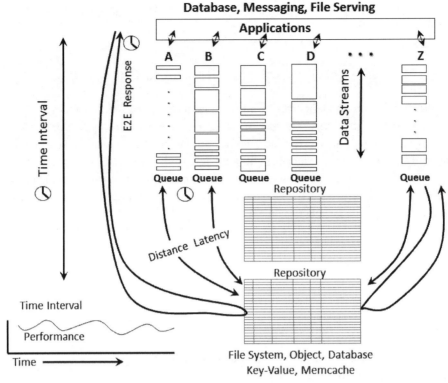

Figure 2.9 Server, storage, I/O performance fundamentals.

- I/O rates usually increase with smaller I/O sizes and vice versa
- Bandwidth increases with larger I/O sizes and vice versa
- Sequential stream access data may have better performance than some random access data
- Not all data is conducive to being sequential stream, or random
- Lower response time is better, higher activity rates and bandwidth are better

Queues with high latency and small I/O size or small I/O rates could indicate a performance bottleneck. Queues with low latency and high I/O rates with good bandwidth or data being moved could be a good thing. An important note is to look at several metrics, not just IOPs or activity, or bandwidth, queues, or response time. Also, keep in mind that metrics that matter for your environment may be different than those for somebody else.

Something to keep in perspective is that there can be a large amount of data with low performance, or a small amount of data with high-performance, not to mention many other variations. The important concept is that as space capacity scales, that does not mean performance also improves or vice versa—after all, everything is not the same.

2.3.2. Availability (Accessibility, Durability, Consistency)

Just as there are many different aspects and focus areas for performance, there are also several facets to availability. Note that applications performance requires availability and availability relies on some level of performance. Availability is a broad and encompassing area that includes data protection to protect, preserve, and serve (backup/restore, archive, BC, BR, DR, HA) data and applications. There are logical and physical aspects of availability including data protection as well as security including key management (manage your keys or authentication and certificates) and permissions, among other things.

Availability = accessibility (can you get to your application and data) + durability (is the data intact and consistent). This includes basic Reliability, Availability, Serviceability (RAS), as well as high availability, accessibility, and durability. "Durable" has multiple meanings, so context is important. Durable means how data infrastructure resources hold up to, survive, and tolerate wear and tear from use (i.e., endurance), for example, Flash SSD or mechanical devices. Another context for durable refers to data, meaning how many copies in various places.

Server, storage, and I/O network availability topics include:

- Resiliency and self-healing to tolerate failure or disruption
- Hardware, software, and services configured for resiliency
- Accessibility to reach or be reached for handling work
- Durability and consistency of data to be available for access
- Protection of data, applications, and assets including security
- Backup/restore, replication, snapshots, sync, and copies
- Basic Reliability, Availability, Serviceability, HA, failover, BC, BR, and DR
- Alternative paths, redundant components, and associated software
- Applications that are fault-tolerant, resilient, and self-healing
- Nondisruptive upgrades, code (application or software) loads, and activation
- Immediate data consistency and integrity vs. eventual consistency
- Virus, malware, and other data corruption or loss prevention

From a data protection standpoint, the fundament rule or guideline is *4 3 2 1*, which means having at least four copies consisting of at least three versions (different points in time), at least two of which are on different systems or storage devices and at least one of those is off-site (on-line, off-line, cloud, or other). There are many variations of the *4 3 2 1* rule (Figure 2.10) along with approaches on how to manage technology to use. We will go deeper into data protection and related topics in later chapters. For now, remember:

4 At least four copies of data (or more)—Enables durability in case a copy goes bad, deleted, corrupted, failed device, or site.

3 The number (or more) versions of the data to retain—Enables various recovery points in time to restore, resume, restart from.

2 Data located on two or more systems (devices or media/mediums)—Enables protection against device, system, server, file system, or other fault/failure.

1 With at least one of those copies being off-premise and not live (isolated from active primary copy)—Enables resiliency across sites, as well as space, time, distance gap for protection.

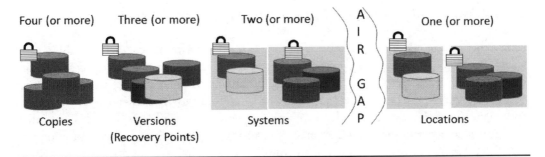

Figure 2.10   *4 3 2 1* data protection with air gap.

2.3.3. Capacity and Space (What Gets Consumed and Occupied)

In addition to being available and accessible in a timely manner (performance), data (and applications) occupy space. That space is memory in servers, as well as using available consumable processor CPU time along with I/O (performance) including over networks. Data and applications also consume storage space where they are stored. In addition to basic data space, there is also space consumed for metadata as well as protection copies (and overhead), application settings, logs, and other items. Another aspect of capacity includes network IP ports and addresses, software licenses, server, storage, and network bandwidth or service time.

Server, storage, and I/O network capacity topics include:

- Consumable time-expiring resources (processor time, I/O, network bandwidth)
- Network IP and other addresses
- Physical resources of servers, storage, and I/O networking devices
- Software licenses based on consumption or number of users
- Primary and protection copies of data and applications
- Active and standby data infrastructure resources and sites
- Data footprint reduction (DFR) tools and techniques for space optimization
- CDN, bandwidth optimization, load balancers
- Policies, quotas, thresholds, limits, and capacity QoS
- Application and database optimization

DFR includes various techniques, technologies, and tools to reduce the impact or overhead of protecting, preserving, and serving more data for longer periods of time. There are many different approaches to implementing a DFR strategy, since there are various applications and data. Some common DFR techniques and technologies include archiving, backup modernization, copy data management (CDM), clean up, compress, and consolidate, data management, deletion and dedupe, storage tiering, RAID (including parity-based, erasure codes, local reconstruction codes [LRC], and Reed-Solomon, among others), and protection configurations along with thin-provisioning, among others.

DFR can be implemented in various complementary locations from row-level compression in database or email to normalized databases, to file systems, operating systems, appliances, and storage systems using various techniques. Also, keep in mind that not all data is the same; some is sparse, some is dense, some can be compressed or deduped while others cannot. Likewise, some data may not be compressible or dedupable. However, identical copies can be identified with links created to a common copy.

2.3.4. Economics (People, Budgets, Energy, and Other Constraints)

If one thing in life and technology that is constant is change, then the other constant is concern about economics or costs. There is a cost to enable and maintain a data infrastructure on premise or in the cloud, which exists to protect, preserve, and serve data and information applications. However, there should also be a benefit to having the data infrastructure to house data and support applications that provide information to users of the services. A common economic focus is what something costs, either as up-front capital expenditure (CapEx) or as an operating expenditure (OpEx) expense, along with recurring fees.

If one constant in life and technology is change, then the other constant is concern about economics or costs. There is a cost to enable and maintain a data infrastructure—on-prem or in the cloud—which exists to protect, preserve, and serve data and information applications. However, there should also be a benefit to having the data infrastructure to house data and support applications that provide information to users of the services. A common economic focus is what something costs, either as up-front capital expenditure (CapEx) or as an operating expenditure (OpEx), along with recurring fees.

Over the past decade, there has been a focus on shifting IT and data infrastructure spending from CapEx to OpEx, along with hardware consolidation, shift to clouds, and other cost-cutting initiatives. For some environments today, users are finding that hardware and CapEx are not the budget issue of a decade or more ago; instead, they now have a growing OpEx, software, and cloud cost issue.

One approach is to cut or reduce spending (OpEx or CapEx), while another is to get more value or return on your investment. For example, similar to how hardware gets consolidated, look for ways to maximize and combine software licensing. Another strategy is to get more transactions, work, or productivity per software license unit cost to reduce the number of new licenses.

Cloud spend can also be optimized by looking into what is being subscribed to and invoiced vs. what is being used. For example, are there cloud compute instances or VMs that are subscribed to and powered on, or off, yet taking up space and other resources? Another cloud strategy is to bring you software licenses and leverage your enterprise license agreements (ELA) where applicable to reduce cost and get more value out of your software investment.

Some other techniques for removing cost is to reduce overhead complexity, eliminate waste, rework, retransmit—performance or availability issues that cause disconnects along with resulting loss of productivity. Also keep various purchase, lease, and subscription options in mind for hardware, software, services, and cloud. For example, with the cloud, are you paying for on-demand (e.g., last minute, full walk-up fare) type pricing or reserved instances with one or three-year pre-pay and larger discounts?

For environments that are cash-flow sensitive, paying the higher monthly fee might be more expensive, although easier than paying up front for a more significant discount. On the other hand, some environments may seek out a lower cost service with less availability, resiliency, performance, and service levels.

Whether legacy, software-defined, container, virtual, cloud, or converged data infrastructure, knowing your applications workloads PACE characteristics and resource needs, how your resources are being used, and the cost of services is essential. Gain insight and situational awareness into your data infrastructure environments to avoid flying blind.

In general, economic considerations include:

- Budgets (CapEx and OpEx), both up front and in recurring fees
- Whether you buy, lease, rent, subscribe, or use free and open sources
- People time needed to integrate and support even free open-source software
- Costs including hardware, software, services, power, cooling, facilities, tools
- People time includes base salary, benefits, training and education

2.4. Where Applications and Data Get Processed and Reside

Data habitats or repositories reside in various locations involving different software along with hardware and services spanning cloud, virtual, and physical environments. A trend today is to place data either closer to the server or where the applications run, or move the applications close to where the data is. For some, this may be a new concept, for others evolutionary, yet for some it will also be *déjà vu* from "back in the day."

What is common across those scenarios is a locality of reference. The locality of reference involves keeping data close to the application and server, or applications as close to the data as possible, to reduce overhead and the time delay of moving or accessing data. Keep in mind that the best I/O is the one that you do not have to do: More data in main memory, larger capacity and faster main memory, as well as faster access to NVM and other fast storage, all help to reduce the overhead of I/Os and subsequent application impact.

Leveraging information about applications and data helps to determine where best to house data and applications, including data infrastructure resources, as well as on-site or on-premise, off-site, cloud, managed server, or other options. Some applications and data lend themselves to being centralized, while others are distributed and rely on collaboration and data synchronization or coordination tools.

Where is the best place to locate applications and data, along with the type of servers, storage, I/O networking hardware, and software, depends on your organization needs and preferences. Some applications and environments have shifted over time from centralized to distributed, to centralized, and so forth, following technology trends, while others adapt to organizational needs and preferences.

Applications and data can reside and be processed on or at:

- Dedicated or shared resources (server, storage, I/O networking)
- Serverless, FaaS, PaaS-based services
- Converged, hyperconverged, cluster-in-box, or unbounded solutions
- Physical (bare metal), virtual machine, or container-based solutions
- Legacy mainframe and proprietary, open systems, *nix or Windows
- Best-of-breed components converged or hyperconverged solutions
- Locally on-site, on-prem, private or public, hybrid, multi-cloud

- Remote at a secondary site, colocation facility
- Hosted, managed services, or cloud provider
- Tightly or loosely coupled or decoupled compute and storage

2.5. Application Data and Data Infrastructure Strategies

Data infrastructure management strategies for application and data topics discussed in this chapter include gaining insight and awareness to avoid flying blind. By having insight and awareness—topics that are discussed further in the following chapters—you, along with AI, ML, DL, and other cognitive software, can make informed decisions and define new policies and procedures for automation. This means having insight and awareness into your workloads, both applications and data at various layers or levels of altitude in the IT and data infrastructure stack (from high to low, low to high).

Keep in mind that everything is not the same across different environments, data centers, and the data infrastructures that exist inside them supporting diverse application workloads. Likewise, all application workloads have various PACE resource and service requirements. Aligning the appropriate resources to workload needs means looking beyond lowest cost, or lowest cost and highest capacity, also considering performance and availability. What this means is making sure that application workloads have enough resources to get their job done, enabling productivity while eliminating waste or overcommit of resources and their cost.

Having insight and awareness about what resources are being used, their cost, and the cost for services provided, along with customer satisfaction, also enables smart decision making. Besides intelligent decision making, applicable apples-to-apples comparisons can be made between local on-site, on-prem-based resources (CapEx or OpEx) and cloud- or other-based services. Tying this all together, have a strategy in which the focus on software-defined anything has the emphasis not on the software, hardware, or service, but on how those are defined to enable the desired business outcome that is flexible, scalable, resilient, efficient, and effective to boost productivity.

2.6. Common Questions and Tips

Part of developing or expanding your tradecraft is practicing and applying what you learn.

Why not keep all data? If the data has value, and you have a large enough budget, why not? On the other hand, most organizations have a budget and other constraints that determine how much and what data to retain.

Why would you put data infrastructure resources, including compute, storage, network, hardware, and software at the edge when the objective is to move them to the cloud? For some environments and scenarios, moving all your applications to a public cloud might make sense. Major public cloud providers such as AWS and Azure, among others, support various data infrastructure services, including IoT hubs, gateways, and management capabilities.

Likewise, primary cloud services have options for bulk data movement and ingest from remote sites into the cloud. However, for other scenarios in which more control or site-specific requirements exist, placing data infrastructure at the edge makes sense. Edge data infrastructure can be small hyper-converged, converged, cluster, and cloud in a box or scale out to meet different workload needs.

What is fog computing? Fog data infrastructures are essentially mini clouds whose architectures, operations, and enablement are similar to more massive core clouds, except that they are at the edge of networks close to where they are used. Think of fog and cloud as a two-tier data infrastructure model, similar to the traditional core or central data centers along with ROBO environments.

With fog, compute, network, storage resources are located close to where the applications are accessed, as well as where data is generated, processed, and used. The difference between fog and traditional ROBO is that the distributed data infrastructure resources are managed similarly to that of a more massive central or core cloud. The benefits of fog are that data infrastructure resources are close to where they are used, reducing time and network latency delays and the burden of moving larger amounts of data for quick analysis.

Good candidates for fog are similar to those of traditional ROBO or remote sites, including energy exploration, IoT, distributed sites that need access to or generate large amounts of data requiring fast analysis, etc. The downside to fog is similar to traditional ROBO or other distributed in that there are more locations and resources to manage.

What is a Lambda architecture? Some usage scenarios have applications with low latency fast analysis, such as clickstream analytics of current operational data and a subset of referential material. Meanwhile, other usage scenarios have applications that need deeper thinking on a more substantial volume of data including recent operational as well as expanding historical data. Lambda architectures provide a hybrid, using two parallel data and processing streams where one is focused on quick, fast analytics processing on smaller amounts of data, the other on longer running, more involved processing, whose results may be used to update fast processing referential data.

What does it mean to have on-prem data centers as a cache? For environments that have moved the authoritative copy of their data to clouds, as well as having a mix of applications running on-prem as well as in the cloud, there can be a locally cached copy of data to boost performance. Data updated on-prem gets sent to cloud at some variable interval for consistency, while local applications performance is benefited by having a cached copy.

What this means is that while there is still local storage, the data center and, more importantly, the data infrastructure are functioning as a cache for the cloud-based data and or application services. Some considerations include data access (block, file, object or blob, table service or database) as well as locking and coherency for data integrity, security, and encryption, along with access controls with audit logs.

What is a data lake? Historically, a data lake might have been called a data warehouse, a large bulk file share or file system, or another repository. A data lake is a repository that holds a significant amount of data, usually unstructured files, images, videos, logs, telemetry and event data, objects, blobs, and other items. These items are used to curate new data via big data and additional analytics processing, AI, ML, DL training learning models, among other uses. A smaller data lake might be a data pond or pool, while a larger one might be a sea or ocean of data. The data lake might be a scalable file system or another storage repository with the flexibility to support NAS file, object, blob, and API, among other access and data types.

Is it true that IoT data does not need to be retained? Keep in mind that everything is not the same across the different organizations, data centers, data infrastructure, applications, and IoT devices. Some IoT devices, such as temperature or other sensor data, can be aggregated and kept in summary form, while others may have data discarded within a short period. For other IoT devices, the metadata might be worth retaining for a period or disposed of, depending what the devices do—for example, a traffic light, intelligent sign, or similar.

On the other hand, an IoT device that is capturing and recording video, audio, or other digital data may need that information along with its metadata retained for long periods of time. Likewise, medical IoT data may need to be kept for different periods, depending on what that information pertains to. Thus, when somebody says IoT data does not need to be saved, ask them for a side of context on what they are talking about.

What is the difference between cost cutting and cost savings? They sound the same. Both are focused on a result of reducing spending. However, they differ in approach and outcome. While both look to reduce the amount spent, cost-cutting is just that, looking for ways to reduce spending without regard to service or other impact. On the other hand, cost savings can be the result of finding and removing complexity and overhead while boosting activity.

Even though the same might be spent, with more productive work being done and hopefully better customer satisfaction, the result is cost savings, also known as *removing cost.* The approach of removing costs can be more involved than merely cutting something from a budget; on the other hand, by eliminating complexity and overhead and streamlining cost per service with improvements, as you scale, your costs go down as you do more activity.

What is meant by using new and old things in new ways? A common trend is that something new, such as an SSD storage system, is used to replace an older HDD or tape device for backup. Instead of using the SSD in new ways, such as for snapshots, flexible point-in-time copies, and restores, it is used in traditional backup and restore mode (e.g., used in old ways).

Using something old in new ways includes front-ending tape with HDD and SSD in a tiered storage model, or using the cloud as a peer-to-peer hybrid high-availability solution instead of as a backup or archive target. Another example is using servers with hypervisors to run different software-defined solution stacks from storage to network, to compute containers. Another approach to using something old in a new way is leveraging Metal as a Service technology to provision bare metal servers in a more straightforward way, effectively virtualizing the management of them.

Where is the best place for a data infrastructure? The best place for your data infrastructure is close to where applications and data will be used, which meets your performance, availability, capacity, economic, and other requirements.

Are converged, hyper-converged, clusters, and cloud in a box data centers in a box or data infrastructures? Yes, although they are often referred to as *data centers in a box* or *software-defined data centers.* Keep in mind that it is the data infrastructure, comprising a server, storage, I/O networking hardware, software, and tools defined by policies and procedures to support applications, that exists inside physical data centers.

Does serverless eliminate servers? FaaS and serverless data infrastructure models still rely on physical servers somewhere. However, they and their operation, use, and management are masked from those who use them. The key point with FaaS and serverless data infrastructure architectures is not whether they have physical servers, but how they enable productivity, flexibility, and ease of application deployment without having to worry about the underlying data infrastructure. On the other hand, if a vendor, service provider, or one of their pundits tell you that they are indeed 100% physical server free for their service, not relying on any other third-party service, say congratulations, and run . . .

How can software-defined networks (SDN) and software defined wide area networks (SD-WAN) help move more data and support IoT devices? SDN and SD-WAN still rely on underlying physical networks and their hardware as well as services; however, they can also help reduce the overhead of data movement and management. For example, leveraging smart cache, bandwidth, and data footprint reduction including compression, protocol acceleration, lowering retransmissions or dropped packets and sessions help to boost productivity and move more data.

Where is the best place to store a large number of videos? How many videos do you have, how big are they, how many are created new each day and from where? What are your retention requirements, including for how long, and how quickly, do you need to access them? What are your metadata management criteria? Do you need lossless retention end to end, or can you support lossy previews and thumbnails with a lossless authoritative copy?

What are your budget requirements? Are you just looking to store the largest amount of digital data at the lowest cost without concern of some protection copies, or do you need a given service-level objective (SLO) and availability requirement? The answers range from using one or more large public clouds and their file, object, and blob services, as well as local on-prem storage solutions, to small NAS and other options.

Isn't the objective to keep less data to cut costs? If the data has no value, then get rid of it. On the other hand, if data has value or unknown value, then find ways to remove the cost of keeping more data for longer periods of time so its value can be realized.

On a server in an environment where there is a good response time and high I/O rate, a large or high queue depth and a relatively low amount of server CPU time being spent on system time or overhead would indicate what? There is a lot of work being done with a large arrival rate, yet the system can keep up with the work. However, if the response time increased, that could indicate a bottleneck somewhere. An increase in CPU time might occur if there are many small I/Os being handled.

An application is doing very large sequential reads (256 KB or larger) across a 15-TB device, and the system is showing a low CPU usage with a high queue depth and large response time. The amount of data being transferred is indicated as 21 Gbps; is this a problem? It depends on what the storage system and its I/O network are capable of, but at 21 Gbps that equates to about 2.6 GB or about half of what a 40-GbE network line rate is capable of. Keep in mind that with large data transfer, your I/O rate or activity will tend to decrease and response time increase. Likewise, less CPU is needed to handle a few larger I/Os than many smaller ones.

2.7. Chapter Summary

Everything is not the same, from businesses, organizations, or institutions (as well as consumers) to their applications and data. Having insight into the applications, data, and their characteristics help to determine where they should run and on what, vs. simply based on what is the newest trend or technology. The data infrastructure might be more flexible to change as long as it can support the upper-level applications and information infrastructure. Be mindful of how or what the upper layer applications depend on. The upper level might be more agile than the lower-level data infrastructures; the key is knowing what to do when, where, why, and how for different situations.

General action items include:

- Expand your tradecraft, balancing technology and business insight.
- Gain insight into the organization, its applications, and the data characteristics.
- Learn about applications and their PACE characteristics.
- Use tools to understand different attributes of data including changing value.
- Understand how to align technology with business needs and vice versa.
- Explore new technologies as well as habitats for technologies.
- Use new and old things in new ways.

That wraps up this chapter and Part One. The bottom line for now is to keep in mind that applications are programs and data structures, and programs = algorithms plus data structures that rely on a server, storage, I/O hardware, and software that are defined into a data infrastructure that enables a business outcome benefit.

Part Two

Data Infrastructure Management

Part Two comprises Chapters 3 through 5. This part leverages what you have learned as part of expanding (or refreshing) your data infrastructure server, storage, I/O networking, and related management services tradecraft skills.

Buzzword terms, trends, technologies, and techniques include habitats for technologies, data centers, availability zones (AZs), cloud, dashboards, portals, reporting, analytics, troubleshooting, and repair, among other topics.

Chapter 3

Data Infrastructure Management

What You Will Learn in This Chapter

- Knowing what tools to have and how to use them as well as when to use them

The focus is on common data infrastructure (both legacy and software-defined) management topics. Key themes, buzzwords, and trends addressed in this chapter include troubleshooting, server, storage, I/O network, hardware, software, services, CI, HCI, software-defined, cloud, virtual, serverless, FaaS, container, and various applications, data protection and security, among others topics.

3.1. Getting Started

All applications have some performance, availability, capacity, and economic (PACE) attributes that vary by type of workload, environment, size, scale, and scope, among other considerations. Different environments, applications, subapplications, or application component workloads also vary, having diverse PACE needs along with different service-level objectives (SLOs). Similarly, the applications, data, and metadata along with the configuration of and the data infrastructure resources they depend on also need to be managed.

There are different focuses and domains of interest when it comes to data infrastructure along with related applications and data center facilities infrastructure management. Management spans automation, processes, procedures, policies, insight (awareness, analytics, metrics) and practices, along with people skillsets and experience (i.e., tradecraft). In addition, management includes tools, technologies, as well as techniques across different legacy and software-defined data infrastructure (SDDI) IT focus areas.

Keep in mind that SDDI and software data infrastructures are what are housed in physical (and cloud) data centers and are generically referred to as software-defined data centers

(SDDC). Does that mean SDDI = SDDC = SDI? Yes. However, SDDI can also mean leveraging software-defined management applied to cloud, virtual, container, and other environments.

Tip: The context of domain means different things, such as networking and URI, URL domain names for endpoints, or security domains such as with active directory (AD) and domain controllers (DCs). Another use of "domain" refers to areas of focus such as higher-level applications, databases, file systems, repository, servers, storage, or I/O networking, along with facilities infrastructure. Yet another use of "domain" refers to an area of knowledge, expertise, experience, or your tradecraft.

There are domains of focus and tradecraft specialty, such as database administration, storage management, hypervisors, VMware, Microsoft, OpenStack, Docker containers, data protection, security, performance, and capacity planning, among others. For example, "cross-domain management" can mean managing across different network or security domains, but it can also refer to managing across applications, server, storage, and data protection.

As you have read throughout this book, some recurring themes include:

- Everything is not the same in various data centers, data infrastructures, and environments.
- There are different sizes, scopes, and scales, with diverse applications along with workloads.
- While things are different even across industries or applications, there are similarities.
- Management involves different tasks, functions, and domains of focus and tradecraft.
- People define software to manage other software, hardware, and services such as cloud.
- SDDI management spans legacy, virtual, container, and cloud environments.

3.2. Data Infrastructure Management and Tools

Figure 3.1 shows some data infrastructure–related tools spanning hardware, software, and services. However, as we have discussed throughout this book, other tools include your experience, skills, and tradecraft, including what to use when, where, why, and how for different scenarios.

Recall Chapter 1, where I provided a sample of various toolbox items for SDDI and SDDC as well as legacy environments including hardware and software. These items, among others in Figure 3.1, are what define, configure, diagnose, monitor, report, protect, secure, and provision resources, among other data infrastructure functions. Some tools focus on hardware, others on software, services, virtual, container, cloud, file systems, databases, backup and data protection, specific products or vendors, as well as other functionality.

Tip: In addition to object, bucket, and other bulk cloud storage, I have a regular volume (EBS) with an image configured with common tools as well as preferences. When I start an instance, I attach that volume to it. It is like moving an HDD or SSD from one physical server to another for a jump start or other activity. In other words, I have a virtual toolbox with different tools that I keep in the cloud.

Apt, Yum, Vum, wget, curl, cyberduck, cloudberry, ycsb, rufus, gpart, fdisk, wmic, esxtop, SAP, Hadoop, Oracle, Microsoft, Cassandra, MongoDB, Hbase, vdbench, diskspd, BMF, TokuDB, OpenStack, diskpart, sysbench ,Enmotus-FuzeDrive, Graphviz, caspa, CPU-Z, datadog, DPA, JAM Treesize, blkdid, nttcp, iperf, iotop, htop, lscpu, ntop, netstat, sar, hdparm and ping among others

Physical, Virtual, Containers
Cloud and Software Defined

Hardware, Physical Tools, Cables
Connectors, Adapters, Storage
Servers and Management Software

Data Infrastructure Tool Box

Figure 3.1   Data infrastructure toolbox items (hardware, software, and services).

In addition to the hardware, software, and services such as cloud found in the data infrastructure toolbox, there are different techniques and approaches for using them in various ways. Companions to the tools and techniques, along with policies and best practices leveraging tradecraft experiences, are people with different roles, focuses, and skills across various domains.

Additional terms and context for this chapter include the context of different application and workload environments. This includes applications such as SAP, M1, and other ERP, financials, Cachè medical and Dexis Dental healthcare; statistical analysis software (SAS), Tensorflow, Hadoop, and MapReduce-enabled big data analytics. Additional application workloads include IoT, AI/ML, cognitive, Oracle, Microsoft SQL Server, Cassandra, MongoDB, HBase, and TokuDB, among many other databases and repositories. Still another context for landscapes refers to *greenfield* (i.e., starting from scratch, brand-new, nothing exists so start fresh) as well as *brownfield* (i.e., something exists, needs to evolve, be migrated, be converted).

Host is another term that requires some context. Host can refer to a physical server configured with a hypervisor that hosts guest virtual machines; or it can be a nonvirtualized server that hosts different applications, also known as a server. Another variation is that some people use the term for the cloud, the web, or other services hosting, or even as a variation of co-location or where your servers, storage, network, and other data infrastructure resources are housed. Thus context matters for the host.

We have discussed efficiency (e.g., utilization, space optimization, data footprint reduction, and savings) as well as effectiveness (e.g., productivity, performance, doing more work, removing waste) as being different yet complementary. Something similar is the idea of needs and wants, two items that often get interchanged along with requirements.

Tip: Think of needs as what you must have, i.e., mandatory requirements, while wants are what you would like to have, secondary or lower on the requirement list. Also keep in mind what are your needs and must have requirements vs. what are the wants of others (what they want or perhaps need you to have). Where wants and needs come into play is across various data infrastructure management activities including configuration and resource decision making among others.

Another distinction to mention here is vertical and horizontal integration. Vertical integration means that resources, tools, and technologies are aligned, with interoperability up and down the data infrastructure stack, from high to a low level (or altitude) and vice versa. Horizontal integration, on the other hand, as its name implies, spans across different resources tightly or loosely integrated including federated. Context matters in that technology and tools can be vertically (or horizontal) aligned. However, some vendors also have vertical integration. Vertical integration for a vendor or supplier simply means they have streamlined their own resources and supply chain, removing complexity and costs while simplifying things for their customers across different layers.

Automation, orchestration, data infrastructure and IT coordination of resources may exist across vertical or horizontal and federated resources and across different application landscapes and environments. Later in the chapter, we will look at some of the sources for data and metrics that matter as well as provide insight awareness. These telemetry data (i.e., metrics) come from various hardware, software, and services with a different focus. Sources of metrics that matter can come from servers, storage, I/O networking, application or data infrastructure, and event logs. Additional insight and metrics sources include shims, sniffers, analyzers, trace, collectors, drivers, hardware, and probes as well as taps. Speaking of telemetry, as a refresher, the term refers to an event, activity, or other data such as logs, performance, availability, access, or security, among others.

Framework, orchestration, dashboards, and key performance indicators (KPI) can align to different resource layers and functionality. In some situations, tools such as Splunk and others are used for enabling big data analytics along with the correlation of telemetry and other data infrastructure as well as broader data center events. Data infrastructure analytics, Artificial Intelligence (AI), deep and machine learning, along with IT service management (ITSM), performance management databases (PMDB), configuration and change management databases (CMDB), along with other data center infrastructure management (DCIM) tools, are essentially the IT systems used by data infrastructures, data centers, and information factories. These various tools and insight metrics track the productivity, resource inventory, costs, quality, on-time, and customer satisfaction of services.

A few more terms and context include *day one* and *day two* nomenclature, which refers to the user or customer experience at different points in time. For example, on day one a technology is delivered, with perhaps initial setup, configuration, and integration along with various integrity and health checks. Day two can refer to what's next: The technology or solution is made ready for use and broader deployment, advanced configuration, provisioning as part of the data infrastructure. Depending on the size, scope, and complexity, some things may be accomplished on day one or day two, while others might span additional days, weeks, or months.

Considerations, tips, and recommendations include:

- *Customer* and *user* can mean different things at various levels of the data infrastructure.
- What is below a given level (or altitude) is considered infrastructure to those above it.
- Those above a given altitude can be thought of users or customers of that layer.
- Understand the context of different terms, as everything is not the same.
- Good management and decisions need insight and awareness via metrics.
- The best metrics are those applicable to your needs vs. somebody else's wants.
- Data infrastructures reside in data centers and other habitats for technology facilities.

3.3. Data Infrastructure Habitats and Facilities

Data infrastructure is the collection of hardware, software, services, people, processes, practices, and policies that combine to support different application workloads. Data centers, also known as habitats of or for technology, are where data infrastructures reside. If you prefer the stack or layering model, data infrastructures sit below information infrastructures (e.g., business applications), and on top of data center facilities and their associated infrastructures.

Similar to a traditional factory, information factories are the collection of application workloads and their data supported by a data infrastructure that resides in a data center. Often the broad term *data center* (aka availability zone [AZ]) is used to refer to data infrastructures, while to others it can be the applications and data infrastructure, yet for others it is a facility physical (or cloud) focus.

Tip: When you hear the term or expression *software-defined data center* (SDDC), its context is the data infrastructure (i.e., SDDI or software-defined data infrastructure). Note that in Figure 3.2, the physical data center (i.e., the habitat for technology) is where data infrastructures are deployed into or hosted from. Collectively, the physical data center, data infrastructure, and applications along with the data they support are *information factories* whose product is information and services.

IT, service provider (SP), and cloud data centers are habitats housing data infrastructure (servers, storage, networks, hardware, software, and applications), also known as information factories. These technologies are defined to support various business applications that transform data into information services.

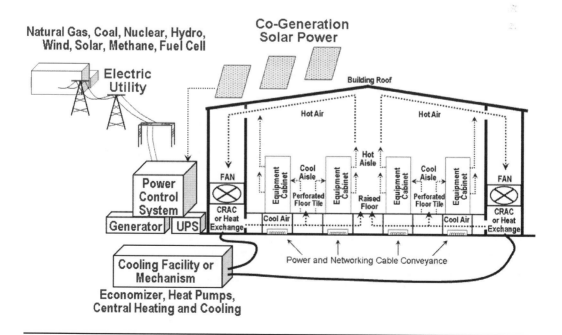

Figure 3.2   Data centers, availability zone (AZ), and habitats for technology.

Similar to a traditional factory that transforms material and components using various tools, technologies, and processes housed inside a facility, data centers or AZ and their data infrastructure, plus information infrastructures and their applications, enable a similar capability (e.g., function as an information factory to deliver information services). While the goods and services that are delivered differ between traditional and information factories, what is common to either is having insight and awareness. The common insight and awareness is into available resources, productivity (effectiveness), utilization (efficiency), errors and rework, quality, cost, service delivery, and customer satisfaction.

Tip: Factories rely on insight, awareness, and metrics to know whether resources are being used cost-effectively (productive) and efficiently (eliminate waste, remove costs). Having insight also enables knowing how to reconfigure technology, implement new services and processes, as well as boost productivity, deliver services on-time, and return on investment, while improving customer satisfaction.

Habitats for technology include physical, cloud, co-located, shared, your own or others, big or small. Technology topics for data center facilities (i.e., habitats for technology) include primary and secondary electrical power, switching, floor space and floor weight loading, cabinet and rack height, as well as cable (I/O and networking along with power) conveyance. Additional topics include heating, ventilation, and air conditioning (HVAC), smoke and fire detection, notification and suppression, humidity and antistatic resources, and physical security.

Considerations, tips, and recommendations include:

- Understand the relationship between data infrastructure resources and facilities.
- Work with data center and facilities staff to understand each other's needs (and wants).

3.4. Data Infrastructure Management

For some, the focus of management is analytics, AI/ML/DL, automation, cloud-based, DevOp centric, GUI, CLI, SSH, PowerShell, API, HTML5, and other interfaces for doing and monitoring things. For others, the focus is broader, including what needs to be done, as well as how it is (or can be) done, along with associated tools. Management tasks, tools, techniques, technologies, trends, and topics focus areas include many things that start with "R" and "Re" (among other letters). For example, RAID, RAIN, re-balance, re-build, re-construct, re-cover, re-host, re-inflate, reliance, reload, repair, re-platform, replicate, resiliency, resolve, resources, restart, restore, resume, re-sync, re-transmit, review, revoke, risks, roll-back, roll-forward, and roll-out, among others. Note that data infrastructure management tasks, topics, tools, and techniques are not exclusive to things that start with the letter "R," as there are many other activities and focus areas as well.

Examples of common data infrastructure management activities include:

- Portals, dashboards, service offering menus, and catalogs
- Orchestration and coordination, allocation, provisioning (self and automated)

- Monitor, collect, analysis, insight, report on events, alarms, activity, and usage
- Diagnose, detect, analysis, correlate, isolate, or identify real vs. false problems
- Planned and unplanned maintenance, repair, replace, remediation, and fix
- Configure, setup, modify, change, update, reclaim, and clean up
- Resource, application workload and data assessment, classification, optimize, and tuning
- Upgrades, replacement, expansion, refresh, disposition of technology resources
- Protect, preserve, secure, audit, and implement governance of data and resources
- Maintenance, migration, conversion of systems, data centers, applications, and data

Additional tasks include decision making for the above as well as other areas of focus: strategy and planning, performance and capacity planning, architecture and engineering. Other tasks include establishing best practices, automation and physical policies, templates, workflows, deployment or implementation guidelines, and cookbooks or template recipes.

Tip: Different management tasks have various impacts on the data infrastructure, resources, and applications. Monitoring should not have a negative impact: it should be passive. However enabling additional detailed debug, trace, and troubleshooting telemetry and log data could have an impact on performance while benefiting troubleshooting. Making changes to a component, system, service, or some aspect of the data infrastructure may have adverse effects if it is not done properly. Part of data infrastructure management tasks is understanding the impact of doing something along with what granularity that may provide a benefit versus having an adverse impact (and on what items).

Figure 3.3 shows various focus areas for data infrastructure, both legacy as well as software-defined, physical, virtual, and cloud. Note the different layers from higher-altitude application

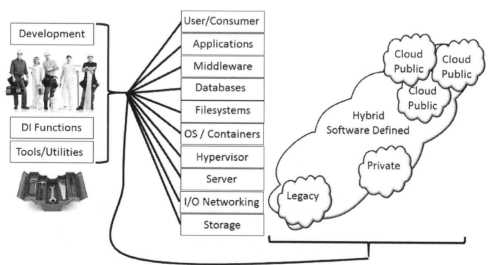

DI Functions = Data Infrastructure Functions (Provision, Define, Remediate, Repair, Plan, Protect, Optimize)

Figure 3.3 Various data infrastructure management focus areas.

Figure 3.4   Dashboard using Datadog software-defined management tools.

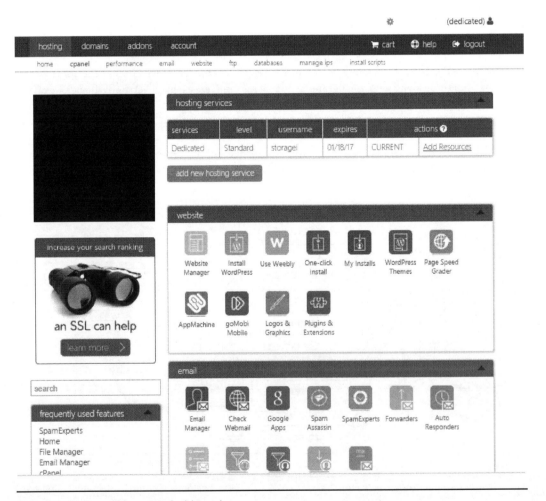

Figure 3.5   Cpanel hosting dashboard.

focus to lower-level data infrastructure resource components spanning different technology domains. Remember that there are different meanings for domains in IT, data centers, and data infrastructures, so context is important.

The next examples move from a higher level to a lower level across technologies.

Figure 3.4 shows a dashboard (Datadog) that spans various layers of data infrastructure resources from lower-level (lower-altitude) virtual machines to higher-altitude (higher-level) applications. With tools such as Datadog, you define the software tool as to what to monitor and collect data about, as well as how and when to display results. In other words, tools like Datadog are software-defined management tools created by people leveraging their tradecraft, skills, and experience to meet the needs of a given software-defined data infrastructure.

Figure 3.5 shows a dashboard (cPanel) for hosting such as websites, blogs, email, and other items. This could be a shared hosting dashboard view, serverless, bare metal (BM) aka physical machine, Metal as a Service (MaaS), a virtual private server (VPS), or a dedicated private server (DPS). Various management functions from provisioning to configuration, monitoring, reporting, troubleshooting, and diagnostics as new feature enablement can be done from the dashboard.

Figure 3.6 shows another cloud-based dashboard and service catalog, this being Amazon Web Services (AWS). Different regions can be selected, along with account and billing information, health status reporting, as well as resource and service provisioning, configuration, and monitoring—for example, accessing Elastic Cloud Compute (EC2) to set up, start, or access compute instances (virtual machines), or access and use Simple Storage Services (S3) or Route 53 networking, among others.

Other orchestration and management functions that can be done via service dashboards include setting up health and resource checks—for example, setting up a health check to monitor the status of various service endpoints or IP addresses. Should a fault be detected, notification can be sent, and some tools can automatically repair. Other tools can make dynamic

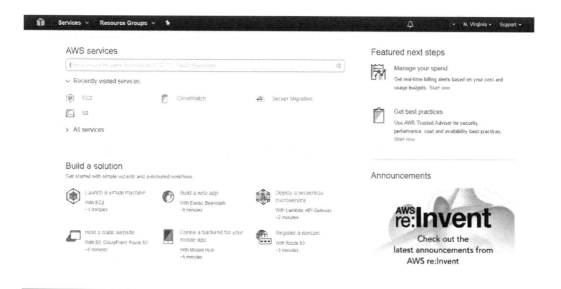

Figure 3.6   AWS service catalog dashboard.

Figure 3.7   Dell EMC Unisphere storage system management.

changes to DNS as well as work with load balancers among other technologies. Additionally, alarms and event notification can be set up for resource usage, activity, performance, availability, capacity consumption, or billing notices. Other tasks include provisioning, remediation, and service management, among others.

Tip: Remember to power down your cloud servers as well as clean up resources when you are done with a project. This can mean taking a snapshot of a server or volume from the primary cloud to object, blob, or other bulk storage. Also remember that if you are done using a database, table, or other resource, clean it up or you might encounter some billing surprises.

Figure 3.7 moves from the cloud to storage, which could be on-site physical hardware-hosted (wrapped) or software-defined. In this example, Dell EMC Unisphere storage management tool accesses and shows the status of a Dell EMC Unity storage array. Note that this particular system is a software-defined virtual storage array (VSA) in which the Unity software is running as a guest virtual machine (VM) on a VMware vSphere host.

The Unisphere software management tools enable orchestration of storage system functions, provisioning, allocation and host access, data protection, and monitoring, among other tasks. From an old-school standpoint, Unisphere and tools like it are sometimes called element or device managers. New-school tools such as Unisphere are sometimes called platform-focused orchestration, federated management, or other software-defined management themes.

Management interfaces and focus include:

- Vendor-specific, third-party, and industry standard interfaces
- A single pane of glass (screen) or multiple views or windows
- Web- and GUI-based, including HTML5-enabled and Wizards
- SSH, CLI, shell, PowerShell, and PowerCLI, among other scripts
- HTTP REST and other API-based, SNMP MIBS, and SMIS, agent and agentless

- MQTT and AMQP, among others, for IoT/IoD scenarios
- Large-scale or small-focused, consumer, SMB, SME, enterprise, or other
- On-premise or cloud-based tools (works on premise but from cloud)
- Cross-technology domain and focus (different layers of the data infrastructure stack)

Note that operating systems, hypervisors, file systems, volume managers, instance, image, databases, software-defined networks, and software-defined storage, among others, are also often considered to be management tools, as well as security, backup, and data protection, among others. Thus context and area of focus for "management software" and tools matter.

Some familiar and perhaps new technologies and tools to add to your toolbox or buzzword vocabulary for various functional areas include Ansible, Apt, AWS cloud watch, Blue Medora, Chef, Curl, Datadog, Docker, dpkg, Uila, Densify, and Komprise. Additional tools include Kubernetes, along with cloud services (AKS-Azure, EKS-AWS, GKE-Google, PKS-VMware/Pivotal). Other tools include MaaS, Mesos, Github, Microsoft MAP, OpenStack Horizon and Ceilometer, PowerShell and PowerCLI, Puppet, Saltstack, Splunk, Swarm, Windows Admin Center, System Center, ARM and WMI, UCS Director, vRealize, VUM and wget, as well as Yarn and Yum, among others. There are also various tools and libraries for cognitive AI/ML/DL, including Tensorflow and mlperf (benchmark) for on-prem as well as cloud based. IoT also has management tools from device control, configuration, and security, as well as deployment, including hubs, gateways, and portals. There are also real-time operating systems from various sources, including AWS and Microsoft, among others, who have created SDK and platforms for developers. Besides the tools (programs), there are also patches, updates, installation and other software kits, including .bin, .ova, .ovf, exe, .iso, .img, .vhdx, .pkg, .zip, .vib, and .msi, among many others.

Considerations, tips, and recommendations include:

- Some tools are for fee and require additional dependent software (or hardware).
- Other tools are for fee, but interoperable with no extra costs for plug-ins.
- There are also free and community as well as other open-source software.
- Do plug-ins, drivers, and modules for interoperability or extra functionality exist?
- There are tools for collecting, analysis, correlating, storing, and visualizing metrics.
- Tools can be installed on physical, virtual, container, or cloud resources.
- Tools can be hosted via clouds, as well as used for managing clouds.

3.5. Troubleshooting, Problem Solving, Remediation, and Repairs

Another aspect of data infrastructure management includes troubleshooting, problem solving, remediation, and repair. This aspect ranges from simple common problems, with easy fixes for known issues, to more complex and involved issues. Some remediation and repairs are in response to problems, others are proactive as well as to implement changes.

General troubleshooting, problem-solving, and diagnostic questions include: Are other data infrastructure and IT personnel or vendors seeing the same issues? Can the problem be forced to occur, or is it transient and random? Are devices and systems on-line, powered on, or need to be reset? Is the problem isolated and repeatable, occurring at a known time or continuously?

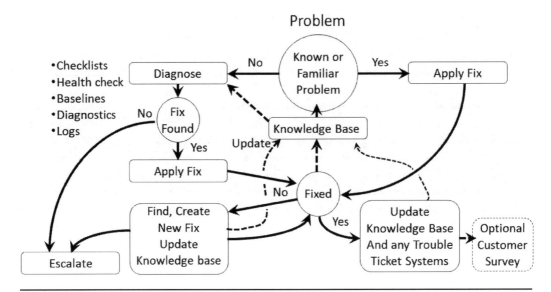

Figure 3.8   Generic simple troubleshooting flow tree.

Is the issue or problem unique to your environment or widespread and affect others? If the hardware or service is ok, what about various data infrastructure or applications software—Is it on-line, available, or need a restart?

Figure 3.8 shows a simple generic troubleshooting decision-making tree that can applied and extended to meet different environment needs.

Additional general troubleshooting and remediation tasks questions include:

- What happens if you force a device rescan or refresh?
- What is working and what is not? Is the problem isolated or widespread?
- Where is the problem? What do your logs and event monitors indicate?
- Who or what is causing the problem? Who is not seeing the problem?
- When did the problem start, or reappear if it has been seen before?
- Are resources up to date with current software, drivers, firmware, and BIOS/UEFI?

Tip: As part of troubleshooting and remediation, as well as being proactive, check with vendors or have them notify you of urgent mandatory updates, as well as recommended upgrades. This should also include resources such as batteries, power supplies, and other not-so-obvious items as well as higher-level software, firmware, and drivers. While it should be obvious and common sense, also have a fall back, fail-back plan with which you can go back to a point in time before problems occurred. Once you have fallen off of the change, reassess and determine where the issue is and plan to try again.

General tips and recommendations include: Is this a now familiar scenario, recurring, transient problem, or something new? What are others seeing and experiencing? What is normal vs. abnormal; do you have a baseline to compare with? What changed; when did something break and stop working? Similarly, something may have been working before but not as well as you thought, and something changed to amplify or make the issue known.

What test and diagnostic tools do you have, and how familiar are you (or somebody in your organization) with using them? Are your different systems and components, from servers to storage, networking, and others, set to the proper data and time? Are license keys, security and authentication certificates, and subscriptions valid and up to date or about to expire? Avoid finger-pointing by having good information, insight, and awareness tools to work proactively with others, or use that information to defend your findings.

Additional general tips and recommendations include:

- Keep good notes, cheat sheets, run books, and other documents.
- Leverage bash, shell, or PowerShell, among other scripts, for common tasks.
- Scripts are also a good way to document processes, and to prevent typos.
- Utilize versioning, snapshots, and PIT copies when doing builds and testing.
- When doing installations, pay attention and watch out for typos (yours and others).

Do you have a problem reporting and trouble ticket tracking system? How about checklists and automated scripts to detect or collect information about known or common problems? What do you have for a preventive and planned maintenance schedule for updates (hardware, software, services)? How frequently do you update software and firmware on various devices?

Are your systems kept at current software and firmware release levels? Alternatively, do your systems stay one or more steps behind current release levels? Are hot fixes applied, or do you wait for regularly scheduled updates if possible? How are software and firmware updates tested and verified before deployment? Will a fix or workaround cause problems elsewhere or a problem to return?

Some I/O- and networking-related topics include: Is the problem local to a server, storage, system, service, or network segment? Is it isolated to a site or facility, location, or geography? Is it all network traffic, or specific ports (TCP, UDP), protocols, or types of traffic? Are there bad cables, physical ports, connectors, interposers, transposers, or other devices?

Tip: Set up a centralized event and activity logging repository where logs are collected and protected (backed up) on some specific time interval to enable later restoration. Leverage log insight and other analysis tools including Splunk, VMWare loginsight, as well as operating system, hypervisor, and third-party or open-source tools. Create an information base (infobase), knowledge base, or other venue for tracking known issues, symptoms, workarounds, and remediation.

It may seem obvious, but check if affected devices along with their ports (physical and logical), adapters, HBA, NIC, switches, or routers are powered off, or not properly configured. Are there issues with software configurations and definitions, such as missing IP gateways, or DNS or DHCP settings? Are the network and I/O issues consistent or intermittent? Is there a pattern to correlate when errors occur? What are the error logs and other telemetry data indicating? Are MTU and jumbo frames set correctly, as well as firewall and iptables ports properly enabled (or disabled)? Also check your virtual private cloud (VPC), virtual private network (VPN), and firewall (local as well as cloud or CDN) to verify that proper ports, protocols, and IP addresses are enabled or being allowed.

Tip: Establish a trouble ticket and tracking system to log, even in a spreadsheet, incidents, what happened, how they were resolved, date and time, along with other information. This log can be used to analyze for trends as well as to plan for future upgrades, remediation, and other changes. Also, establish your health check, status, and diagnostics, including capturing relevant logs, metrics, and configurations to aid in problem resolution. As part of the diagnostics, you can also eliminate what is working and focus on what is not and why the problem is occurring.

Additional I/O and general networking items to look at include:

- What changed, when, and where; what are the event logs indicating?
- What do network traffic displays show or indicate?
- What are your VLAN, VPN, VPC, firewall (or iptables), and load balancer settings?
- For cloud resource access, do you have proper inbound or outbound addresses?
- Are proper security certificates valid and access keys in place?
- Is there a network bandwidth service provider hardware or software issue?

Server-related topics include hardware as well as software configuration, setup and settings, driver or version mismatch, device or driver conflicts, physical and logical connections. Other server considerations include:

- Higher-level software and drivers, including hypervisors and operating systems
- Utilize various hypervisor, operating system, and related tools.
- If a server or VM will not boot, check GPT and MBR, as well as BIOS and UEFI settings.
- Verify software license or subscriptions are valid and have not timed out.

Availability, data protection, security, and backup topics include: Can you restore the contents of a storage device or medium (e.g., SSH, PMEM, SCM, NAND flash, and other SSD, HDD, tape, or optical)? This means can you access the stored data and restore it to some other medium? Are you then able to read and use the restored data, or does it need to be decrypted, security certificates applied? Are permissions, access control, and other attributes preserved and restored to expected settings?

Additional availability and data protection along with security topics include:

- Has a resource to be protected (name, address, endpoint) been moved?
- Is there enough free space on the target device or destination, or is there a quota or limit?
- Are backups or protection copies taking longer than normal due to there being more data?
- Did protection copies run faster than normal even though there was more data?
- Did a backup, snapshot, or other protection task fail due to open files in use?
- Are there network, server, storage, or other issues causing problems?
- What protection and availability tasks worked? Which failed and when?

Can you access files (read and write), local or remote, with firewall enabled or disabled? Can you ping remote devices and endpoints? Can you *nmap–v* a server or storage to see what ports are open or available? What happens if you try to ping the DNS or another known name local or remote? Can you create a local file? If not, can you do more than an *ls* or display of a file or its directory and metadata? What are the file ownership and permissions (i.e., on Linux, do a *ls – al*).

Storage-related problem-solving, troubleshooting, and diagnostics topics span from hardware to software and services, similar to servers and networking. Can you access or see the storage system, device, endpoint, volume, LUN, file system from different systems, or only certain ones? Are you able to log in or access storage systems or software-defined storage software management tools, and what are you able to observe, including any health, status, or error log messages?

Are there any other current issues or problems with networks, servers, or other data infrastructure activities and problems? If the device is not shared, can you reset it, or force a scan from the operating system or hypervisor to see if the device appears? What happens if you reboot the server operating system or hypervisor? Also verify if firmware, BIOS/UEFI, drivers and other software are up to date.

Other considerations include: Is there a device name, address, letter, ID, or mount point conflict? Is there a missing mount point, directory, or folder preventing the device from mounting properly? Is there a problem with incorrect security or permissions? What changed? Did the storage work before? Is the device (hardware or software-defined) stuck in a state that prevents it from being re-initialized, or is software enabled as read-only? (See the Appendix for some possible workarounds.) If an operating system command does not work, what happens if you run in Administrator mode (Windows) or sudo (Linux)? Are permissions and access control as well as ownership configured as expected and needed?

Additional storage-related items include:

- If it is a new device, has the volume or file system been initialized, prepared, exported?
- NAS- and IP-related: Is the DNS working? Can you ping and do other things?
- What is appearing in event and error logs?
- What about access controls and certificates—Are they valid or missing?
- Various tools such as Windows diskpart and Linux fdisk and gparted can be useful.
- How much free space exists on the different storage devices?
- If a Linux command does not work, try running in sudo mode.

Cloud-related items include:

- Do you have a proper endpoint or address for service or resources?
- Do you have the proper access keys and security certificates?
- Are network ports and firewall settings configured for inbound and outbound?
- Are you using HTTP or https as part of your endpoint and applicable ports?

File systems, databases, and other data repository issues include:

- Verify that the database server instance and database are running.
- Check whether network access ports, named pipes, and endpoints are configured.
- Review local and remote access settings, including firewall and user authentication.
- Are the tempdb and other database items full, or on a device that is full?
- Are the main database tables and log files on a slow device or one that is full?

- Does the database server have enough memory allocated to its buffers?
- What are the logs and other telemetry data indicating?
- If you have test SQL queries, what results do they show?

Figure 3.9 shows various data infrastructure and application focus areas as well as layers on the left. On the right of Figure 3.9 is a focus on hypervisors with VMware vSphere using various tools to gain insight into performance, availability, and capacity along with configuration. Different tools provide various levels of detail and insight as well as help correlate what is causing issues, where the problem exists, or perhaps where it does not exist.

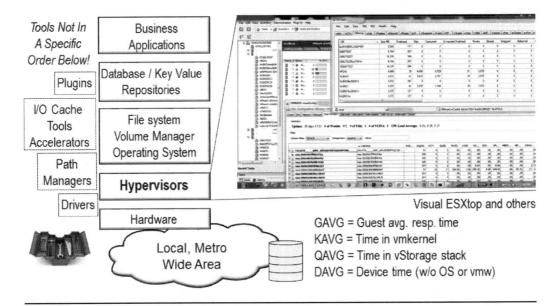

Figure 3.9   Data infrastructure focus layers.

Tip: Sometimes, quickly identifying where the problem does not exist, or where there is no impact, can streamline problem resolution. Eliminating where there is no issue or problem can help bring focus to the area where the problem exists, or what is causing or amplifying it to be an issue. Also pay attention to moving problems—when you fix in one location and something happens elsewhere.

Figure 3.10 shows, on the left, status information for a four-node Ceph software-defined storage cluster using commands such as *ceph health, ceph osd tree,* and *ceph–s.* On the right of Figure 3.10 is a status display from a Microsoft Failover Cluster health and configuration check. The Microsoft Failover Cluster tool checks hardware and software configuration, pointing out issues, problems, and configuration items to address before creating a cluster (or that might prevent a cluster from being created).

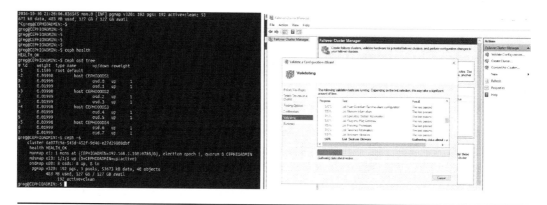

Figure 3.10   Ceph Status (left) and Microsoft Windows Cluster Health check (right).

Figure 3.11 shows a VMware and vSAN health status display. Note that all of the alerts and alarms shown point out abnormal conditions such as when something fails (or introduces a fault for training, or learning). Various alarm conditions via vCenter for a VMware vSAN are shown—for example, where the nodes (hosts) have been disconnected (hence why the errors) due to a network issue.

Figure 3.11   VMware vSAN health and status.

Tip: Are devices properly plugged into electrical power and I/O network connections? Double-check the obvious to make sure components are properly connected or determine loose and weak connections. Sometimes a device may be plugged into power or a network connection and may need to be simply unplugged for 15–30 seconds or a minute, then reconnected—magically, things may start to work (though not always).

Do you have basic and advanced troubleshooting scripts and diagnostics tools? Tools that can check and verify connectivity to services and resources? Ability to investigate performance responsiveness against known behavior? For example, scripts that can access management ports or services to get health, status, and event activity logs or information to help isolate and determine problems. Another example is whether you can ping a device, system, or service locally as well as remotely to verify network connectivity, DNS and routing, as well as firewalls and iptables configurations.

Tip: Make sure not to unplug the wrong device! In addition to making sure power cords, I/O, and network interfaces are securely connected, are they attached to the proper ports, devices, adapters, or network components? Also remember to label cables and devices so you know what they are for.

Tip: Error and event logs for Windows systems can be found in the *%SystemRoot%\system32\winevt\logs* directory folder and accessed via the Event Viewer via Control Panel or the command line using *C:\ eventvwr.* Logs and events for the local system are displayed, as well as access to remote Windows computers activity using the Action Tab from Event Viewer. Note that you may need to do some firewall and other configuration changes to use remote capabilities. Figure 3.12 shows an example of Windows Event Viewer; note the Action Tab at top left, which can be used to access remote computers. Additional troubleshooting activities include:

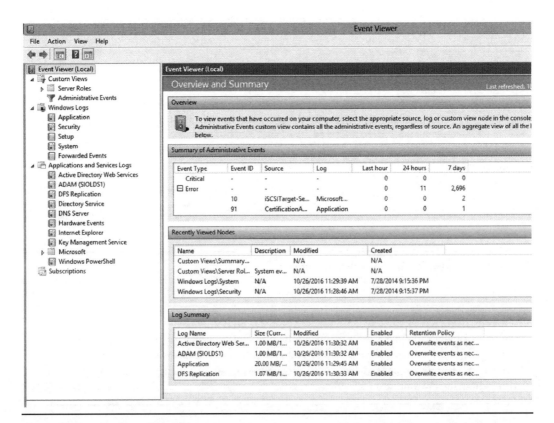

Figure 3.12   Windows Event Viewer.

- Has storage or memory space been exceeded (no free space, or quota limits)?
- Did a resource move to a new location and some task is looking in the old place?
- Are timeouts occurring while a service or resources wait on something?
- What are the symptoms or issues? Is one person or system affected, or everybody?
- What changed, when, where, and by whom?
- What's different now vs. before the problem?
- Is the problem known and isolated, or yet to be determined?
- Is the fault isolated, or is it being triggered by some other event?
- What are your indicators (logs, event notification, error counters) showing?
- Do you have optional debugging and trace modes that generate more telemetry (log and event) data that you can enable for troubleshooting (remember to disable when done)?

Tip: On Linux systems, look in the /var/log directory folder (and subfolders) for various logs. You can use commands such as (among others) *less, grep, more, cat, ls,* and *tail* of a specific log file. For example (unless they have been moved), if you have MySQL installed, look in /var/log/mysql, or for OpenStack, compute /var/log/nova, or /var/log/ceph for Ceph. Figure 3.13 shows a directory listing "*ls /var/log*" of various logs and subfolders, followed by a "*tail /var/log/messages*" to display some log event activity.

```
[greg@centio02 ~]$
[greg@centio02 ~]$ ls /var/log
anaconda   cron        lastlog              pcsd       secure              wtmp
audit      cups        libvirt              pluto      speech-dispatcher   Xorg.0.log
boot.log   dmesg       maillog              ppp        spooler             Xorg.0.log.old
btmp       dmesg.old   messages             qemu-ga    tallylog            yum.log
chrony     gdm         openlmi-install.log  sa         tuned
cluster    glusterfs   pcp                  samba      wpa_supplicant.log
[greg@centio02 ~]$ sudo tail /var/log/messages
Oct 29 17:13:02 centio02 dbus-daemon: dbus[707]: [system] Activating via systemd: servi
ce name='net.reactivated.Fprint' unit='fprintd.service'
Oct 29 17:13:02 centio02 dbus[707]: [system] Activating via systemd: service name='net.
reactivated.Fprint' unit='fprintd.service'
Oct 29 17:13:02 centio02 systemd: Starting Fingerprint Authentication Daemon...
Oct 29 17:13:02 centio02 dbus[707]: [system] Successfully activated service 'net.reacti
vated.Fprint'
Oct 29 17:13:02 centio02 systemd: Started Fingerprint Authentication Daemon.
Oct 29 17:13:02 centio02 dbus-daemon: dbus[707]: [system] Successfully activated servic
e 'net.reactivated.Fprint'
Oct 29 17:13:02 centio02 fprintd: ** (fprintd:26337): WARNING **: fprint init failed wi
th error -99
Oct 29 17:13:02 centio02 systemd: fprintd.service: main process exited, code=exited, st
atus=157/n/a
Oct 29 17:13:02 centio02 systemd: Unit fprintd.service entered failed state.
Oct 29 17:13:02 centio02 systemd: fprintd.service failed.
[greg@centio02 ~]$
```

Figure 3.13   Centos Linux event logs.

Some network tasks for gaining insight, awareness, and testing configurations include:

- What are your event and activity logs indicating?
- Can you ping your known resources by name or IP address?
- Can you ping your DNS servers or another known address such as 8.8.8.8?

- Windows *ipconfig /all* along with *ipconfig /release* as well as *ipconfig /renew*
- On Linux systems, instead of using *ipconfig*, use *ifconfig*, among other tools
- Some additional Linux tools for testing and troubleshooting networks include:
    - Perform an arp scan on a network interface such as eth0: *arp-scan –I eth0 –l*
    - Display network mapping info on a network: *nmap –sP 192.168.0.0/20*
    - *Netstat* along with *lshw –class network* or *arping –I eth0 –c 5 192.168.1.1*
    - *nmap -sS -sU -PN -p 1-500 66.33.99.11* to see open ports on a device

---

Tip: If you are going to ping a resource, make sure that it allows being pinged, to avoid chasing a false error. In other words, if you ping something and it does not support ping (or ping is disabled), you may in fact not have an error, or the error is occurring elsewhere.

As an example, suppose there is a performance problem with the server and storage system such that the application slows down. Someone might say that he has a problem with his database storage server and that he has Cisco, Dell, HPE, IBM, Oracle, or some other. Is he referring to a server, storage system (or appliance), hardware or software, network, or other data infrastructure resource? Context matters!

Let's say some additional questions and insight determines that the application is a database on Linux, and the storage is dual-pathed. However, the application slows down. Ask some questions, such as what type of storage, SAS, NVMe and NVMeoF, Gen-Z, PCIe, iSCSI, or FC. Sometimes the answer might be a specific vendor, make, and model, while at other times the answer might be generic such as a Dell EMC, Fujitsu, HDS, HPE, IBM, NetApp, Nutanix, Oracle, Pure, Quantum, Seagate, or a product from another vendor. If the vendor has only one product, that narrows things down. On the other hand, if, for example, somebody says it is a Dell EMC, then it could be ECS, SC (Compellent), Datadomain, Isilon, PowerMax (formerly known as VMAX), VNX, ScaleIO, Unity, or XtremIO, among others. Another example is if somebody says they have an NVMe or NVMeoF storage. What is the context? Is it a NVMe U.2 (8639) drive, M.2 (e.g., NGFF "gum stick") PCIe card, or NVMeoF using Fibre Channel, RoCE, or IP, among others. Likewise, somebody might say the storage is fiber attached to a server; instead of assuming it is Fibre Channel, verify whether it is Gb Ethernet (or 10 GbE or faster) supporting iSCSI or NAS, or something else.

When running on one path, things are ok; however, when running on both paths, things are not ok. So, what path driver is being used? What happens if you failover to the other path: Can you run on path A ok, or path B, but not on path A and path B at the same time? What do you see in the system and storage error logs? Are IOs being shipped to a different node or controller for processing? What's normal behavior?

Tools, technology, and techniques include:

- Note that, in addition to automating tasks, scripts also serve to document activity.
- Use tools including hardware and software probes, sniffers, tracers, and analyzers
- Leverage change management to fall back or off from a change.
- Use automated tools and scripts including health checks to verify current status.
- Revert to a previous version, PIT snapshot, copy, or backup:

○ Different granularity from application to system or device
○ Application and database checkpoints and consistency points
○ Snapshots and other PIT copies or recovery-point protection

---

Tip: Creating a baseline of your environment can be as simple as having a report, graphic, image, or other information of what is normal vs. abnormal behavior. This can be from an application and workload perspective, such as how many users are normal, amount of CPU, memory, and storage space consumed, network activity, and I/O performance.

Other baseline indicators include normal number of errors or other log entry activity, response time for different application functions, and configuration. Response time can be measured by applications or data infrastructure tools, or as simply as with a stopwatch (real or virtual). The point is that you can start simple and evolve into a more complex baseline. A more complex baseline would include scripts that collect and compare logs, events, resource usage, and activity. For databases, this can include diagnostic or other transactions that can be run to see if they work, and how long they take.

General considerations include:

- Establish a baseline to compare normal and abnormal behavior of the environment.
- Implement test and diagnostics tools along with scripts for automated fault isolation.
- Leverage planning and analytics tools to test and simulate workload changes.
- Utilize automated tools for proactive and reactive problem isolation.
- Do root-cause analysis: what caused the problem, how to fix it, and how to prevent it from reoccurring in the future.

Considerations, tips, and recommendations include:

- Have a test system and lab environment that can be used in support of problem-solving.
- Start with the simple and basic; leverage automation where possible.
- Compare with known experiences; utilize your knowledge base and tradecraft.
- Conduct a failure or fault postmortem to capture insight to prevent future incidents.
- Create a knowledge base, wiki, or cheat sheet of troubleshooting hints and tips.

3.6. Common Questions and Tips

What does scale with stability mean? As you scale up and out to expand resources, this should occur without introducing performance bottlenecks, availability points of failure, or excessive resource overhead and management. In other words, as a result of scaling, your data infrastructure should not become unstable, but rather, more stable across PACE and SLO.

Are chargeback and orchestration required for cloud and software-defined environments? Different types of orchestration tools should be leveraged to help with automation of not only cloud but also other software-defined, virtual, and legacy environments. Depending on your environment needs, a chargeback may be applicable, or a showback as a means of conveying or educating users of those services what the associated costs, as well as benefits, are.

What level of audit trails and logging is needed? Maintain audit trails of who has accessed or made copies of data for event analysis. As important as is what you collect, it is also important how you use and preserve logs for analysis or forensic purposes. Leverage automation tools that can proactively monitor activities and events as well as distinguish normal from abnormal behaviors.

Who should be responsible for security? Some organizations have dedicated security groups that set policies, do some research, and do some forensics while leaving actual work to other groups. Some security organizations are more active, with their own budgets, servers, storage, and software. Security needs to be a part of activity early on in application and architecture decision making as well as across multiple technology domains (servers, storage, networking, hardware, and software) and not just via a policy maker in an ivory tower.

3.7. Chapter Summary

Insight enables awareness so you can avoid flying blind with your data infrastructure, including decision making and other management tasks for on-prem as well as public clouds.

General action items include the following:

- Gain insight and awareness of your application workloads and data infrastructure.
- Leverage new and existing technology in new ways vs. using new things in old ways.
- Balance optimization for efficiency utilization vs. productivity and effectiveness.
- Know your tools and how, as well as when, to use them in different ways.
- Decision making applies to acquisition, planning, configuration, and troubleshooting.
- Leverage your expanded or refreshed tradecraft to know what to use when, where, and why.

Chapter 4

Data Infrastructure Availability, Data Protection, Security, and Strategy

Data infrastructures store, protect, preserve, secure, and serve information.

What You Will Learn in This Chapter

- Reliability, availability, and serviceability (RAS), along with data protection
- Accessibility, availability, durability, security, and consistency
- Importance of 4 3 2 1 data protection rule for enabling availability
- Basic and high availability (HA), clustering, and other resiliency topics
- Applications, data, and data infrastructure security (physical and logical)
- Protecting applications and data at various levels, intervals, and granularities

The focus of this chapter is availability (data protection), management, recovery-point protection (e.g., backup, snapshots), security, and associated strategy. Key themes, buzzwords, and trends addressed in this chapter include availability, durability, security, business continuance (BC), business resiliency (BR), disaster recovery (DR), backup, archive, high availability (HA), reliability availability serviceability (RAS), fault domains, faults (or failures) to tolerate (FTT), fault tolerance mode (FTM), RTO, RPO, snapshots, and versions, among others.

4.1. Getting Started

A recurring theme is that everything is not the same in the data center, information factory, data infrastructure, various environments, and applications. However, there are similarities and commonalities both regarding threat risks or things that can and do go wrong from technology failure, human error including misconfiguration, to accidental and intentional acts of man, as well as acts of nature. Remember, if something can go wrong, it probably will at some point—either on its own or with the help (or neglect or mistake) of somebody.

Keep in mind that the fundamental function of data infrastructure is to store, protect, secure, and serve data for applications that transform it into information.

4.2. Data Protection Fundamentals

Let's start this data infrastructure data protection, availability, and security discussion with *backing store.* Backing store has different context and meanings, but there are common themes. The common themes are some software with a back-end persistent, nonephemeral, non-volatile memory or storage where data is written (stored). Data is stored on different physical media or mediums such as NVM, SCM and other SSD, HDD, tape, and optical. The backing store can also be a system or appliance (physical or virtual) where data is stored, as well as a service such as cloud storage.

Another context for backing store can be the software that provides abstraction via different tools, applications, and associated data infrastructure components. This can range from a backing store driver or plug-in for Docker containers enabling persistent storage to persistent memory and storage for in-memory databases, virtual memory, storage back-ends for databases, volume managers, file systems, key value repositories, and other software.

Context matters to understand what is being discussed—hardware, software, cloud, virtual, or other backing store device, tool, application, or utility.

Beyond backing store, some other context includes remembering that delta refers to change, a point in time or the difference between different times, or copies of data. Coverage has a data protection context in what is protected or skipped (i.e., not covered).

Another term you may hear tied to availability, resiliency, data protection, business continuity (BC), business recovery (BR), and disaster recovery (DR), among other activities, is *belt and suspenders.* This simply means having both a belt and a pair of suspenders to be sure that if either fails, the other should keep your pants from falling. The idea is that for some applications, multiple types of data protection, availability, and resiliency are needed to complement each other, as well as in case something fails—for example, using both higher-level application or server software replication along with lower-level storage system or appliance mirroring and replication.

A number of 9's availability or downtime, for example, 99.99 (four nines), indicates the level of availability (downtime does not exceed) objective. For example, 99.99% availability means that in a 24-hour day there could be about 9 seconds of downtime, or about 52 minutes and 34 seconds per year. Note that numbers can vary depending on whether you are using 30 days for a month vs. 365/12 days, or 52 weeks vs. 365/7 for weeks, along with rounding and number decimal places.

Service-level objectives (SLO) are metrics and *key performance indicators* (KPI) that guide meeting performance, availability, capacity, and economic targets—for example, some number of 9's availability or durability, a specific number of transactions per second, or recovery and restart of applications.

A *service-level agreement* (SLA) specifies the various service-level objectives such as PACE requirements including RTO and RPO, among others. SLA can also specify availability objectives as well as penalties or remuneration should SLO be missed.

Recovery-time objective (RTO) is how much time is allowed before applications, data, or data infrastructure components need to be accessible, consistent, and usable. An RTO = 0 (zero) means no loss of access or service disruption, i.e., continuous availability. One example is an application end-to-end RTO of 4 hours, meaning that all components (application server, databases, file systems, settings, associated storage, networks) must be restored, rolled back, and restarted for use in 4 hours or less.

Another RTO example is component level for different data infrastructure layers as well as cumulative or end to end. In this scenario, the 4 hours includes time to recover, restart, and rebuild a server, application software, storage devices, databases, networks, and other items. In this scenario, there are not 4 hours available to restore the database, or 4 hours to restore the storage, as some time is needed for all pieces to be verified along with their dependencies.

Recovery-point objective (RPO) is the point in time to which data needs to be recoverable (i.e., when it was last protected). Another way of looking at RPO is how much data you can afford to lose, with RPO = 0 (zero) meaning no data loss, or, for example, RPO = 5 minutes being up to 5 minutes of lost data.

Data loss access (DLA) occurs when data still exists, is consistent, durable, and safe, but it cannot be accessed due to network, application, or other problem. Note that the inverse is data that can be accessed, but it is damaged.

A *data loss event* (DLE) is an incident that results in loss or damage to data. Note that some context is needed in a scenario in which data is stolen via a copy but the data still exists, vs. the actual data is taken and is now missing (no copies exist).

Data loss prevention (DLP) encompasses the activities, techniques, technologies, tools, best practices, and tradecraft skills used to protect data from DLE or DLA.

Point in time (PIT) refers to a recovery or consistency point where data can be restored from or to (i.e., RPO), such as from a copy, snapshot, backup, sync, or clone. Essentially, as its name implies, it is the state of the data at that particular point in time.

4.3. Availability, Data Protection, and Security

Threats to data infrastructures along with the applications (and data) they support can be physical or logical, such as a data breach or a virus. Different threat risks require multiple rings or layers of defense for various applications, data, and IT resources, including physical security. Data infrastructures rely on both logical and physical security. Logical security includes access controls or user permissions for files, objects, documents, servers, and storage systems, along with authentication, authorization, and encryption of data.

Another aspect of security is to "bleach" (wipe) servers and storage with digital secure erase that does deep cleaning. Digital erase should also provide verification along with optional documentation for compliance, such as a digital certificate of death for the device and your data.

Tip: Know and understand legal and regulatory requirements for your organization as well as applications and data. This includes what applications and data can be located in different geographies for data privacy, among other regulations. Likewise, there are applicable regulations that require you not only to demonstrate having copies of applications and data off-site, but also to demonstrate a restoration in a given amount of time.

Compliance and governance apply to availability, protection, and security to determine who can see or have access to what, when, where, why, and how. This might require solutions in which systems administrators who have root access to systems are blocked from reading or accessing data or even metadata in secured systems. RTO and RPO can be part of regulations and compliance for applications and their data, as well as retention of data, some number of copies, and location of the copies.

Additional availability, data protection, and security topics include subordinated and converged management of shared resources, including AD. Remember to keep mobile and portable media, tablets, and other devices in mind regarding availability as well as security. How will your solutions work with encryption and data footprint reduction tools such as compression, de-dupe, and eDiscovery?

Also keep in mind: Do you have orphaned (forgotten) storage and data or zombie VM (VM that are powered up but are no longer in use)? Have you assessed and classified your applications along with their data in terms of data protection, availability, and security SLO alignment needs? Do you know the number and diversity of telemetry and log files to monitor and analyze how long they will be retained and who has access to them?

General considerations, tips, and recommendations include:

- Have international and multilanguage support via tools and personnel.
- Implement proactive intrusion detection software (IDS) and systems.
- Manage vendors and suppliers as well as their access or endpoints.
- Utilize secure erase (digital bleach) solutions to wipe clean devices for disposition.
- Track physical and logical assets with printed barcodes as well as RFID and QR codes.
- Leverage health checks, automation, proactive data integrity, and virus checks and repairs.
- Implement Data At Rest Encryption (DARE) via servers, storage, devices, and clouds.
- Talk with your compliance and legal experts about what's applicable for your environment.

Additional availability, data protection, and security considerations include:

- Utilize multiple layers of protection, from application to lower-level component.
- Find a balance between higher-level application and lower-level component protection.
- Safeguard your data protection, security, and availability configurations, settings, and keys.
- What are you looking to protect against and why?
- What are your application PACE needs and RPO, RTO, SLO?
- Keep the 4 3 2 1 rule in mind for your different applications.
- Everything is not the same; do you have the same FTT, RTO, RPO, and other SLO?

4.4. Availability (Resiliency and Data Protection) Services

The A in PACE is *availability*, which encompasses many different things, from accessibility, durability, resiliency, reliability, and serviceability (RAS) to security and data protection along with consistency. Availability includes basic, high availability (HA), BC, BR, DR, archiving, backup, logical and physical security, fault tolerance, isolation and containment spanning systems, applications, data, metadata, settings, and configurations.

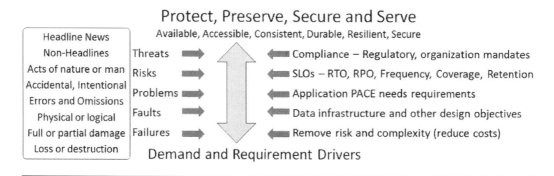

Figure 4.1   Data infrastructure, applications, and data availability points of interest.

From a data infrastructure perspective, availability of data services spans from local to remote, physical to logical and software-defined, virtual, container, and cloud, as well as mobile devices. Figure 4.1 shows various data infrastructure availability, accessibility, protection, and security points of interests (threat risks, threat vectors, attack surface areas and solutions). On the left side of Figure 4.1 are various data protection and security threat risks and scenarios that can impact availability, or result in a DLE, DLA, or disaster. The right side of Figure 4.1 shows various techniques, tools, technologies, and best practices to protect data infrastructures, applications, and data from threat risks.

What this all means is keeping in mind that there are different threat risks or things to protect your data infrastructure, applications and data from, but you also have options. You have the option to treat everything the same or to align the appropriate protection and resiliency to different applications based on their PACE requirements and SLO needs.

There is an industry sales and marketing saying that one should never let a good (or bad) disaster go to waste. This means that when something bad happens and appears in the news, it is no coincidence that you will hear about a need for local or cloud backup, BC, BR, DR, security and antivirus protection, endpoint protection, and resiliency, among other related themes. That is because availability has traditionally been seen as a cost overhead similar to insurance: a necessary expense of doing business rather than a business enabling asset. As a result, some vendors who sell availability and data protection hardware, software, or services tend to do so based on fear of something happening, or what the cost and expense will be if you are left exposed. There is merit to this approach, but so too is selling not just on fear, but also on availability being a business asset and enabler.

Figure 4.2 builds on Figure 4.1 by showing various data infrastructure and application points of interest needing data protection and availability. Also shown in Figure 4.2 are various general techniques that can be used at various data infrastructure layers in combination with others.

4.5. Revisiting 4 3 2 1—The Golden Rule of Data Protection

Everything is not the same; different threat risks require different data protection technologies, tools, and techniques. These tools, technologies, and techniques address threats, risks, and availability concerns at different layers in the data infrastructure stack. Some may be seen as competitive. However, they can also be complementary, for example, using upper-level

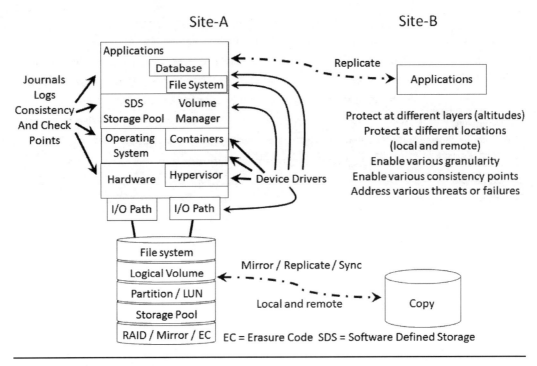

Figure 4.2   Points of availability, accessibility, and durability concerns.

application replication for small, narrow, tight, or synchronous RPOs while using lower-level storage systems, appliances, and software for broader RPOs leveraging asynchronous communications.

Data protection focus is tied to different threat risks or things that can happen, or impact data infrastructure as well as applications and data. For example, things that can go wrong or happen include physical or logical, from damage to deletion and distraction of data or systems. This includes intentional or accidental device and software failures, network and service provider outages, and configuration errors.

Tip: Data loss can be complete (all gone) or partial (some data gone or damaged). Scope, scale, and focus of data protection ranges from geographic region locations to sites and data centers, systems, clusters, stamps, racks, cabinets, shelves, and individual servers or other components (hardware and software). This includes software-defined storage, file systems and volumes, databases, key value repositories, hypervisors, operating systems, and associated configuration settings.

What are your data protection priorities?

- Speed of protection and impact on production work
- Performance impact during recover, rebuild, repair
- Speed of reconstruction, restore, restart, resume service
- Low overhead (performance, space capacity) and cost

- Retention, compliance, regulatory, corporate mandates, disposition
- Least amount of data loss and application impact
- Portability, mobility, flexibility, and relocate ability of data
- Number and types of failures or faults to tolerate (FTT)

Granularity for data protection has different focus areas:

- Application, transaction, database, instance, table, row, or column
- File system, folder, file, bucket or container, blob or object, mailbox
- Data and metadata, application software and settings
- Operating system, virtual machine, hypervisor
- Device, drive, volume, system, appliance, rack, site

Tip: Keep in mind that availability is a combination of accessibility (you can get to the data and applications) and durability (there are good consistent data copies and versions). The *4 3 2 1 golden availability protection rule,* also known by a variation of grandfather, father, son (i.e., generations), encompasses availability being a combination of access, durability, and versions.

What this means is that availability sometimes has a context of simply access: Can you get to the data? Is it there? This is enabled with high availability and fault tolerance, along with mirroring, replication, and other techniques. This might be measured or reported in the number of 9's, or how many hours, minutes, or seconds of downtime per year. Figure 4.3 shows how the 4 3 2 1 rule encompasses and enables SLO, availability and data protection QoS, as well as RTO, RPO, and accessibility.

There are different types of availability data services to enable reliability, accessibility, serviceability, and resiliency (Table 4.1). This means enabling the 4 3 2 1 principle of data protection: having at least four copies (or more) of data, with at least three (or more) versions on two (or more) systems or devices, and at least one of those is off-site (on- or off-line).

One aspect of enabling availability along with facilitating copy management is having multiple copies of data in different locations. However, if those different copies in different locations are all corrupt, damaged, infected, or contain missing or deleted data, then there is a problem—thus the need for multiple versions and timer interval protection.

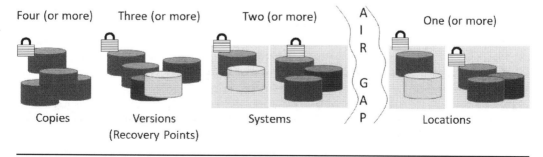

Figure 4.3 The New School 4 3 2 1 data protection best practice rule.

Table 4.1. Fundamental Availability and Resiliency Topics

Reliability, availability, serviceability (RAS)	Power-on self-test (POST), self-healing, automatic failover, active/passive or active/active redundant hardware (servers, controllers, power, cooling, I/O ports and paths, management). Fault isolation and containment, proactive data integrity checks and repairs. Error correction code (ECC), parity, and other protection and integrity for the block, file, object data checksums.
Enabling recovery-point objective (RPO)	Versioning, point-in-time (pit) copies, snapshots, time interval protection, continuous data protection, backup, consistency point, transactional, application, crash, checkpoint, archive, consistency points, log or journal switch
Enabling recovery-time objective (RTO)	High availability, fault tolerance, replication, mirroring, and RAID, including advanced parity such as Erasure Code (EC) and forward error correction, among other approaches.
Data and storage security	Physical, logical, access control, encryption, endpoint protection

4.6. Availability, FTT, and FTM Fundamentals

A component of availability besides access is the durability and consistency of the data. This means that there are versions and copies of data in different places (the 4 3 2 1 rule) that are stateful and have integrity. Something to be aware of is that some cloud and other solution providers might mention 13, 15, or more numbers of 9's of availability. Some people might tell you that is not possible or practical; given the proper context—access only or durable only— that could be true.

Tip: In the context of combined access plus durability, 13, 15, or more 9's are possible and practical, depending on your specific needs. Hence keep context in mind when looking at availability and associated metrics. The fundamental point with data services and features is to keep in mind what are you protecting against, and whether all threat risks are applicable across your different applications.

Another availability topic is the number of faults (or failures) to tolerate (FTT) for an application, site or data center, system, appliance, server, or other data infrastructure component. An FTT = 0 means there is no fault tolerance or resiliency, whereas FTT = 1 (one copy or replica exists, i.e., N + 1) means one fault or failure can be tolerated. Note that FTT can apply to the entire stack from the application to the site, to the system, subsystem, server, appliance, or specific component.

Tip: There can be different FTT for various layers, such as FTT = 1 at the database layer, relying on database replication, and FTT = 2 at the storage system layer. Another option is to use FTT = 0 at the database layer while the underlying storage system might have a FTT = 2 or 3. Another variation is converged infrastructure (CI) and hyper-converged infrastructure (HCI) solutions, where FTT applies to application servers as well as underlying storage and networks.

Tip: Knowing the data protection priorities, requirements, granularity, and focus helps to determine what type of fault or failure-tolerant method (FTM) and data protection technique to use. For some scenarios, there will be an application, database, host or upper-level protection focus using replication and other techniques. Other scenarios will place more emphasis on the lower-level storage system, server clustering, and other FTM and data protection techniques. Still others will use hybrid approaches across different applications and service needs.

Tip: There are different FTM and data protection availability techniques and technologies that can be used in various ways. For example, is your primary focus on protecting against a device (PNEM, SCM, SSD, HDD) failure, bit error rate (BER), recoverable BER (RBER), or unrecoverable BER (UBER), among other considerations. There can be a focus on RAID or erasure code for protection and availability, including for normal operations or when something fails.

Bit rot can occur on magnetic or NVM-based storage mediums (e.g., PNEM, SCM, Flash SSD), as well as in virtual and logical file systems, databases, and among solutions. This phenomenon results in bits degrading or being damaged over time, compromising data integrity. The solution is to have file systems, databases, and other software-defined storage perform background data integrity checks and repair as needed. Another approach is to perform E2E data integrity checks including write verification.

For example, there can be the primary focus on a particular RAID approach such as RAID 10, or, a combination of techniques using different RAID levels along with replication or snapshots. Alternatively, if your focus is on protecting against device failures, also look into using better drives or devices and components along with software tools.

Tip: There should be a focus on having protection copies, replicas, and other approaches for when other things fail, from file systems to object stores, front-ends, gateways, networks, and so forth. Not to mention supporting different granularity. In other words, are you building a data protection approach focused around something failing; then, as part of the solution, look at what is going to fail and what alternatives may exist to using that technology. For example, what are your needs and requirements for all applications and data, or different categories and tiers such as faults to tolerate, to determine the applicable fault tolerance mode (FTM)?

Faults to tolerate (FTT) can be specified for a component device, system, rack, cabinet, cluster, or site (i.e., the fault domain) with varying values. For example, some components or layers in the data infrastructure stack may have higher FTT vs. others, such as a number of HDD or SSD that can fail, or host adapters or servers, among other resources. This also applies to what types of failures and their locations to be resilient toward and protect against. The FTM indicates what type of protection techniques and technologies to use to support FTT as well as RPO and RTO.

Considerations include:

- Where to implement availability and data protection
- What FTM to use when and where to meet FTT needs
- How much availability (or tolerance to downtime) is needed
- Keep availability regarding accessibility and durability in mind
- Keep in mind that if something can go wrong, it probably will, so be prepared

4.7. Common Availability Characteristics and Functionalities

When it comes to availability, including access, durable data protection (backup, BC, BR, DR), and resiliency, no one approach (other than common sense and tradecraft experience) fits all environments, applications, and scenarios. There are different applications with various

PACE attributes and QoS requirements, and there are big and small environments. Likewise, there are different threat risks that have various applicability and impact (i.e., what matters to your specific needs).

In addition to various threat risks (things that can go wrong) impacting data infrastructure, the application, as well as data availability (and security), there are also different approaches for protection. Some approaches leverage more resiliency in the underlying server and storage layers, while others rely on applications and upper levels of protection.

Tip: Another approach is hybrid, using the best of an upper-level, higher-altitude application, along with a lower-level storage system, as well as network techniques and technologies for data infrastructure reliability, availability, and serviceability (RAS).

What this means is that since everything is not the same, yet there are similarities, different techniques, technologies, tools, and best practices should be leveraged using your tradecraft experience. In other words, use different approaches, techniques, tools, technologies, and solutions for various applications, environments, and scenarios.

Still another approach is use many lower-cost, less reliable components and subsystems instead of relying on upper-level applications, database, and/or software- defined storage for resiliency. Another is a hybrid of the above on an application or system-by-system basis.

What are you protecting for/from?

- Location impact based (geographic region, metropolitan, local site)
- Physical facility damage or loss of access (physical or logical network)
- Logical, full or partial impact (loss, corrupted, deleted, inconsistency)
- Data loss event (DLE) or lost access (DLA) to safe, secure data
- Data intact and consistent, data infrastructure or application software damaged
- Technology failure or fault (hardware, network, electrical power, HVAC)

Additional considerations that determine what type of availability and resiliency mode or method to use include planned (scheduled) downtime, unplanned and unscheduled downtime, recurring or transient failures and issues (problems), application service PACE requirements, and SLO, RTO, and RPO needs.

Availability and protection quality of service (QoS) is implemented via:

- Reduced and standard redundancy along with high-availability
- Redundant components (hardware, software, power, cooling)
- Clusters and failover (active or standby, local and remote)
- Archives, clones and copies
- Backups, snapshots, CDP, and backdating
- Replication, mirroring, RAID, and erasure codes

Availability, resiliency, and data protection management includes:

- Testing and verification of processes, procedures, and copies made

- Grooming and cleanup, removing expired protection copies
- Change management, planning, implementation, and fallback
- Contingency planning and preparing, testing, remediating, communicating
- Priority of queues, tasks, jobs, and scheduling of protection
- Support for various data sizes, data volumes, data values, and applications
- Insight and awareness into data access patterns and usage

Availability, resiliency, and protection solutions, in general, should support:

- Long and complex file names along with deep directory folder paths
- Application integration, open files, plug-ins, and pre-/postprocessing
- Consistency checkpoints, quiescence of applications or file systems
- Filters to select what to include, exclude, and schedule for protection
- Options on where to protect data along with different format options
- Support for multiple concurrent data protection tasks running at the same time

Figure 4.4 shows how data is made durable and protected by spreading across different resources to eliminate single points of failure (SPOF). The top left shows (A) an application leveraging a data infrastructure configured and defined for resiliency. Data is spread across storage shelves (B1) with redundant power supplies, cooling fans, dual-path I/O and network interfaces, and management ports. The storage devices themselves (B2) have various resiliency and fault isolation and repair capabilities, combined with data infrastructure and software-defined

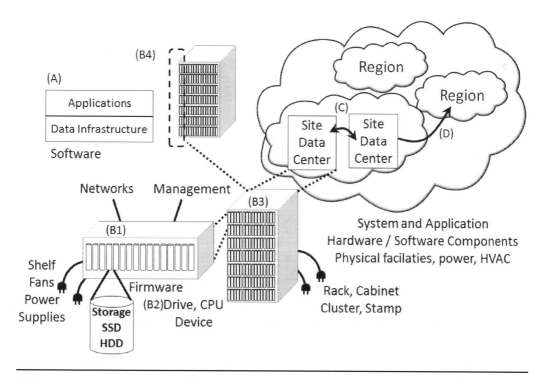

Figure 4.4   Fault domains and availability considerations.

storage tools. Multiple shelves exist in a cabinet or rack (B3) as a fault domain, with data being placed on different shelves (B4) for resiliency.

Tip: For additional resiliency, data can be spread across multiple racks or cabinets, across data centers as a higher-level fault-domain and across sites (Figure 4.4). Data can also be spread across systems, clusters, or stamps spanning data centers, sites, and regions for geographic dispersal. How much resiliency and number of faults or faults to tolerate (FTT) will depend on different application PACE and SLO requirements.

Data infrastructure availability can be implemented in various places, including:

- Applications, databases, middleware, file systems, and repositories
- Volume managers and other software-defined storage places
- Operating systems, hypervisors, and third-party add-on software
- Storage systems, appliances, networks, cloud, and service providers

Considerations include:

- Restore to alternate locations and formats (P2V, V2V, V2P, V2C)
- Protect against accidental overwrite and selection filters
- Test and dry-run modes to verify intended operations
- Proactive, preventive, pre-emptive vs. reactive or after-the-fact protection
- Granularity of protection and application integration
- Probability of system and component failures or subsequent faults
- How to protect against full vs. partial data loss or damage
- Workspace capacity for logs, backup staging, import/export, catalogs, conversions

4.8. Enabling Availability, Resiliency, Accessibility, and RTO

Tip: Key to resiliency is being able to isolate and contain faults (hardware, software, services, technology, and configuration) from spreading and resulting in larger-scale issues, problems, or disasters. As part of resiliency, how is cached or buffered data rewarmed (reloaded) from persistent storage after a system shutdown or crash? Can you resume a stopped, paused, or interrupted operation (snapshot, copy, replica, or clone) from where it last left off, or do you have to start over again from the beginning?

Another variation is the ability to resync data and storage based on some rules or policies to add changes (or deletions) without having to recopy everything. This could be to resynchronize a mirror or replica after a system or device is removed for planned or unscheduled maintenance, hardware, or software failure. As part of resiliency and failover to another system, do applications have to roll back (go back to a given RPO) to a consistency point, or can they simply resume operations where they left off?

Still another consideration is what type of fallover is required—for example, a system or application restart, or can it resume from the last transaction (i.e., is there application

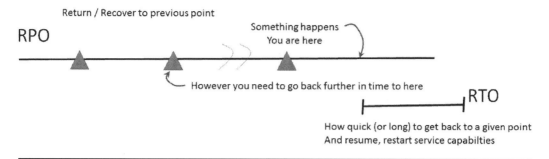

Figure 4.5   Resiliency including availability, RTO, and RPO.

and transaction consistency)? What is required, for example, simple, quick repairs or more extensive rebuild and reconstruction to file systems, other software-defined entities along with failed RAID, mirrors, replicas, and erase coded automated using spares, or is manual intervention necessary?

In addition to automated or manual attention, what is the repair or rebuild overhead in terms of space or systems capacity, network, server, and storage I/O performance, and impact on applications? Figure 4.5 shows points in time where data is changed as well as protected (i.e., consistency, checkpoint or recovery point), also known as delta (i.e., something changes).

Also shown in Figure 4.5, besides the RPO or points in time from where data can be recovered, or applications and systems rolled back to resume processing, are times to recover (or restore). The time to recover or restart represents the RTO of how much time is needed to resume, restart, restore, rebuild, or recover, along with several other things that start with R (e.g., repair, reload, reconstruct, rollback, or roll-forward).

Tip: Keep in mind that RTO needs to be seen in context: Is it end to end (E2E) for all data infrastructure components, or is it for a single item. For example, a single component might have an RTO for just storage or just database or servers, where E2E includes total time for applications, database rollback, data restore, storage, or other configuration and repairs.

Availability and resiliency topics, technologies, and techniques include:

- Redundant components and paths (hardware, software, services)
- Power, cooling, I/O, and management network access
- Configuration for RAS, basic and HA, to meet FTT and PACE needs
- Active/active or active/passive (standby) failover capabilities
- Manual, semiautomatic, and automatic failover (and failback)
- Mirroring, replication, sync, and clone
- RAID (mirror, parity, Reed-Solomon erasure code)
- Rebuild, reconstruction, restore, restart, repair, recovery
- Combine and complement with point-in-time protection techniques

Figure 4.6 shows resiliency- and availability-enabling technologies along with techniques used at different layers as well as locations to meet data infrastructure and application PACE

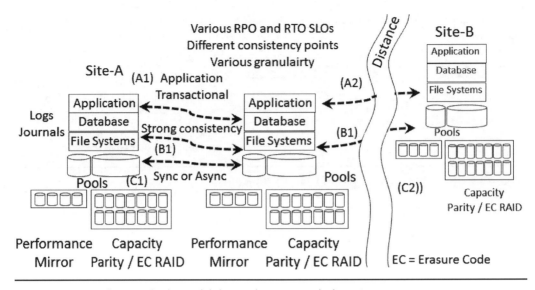

Figure 4.6   Combing multiple availability techniques, including air gaps.

needs. This includes local (Site-A) resiliency across systems and applications using different techniques that in turn protect to a secondary site (Site-B).

Some of the systems in Figure 4.6 implement application-level protection using local as well as remote replication. Other applications rely on lower-level replication via database, file systems, operating system, hypervisor, and storage system or appliances. Data is also protected at different levels for various granularities using snapshots, backups, versions, and other point-in-time techniques. For example, application- or database-level point-in-time protection enables application and fine-grained transaction consistency.

On the other hand, lower-altitude data protection in the data infrastructure stack such as a file system, operating system, hypervisor, or storage represents context and coarser granularity for those given levels. Figure 4.6 is an example of how different techniques should be combined to address different needs aligned to your environment.

Considerations include:

- What threat risk scenarios your data infrastructure needs to protect against
- Application PACE characteristics requirements for normal and abnormal times
- Balancing speed of restore or restart with protection overhead
- Heterogeneous mixed vendor, hardware, software, services, and technology
- Geographical location needs to meet SLO and other requirements
- Whether you will treat all applications and systems the same or use various techniques

4.9. Reliability, Availability, and Serviceability (RAS)

A resilient data infrastructure (software-defined, SDDC, and legacy) that protects, preserves, and serves information involves various layers of technology. These technologies enable various layers (altitudes) of functionalities, from devices up to and through the applications themselves. Some applications need a faster rebuild; some need sustained performance (bandwidth, latency, IOPs, or transactions) with the slower rebuild; some need lower cost at the expense of performance; others are ok with more space if other objectives are meet. The result is that since everything is different yet there are similarities, there is also the need to tune how data infrasture protects, preserves, secures, and serves applications and data.

General reliability, availability, serviceability, and data protection functionality includes:

- Ability to manually, or automatically via policies, start, stop, pause, and resume protection
- Adjust priorities of protection tasks, including speed, for faster or slower protection
- Fast-reacting to changes, disruptions or failures, or slower cautious approaches
- Workload and application load balancing (performance, availability, and capacity)

RAS can be optimized for:

- Reduced redundancy for lower overall costs vs. resiliency
- Basic or standard availability (leverage component plus)
- High availability (use better components, multiple systems, multiple sites)
- Fault-tolerant with no single points of failure (SPOF)
- Faster restart, restore, rebuild, or repair with higher overhead costs
- Lower overhead costs (space and performance) with lower resiliency
- Lower impact to applications during rebuild vs. faster repair
- Maintenance and planned outages or for continues operations

RAS techniques, technologies, tasks, and topics include:

- Automatic fault detection, isolate, contain, and repair where possible
- Protected journal and log files for transactional (or system) integrity
- Data infrastructure and component health status check
- Data integrity and checksums at various locations
- Local, remote, physical, virtual, cloud, and hybrid across all of them

Additional RAS functionality and topics include:

- Power-on self-test (POST) for hardware, software, networks, and services
- Redundant $N + 1$ power supplies, cooling, I/O connections, and controllers
- Mirrored cache with battery backup (BBU) power protection
- Background data integrity and consistency checks and repairs (self-healing)
- Hot and on-site spare components such as HDD, SSD, and server cluster nodes
- Nondisruptive code load (NDCL) and nondisruptive code activation (NDCA)

A technique and technology for enabling resiliency, as well as scaling performance, availability, and capacity, is clustering. Clusters can be local, remote, or wide-area to support different data infrastructure objectives, combined with replication and other techniques.

Another characteristic of clustering and resiliency techniques is the ability to detect and react quickly to failures to isolate and contain faults, as well as invoking automatic repair if needed. Different clustering technologies enable various approaches, from proprietary hardware and software tightly coupled to loosely coupled general-purpose hardware or software.

Tip: Care should be taken to configure clusters for resiliency; that is, in addition to the cluster enabling data infrastructure resiliency, make sure the cluster is not an SPOF. For example, make sure there are adequate and redundant components, I/O and network paths for east–west traffic including heartbeat and health status, repair, and other functions, along with general north–south access. Other considerations include the ability to tune for faster failover and repair, balanced with how to fallback when things return to normal.

Another clustering topic is partitioning, for which some context is needed. To enable resiliency and data integrity, the cluster needs to be protected from split-brain (the cluster divides into two or more independent clusters) or partitioned mode. In a cluster context, *partitioned* refers to how the cluster operates as a single entity, as opposed to how a disk is subdivided and formatted.

Most clusters require some number of member nodes with a vote to establish a quorum (i.e., the cluster can exist). Some clusters require an odd number such as three or more nodes to function, although this attribute varies by implementation. Additional proxy, witness, or surrogate quorum voting nodes (or devices) can be used to create a cluster quorum and prevent a partition or split-brain scenario.

Clustering characteristics include:

- Application, database, file system, operating, hypervisor, and storage-focused
- Share everything, share some things, share nothing
- Tightly or loosely coupled with common or individual system metadata
- Local in a quad (or larger) server chassis (e.g., multiple unique nodes in a box)
- Local in a cabinet or rack as part of a CI, HCI, CiB, or stamp
- Local in a data center, campus, metro, or stretch cluster
- Wide-area in different regions and availability zones
- Active/active for fast failover or restart, active/passive (standby) mode

Additional clustering considerations include:

- How does performance scale as nodes are added, or what overhead exists?
- How is cluster resource locking in shared environments handled?
- How many (or few) nodes are needed for quorum to exist?
- Network and I/O interface (and management) requirements.
- Cluster partition or split-brain (i.e., cluster splits into two)?
- Fast-reacting failover and resiliency vs. overhead of failing back.
- Locality of where applications are located vs. storage access and clustering.
- Does the clustering add complexity or overhead?

RAS considerations:

- Application higher-level, fine-grained, transactional consistency protection
- Lower-level, coarse crash consistency protection
- Leverage good-enough components with higher-level resiliency
- Leverage more reliable components with less higher-level resiliency
- Use a combination of techniques and technologies as needed
- Leverage lower costs to have more copies and resiliency
- How you will protect applications, data, and data infrastructure metadata settings

---

Tip: The tradecraft skill and trick is finding the balance, knowing your applications, the data, and how the data is allocated as well as used, then leveraging that insight and your experience to configure to meet your application PACE needs.

4.10. Enabling RPO (Archive, Backup, CDP, Snapshots, Versions)

RAID, including parity and erasure code along with mirroring and replication, provide availability and accessibility. These by themselves, however, are not a replacement for backup or sufficient for complete data protection. The solution is to combine resiliency technology with point-in-time tools that enable availability and facilitate going back to a previous consistency time.

Recovery-point protection is implemented within applications using checkpoint and consistency points as well as log and journal switches or flush. Other places where recovery-point protection occurs include in middleware, database, key-value stores and repositories, file systems, volume managers, and software-defined storage, in addition to hypervisors, operating systems, utilities, storage systems, appliances, and service providers.

Tip: There are different approaches, technologies, techniques, and tools, including archive, backup, continuous data protection, point-in-time copies, or clones such as snapshots, along with versioning.

In the context of the 4 3 2 1 rule, enabling RPO is associated with durability, meaning number of copies and versions. Simply having more copies is not sufficient because if they are all corrupted, damaged, infected, or contain deleted data, or data with latent nefarious bugs or rootkits, then they could all be bad. The solution is to have multiple versions and copies of the versions in different locations to provided data protection to a given point in time.

Timeline and delta or recovery points are when data can be recovered from to move forward. They are consistent points in the context of what is/was protected.

Tip: Simply having multiple copies and different versions is not enough for resiliency; some of those copies and versions need to be dispersed or placed in different systems or locations away from the source. How many copies, versions, systems, and locations are needed for your applications will depend on the applicable threat risks along with associated business impact.

PIT intervals enable recovering or access to data back in time, which is a RPO. That RPO can be an application, transactional, system, or other consistency point, or some other time interval. Some context here is that there are gaps in protection coverage, meaning something was not protected.

Another gap in protection coverage can be a time interval enabling RPO, or simply a physical and logical break and the distance between the active or protection copy, and alternate versions and copies. For example, a gap in coverage means something was not protected. A PIT gap occurs when a snapshot, copy, or version is made on some time interval—for example, hourly.

A protection air or distance gap is having one of those versions and copies on another system, in a different location and not directly accessible. In other words, if you delete, or data gets damaged locally, the protection copies are safe. Furthermore, if the local protection copies are also damaged, an air or distance gap means that the remote or alternate copies, which may be on-line or off-line, are also safe. Hence context is important when discussing data protection gaps.

Data services and features for enabling RPO and time-interval copies include:

- Application, AD/DC/DNS and system restore points or backups
- Point-in-time snapshots, CDP, and back-dating
- Scheduled, ad-hoc, on demand and dynamic
- Checkpoints, consistency points, scheduled
- Archives, backups, clones, and copies
- Versioning, journals, transaction and redo logs
- Backup, protection, and consistency groups

Point-in-time copies can be implemented in different locations from applications, databases, key-value and object repositories, file systems, volume managers, operating systems, and hypervisors to storage systems, appliances, and cloud services.

In addition to where the functionality is located, how those capacities are delivered also varies. For example, some are bundled as part of an application, database, operating system, hypervisor, or storage system, while others are add-ons, either for a fee or free. Some approaches implement these features as an add-on software module, or in a storage system or appliance. Other implementations are delivered via a software appliance model that is provided as a virtual appliance, cloud appliance, or as tin-wrapped software (software delivered with hardware).

Another variable is the granularity, consistency point, and application integration of PIT copies. Some approaches are tightly integrated with an application for transactional data consistency, others with databases or file systems. This means that the granularity can vary from fine-grain application transaction consistent, time interval, entire database or file system, volume, or system and device basis for crash consistency.

Tip: Simply having a snapshot, for example, of a particular time, may not be sufficient even if 100% of what is written to disk is protected if 100% of the data has not been written to disk. What I mean by this is that if 5% of the data, including configuration settings, metadata, and other actual data, is still in memory buffers and not flushed to disk (made consistent), and that data is not protected, then there is not a consistent copy. You might have a consistent copy of what was copied, but the contents of that copy may not be consistent to a particular point in time.

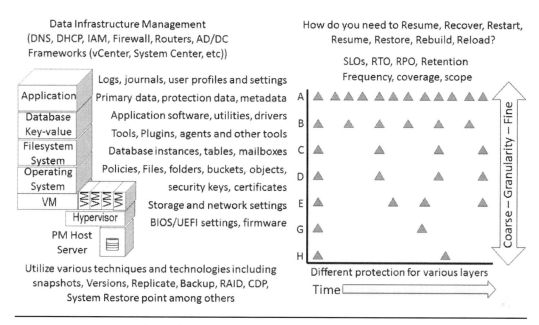

Figure 4.7   Protecting data infrastructure and enabling resiliency at various layers.

What's your objective: to resume, roll back or roll forward, restore, reload, reconstruct or rebuild, restart, or some other form of recovery? Different applications (or portions of them) along with various environments will have different PACE criteria that determine RTO and RPO as well as how to configure technologies to meet SLOs.

Figure 4.7 shows on the left various data infrastructure layers moving from low altitude (lower in the stack) host servers or PM and up to higher levels with applications. At each layer or altitude, there are different hardware and software components to protect, with various policy attributes. These attributes, besides PACE, FTT, RTO, RPO, and SLOs, include granularity (full or incremental), consistency points, coverage, frequency (when protected), and retention.

Also shown in the top left of Figure 4.7 are protections for various data infrastructure management tools and resources, including active directory (AD), domain controllers (DC), group policy objects (GPO) and organizational units (OU), network DNS, routing and firewall, among others. Also included are protecting management systems such as VMware vCenter and related servers, Microsoft System Center, OpenStack, as well as data protection tools along with their associated configurations, metadata, and catalogs.

The center of Figure 4.7 lists various items that get protected along with associated techniques, techniques, and tools. On the right-hand side of Figure 4.7 is an example of how different layers get protected at various times, granularity, and what is protected. For example, the PM or host server BIOS and UEFI as well as other related settings seldom change, so they do not have to be protected as often. Also shown on the right of Figure 4.7 are what can be a series of full and incremental backups, as well as differential or synthetic ones.

Figure 4.8 is a variation of Figure 4.7 showing on the left different frequencies and intervals, with a granularity of focus or scope of coverage on the right. The middle shows how different layers or applications and data focus have various protection intervals, type of protection (full, incremental, snap, differentials), along with retention, as well as some copies to keep.

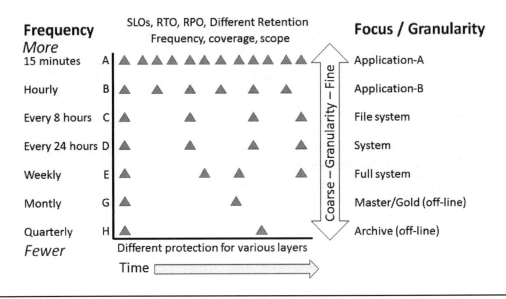

Figure 4.8   Protecting different focus areas with various granularities.

Protection in Figures 4.7 and 4.8 for the PM could be as simple as documentation of what settings to configure, versions, and other related information. A hypervisor may have changes, such as patches, upgrades, or new drivers, more frequently than a PM. How you go about protecting may involve reinstalling from your standard or custom distribution software, then applying patches, drivers, and settings.

You might also have a master copy of a hypervisor on a USB thumb drive or another storage device that can be cloned, customized with the server name, IP address, log location, and other information. Some backup and data protection tools also provide protection of hypervisors in addition to the VM, guest operating systems, applications, and data.

The point is that as you go up the stack, higher in altitude (layers), the granularity and frequency of protection increases. What this means is that you may have more frequent smaller protection copies and consistency points higher up at the application layer, while lower down, less frequent, yet larger full image, volume, or VM protection, combining different tools, technology, and techniques.

Management considerations for enabling recovery-point protection include:

- Manual and policy-enabled automated tools
- Insight, awareness, analytics, reporting, and notification
- Schedules, frequency, coverage, clean-up, grooming, and optimization
- Monitoring, diagnostics, troubleshooting, and remediation
- Interfaces, plug-ins, wizards, GUIs, CLI, APIs, and management tools

Figure 4.9 shows how data can be made available for access as well as durability using various techniques combined on a local, remote, physical, and virtual and cloud basis. This includes supporting recovery points in time as well as enabling RTOs.

Considerations include:

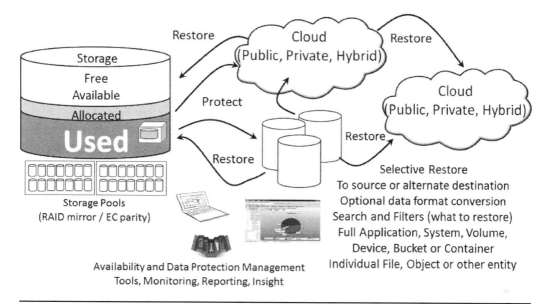

Figure 4.9   Protecting and restoring data to/from various locations.

- Local and remote as well as geographic location requirements
- Change block tracking, fast and intelligent scans to determine what data changed
- Impact of protection on normal running systems and applications
- Impact on applications during degraded or rebuild scenarios
- Heterogeneous mixed vendor, technology, tool, and application environments
- Hardware, software and services dependency and interoperability
- How many concurrent copies, clone, mirror, snap, or other protect jobs

4.11. Point-in-Time Protection for Different Points of Interest

Figure 4.10 shows backup and data protection focus, granularity, and coverage. For example, at the top left is less frequent protection of the operating system, hypervisor, and BIOS/UEFI settings. At the middle left is volume- or device-level protection (full, incremental, differential), along with various views on the right ranging from protecting everything, to different granularities such as file system, database, database logs and journals, and OS and application software, along with settings.

In Figure 4.10, note that the different focus points and granularities also take into consideration application and data consistency (as well as checkpoints), along with different frequencies and coverage (e.g. full, partial, incremental, incremental forever, differential) as well as retention.

Tip: Some context is needed about object backup and backing up objects, which can mean different things. As mentioned elsewhere, objects refer to many different things, including cloud and object storage buckets, containers, blobs, and objects accessed via S3 or Swift, among other APIs. There are also database objects and entities, which are different from cloud or object storage objects.

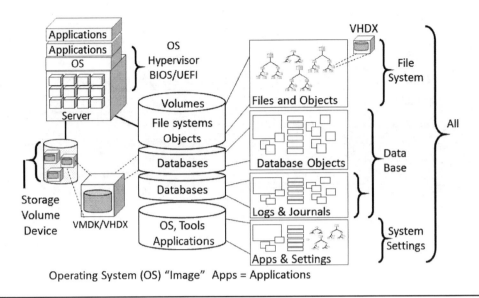

Figure 4.10   Backup and data protection focus, granularity, and coverage.

Tip: Another context to keep in mind is that an object backup can refer to protecting different systems, servers, storage devices, volumes, and entities that collectively comprise an application such as accounting, payroll, or engineering, vs. focusing on the individual components. An object backup may, in fact, be a collection of individual backups, PIT copies, and snapshots that combined represent what's needed to restore an application or system.

On the other hand, the content of a cloud or object storage repository (buckets, containers, blobs, objects, and metadata) can be backed up, as well as serve as a destination target for protection.

Backups can be cold and off-line like archives, as well as on-line and accessible. However, the difference between the two, besides intended use and scope, is granularity. Archives are intended to be coarser and less frequently accessed, while backups can be more frequently and granularly accessed. Can you use a backup for an archive and vice versa? A qualified yes, as an archive could be a master gold copy such as an annual protection copy, in addition to functioning in its role as a compliance and retention copy. Likewise, a full backup set to long-term retention can provide and enable some archive functions.

Backup functionality and features include:

- Hot, open file, snapshot, application integration
- Read verification and data integrity checks
- Path to tape and tape as well as optical, HDD, or cloud migration
- Encryption and compression, various formats
- Application integration with databases, email, file systems, hypervisors
- Clones of backups and protection copies
- Management tools and interfaces from GUI, Wizard, CLI, and PowerShell

Additional backup and protection performance topics include:

- Proprietary or open format (tar, gzip) or native file system
- S3, Swift, and other cloud or objects, buckets, and containers
- Targets, including block, file, object, and API
- Virtual tape library, disk library, or optical library
- Physical and logical labels, RFID and tracking
- Throttling and performance priorities to enable protection quality of service
- Processing offloads and drivers for compression, de-dupe, and other functions
- Cloud, object, API, chunk and shard size issues, file split

4.12. Snapshots, Consistency, and Checkpoints

Part of backup or data protection modernization that supports data footprint reduction includes space-saving snapshots. Space-saving or space-efficient PIT copies can be used for more than data protection. As part of CDM, PIT copies also support making copies of production data that can be used for quality assurance or testing, development, decision support, and other uses.

Tip: A fundamental premise of recovery-point protection is that at some point in time a copy of the data is made so that recovery can be accomplished to that point. What varies is how those copies are made, for example. like with traditional backups, or with snapshots among other techniques. Another variation besides the time interval or frequency is granularity, along with whether data is quiesced (i.e., quiet) or changing.

PIT copies include:

- Backups (full, incremental, differential)
- Snapshots, consistency points, and checkpoints
- Versioning, journaling, and CDP
- Change management of applications and data infrastructure software

PIT copies can be done via:

- Applications, databases, key-value repositories, email systems
- File systems, volume managers, operating systems, hypervisors
- Storage systems, appliances, cloud services

Tip: The importance of a space-saving snapshot is to reduce the overhead of extra space needed every time a copy or snapshot of a snapshot is made. First-generation snapshots, which have been deployed in various systems for many years, if not decades, have continued to improve in terms of performance and space efficiency. The next wave was to enable copies of copies using change tracking and redirection on write tehniques to reduce the amount of storage required while enabling fast copies to be made. The importance of space-saving, as well as traditional, snapshots is that, as part of a data protection modernization, changing the way information is copied can reduce the overhead of storage needed, enabling a smaller data footprint. The object is to be able to store and retain more data in a smaller, more economical footprint.

Another aspect of PIT copies including snapshots, checkpoints, and consistency points (and for that matter, backups) along with versions is time interval (i.e., how often they are done). The time interval can be a defined fixed schedule or ad-hoc. The interval might be monthly, weekly, daily, end of shift, hourly, or every few minutes (or more often). A longer interval between PIT copies is referred to as coarse recovery points, narrower or shorter intervals being fine-grained.

Tip: Why not just have continuous replication or mirroring? Replication and mirroring provide a continuous update of what has changed. Recall that the good news here is that if something good gets changed, the copy is instantly (or with only a slight time delay with asynchronous mode) made. The bad news is that if something bad happens, then that also occurs to the mirror or replica unless there is some form of PIT recovery point.

A variation of snapshots is known as CDP, which combines the best of replication and mirroring along with PIT RPO copies and the ability to run at a fine grain with low overhead (e.g., under a minute). For many environments, simply running frequent snapshots—every few to several minutes—is sufficient and what some refer to as near-CDP.

Tip: With some CDP and other PIT-based solutions, besides fixed static intervals, there is also the ability to back-date to dynamically create a recovery point after the fact. What is best for your environment and applications will vary depending on your SLOs including RPOs and PACE requirements.

Besides frequency and time interval, another aspect is granularity of the protection, similar to backup disused in the previous section. Granularity includes from an application transactional perspective, database instance or table, file system, folder or file, virtual machine, and mailbox, among other resources, as well as software change management. Granularity also connects to what you are protecting against, as well as the level of data consistency needed. As with backup, application interaction, is another consideration, for example, how snapshots, CDP, and consistency points are integrated with databases such as SQL Server and Oracle, among others.

Databases also leverage their own protection scheme using checkpoints or consistency points to a checkpoint, journal, or log file. These checkpoints, consistency points, or log switches are timed to the desired RPO. The checkpoint, consistency point, and log or journals can be used as part of database recovery to roll back transactions or the database to a known good point.

DBAs will find a balance between too many, too long a consistency point that meets RPO requirements as well as space along with performance implications. Note that as part of a data protection scheme; a database can be replicated as well as backed up to another location. So too can its log files, which, depending on the database and configuration, can be applied to a standby copy as part of a resiliency solution.

Snapshots, checkpoints, and consistency points can be organized into groups that refer to the resources for an application or some other function. For example, a consistency group of different snapshots, versions, or PIT copies spanning various times and multiple volumes or file systems can be created for management purposes.

Functionality varies with different solutions and where they are implemented. However, there are some common considerations, including application, server, storage, and cloud services integration via plug-ins or other interfaces; granularity by system, application, database, table, file, folder, or device; performance impact when copies are made, along with how many concurrent operations, as well as total number of copies per item protected, and in total. Other commonalities include scheduling, retention, the scope of what to protect, and security in terms of who can access the data.

PIT copy considerations include:

- Snapshot, CDP, and consistency-point functionality
- DFR, including compression and de-dupe
- Whether and how log or journal files for databases can be copied to other systems
- Integration with mirroring, replication, and other data protection tools
- Whether there are space reservation requirements for the copies, and what the overhead is
- Whether the snapshots or versions can be accessed for read/write, or marked as WORM
- What are the dependencies and prerequisite software or hardware and management tools
- Import and export of snapshots, repair, rebalance, and integrity checks

4.13. Data Infrastructure Security (Logical and Physical)

The why of data infrastructure security is to protect, preserve, and secure resources, applications, and data so that information services can be accessed and served. This means protecting and repelling various threats against unauthorized access to applications and data infrastructure components along with associated data, as well as metadata.

Examples of why and what data infrastructure security addresses include:

- Enabling privacy of information, applications, and configuration
- Protecting against nosey neighbors, eavesdropping, and unauthorized access
- Guarding against theft, damage, or destruction of data and applications
- Defending against ransomware, malware, viruses, and rootkits
- Deterring hackers, intruders, ransomware, malware, viruses and rootkits
- Facilitating regulatory, industry, self- and compliance requirements

Data infrastructure security includes both physical as well as logical and software-defined as well as being associated with data protection (backups, BC/DR/BR).

Data infrastructure and related application security occurs in or at:

- Physical, software-defined virtual, cloud, container, and converged resources
- Servers, storage, I/O, and networking devices along with associated protocols

- Hypervisors, operating systems, file systems, volume managers, and device drivers
- Data infrastructure applications including DNS, DHCP, AD/DC, and other components
- Local, remote, mobile across various devices including tablets and phones
- Utilities, databases, repositories, middleware, and applications
- Facilities, including on-premise as well as third-party or managed cloud services

Security tasks and activities are ongoing, performing checks, virus, and other data integrity safety scans, leveraging digital forensics to determine what happened, why, and how—for example, looking for digital (or physical) fingerprints of what happened, perhaps by whom, or, in some cases, looking at or for the absence of fingerprints vs. known and what should exist to determine that something happened.

Security is implemented when:

- Before something happens (proactive and preventive)
- While something is happening
- After something happens

Security is implemented via:

- Access control, identity management
- Encryption and checksums
- Physical and logical

4.13.1. Data Infrastructure Security Implementation

There are several different security focus areas for data infrastructures. These include physical as well as logical, spanning legacy, software-defined, virtual, cloud, and container data infrastructures. Similarly, security topics span from applications to the database, file systems and repository, mobile and fixed devices for accessing application and data infrastructure resources. Additional focus areas include servers, storage, I/O networks, hardware, software, services, and facilities, among others.

Logical data infrastructure security topics include:

- Identity access management (IAM) controls, roles and rights management
- Username, password, PIN, roles and access controls
- Controlling access for create, read, update, and delete (CRUD) of data and metadata
- Securing primary, secondary, and protection copies of data and applications
- Audit, event, and activity logs for analysis, reporting, monitoring, and detection
- Encryption of data-at-rest and in-flight (when moved), key management
- Grant, remove, suspend, configure rights, roles and policies
- Intrusion detection alert, notification, remediation
- Policies, logical organizational units (OU), single sign-on (SSO)

4.13.2. Physical Security and Facilities

As its name implies, physical security spans from facilities to access control of hardware and other equipment along with their network and management interfaces. Physical data infrastructure security topics include:

- Biometric authentication, including eye iris and fingerprint
- Locks (physical and logical) on doors, cabinets, and devices
- Asset-tracking tags including RFID, barcodes, and QR codes
- Tracking of hardware assets as well as portable media (disk, tape, optical)
- Logging and activity logs, surveillance cameras

Physical security items include:

- Physical card and ID if not biometric access card for secure facilities
- Media and assets secure and safe disposition
- Secure digital shredding of deleted data with appropriate audit controls
- Locked doors to equipment rooms and secure cabinets and network ports
- Asset tracking, including portable devices and personal or visiting devices
- Low-key facilities, absent large signs advertising that a data center is here
- Protected (hardened) facility against fire, flood, tornado, and other events
- Use of security cameras or guards

Physical security can be accomplished by addressing the above items, for example, ensuring that all switch ports and their associated cabling and infrastructure including patch panels and cable runs are physically secured with locking doors and cabinets. More complex examples include enabling intrusion detection as well as enabling probes and other tools to monitor critical links such as wide-area interswitch links (ISLs).

For example, a monitoring device could track and send out alerts for certain conditions on critical or sensitive ISLs for link loss, signal loss, and other low-level events that might appear as errors. Information can then be correlated with other information to see whether someone was performing work on those interfaces, or whether they had been tampered with in some way.

4.13.3. Logical and Software-Defined Security

Fundamental security and permissions include account, project, region, availability zone (AZ) or data center location, group, and user, among others. Additional permissions and roles can be by company, division, application, system, or resource, among others. Basic permissions to access files, devices, applications, services, and other objects should be based on ownership and access. In addition to standard access, roles can be assigned for elevated permissions via the Linux *sudo* command and administrator user modes for performing certain functions needing those rights.

Basic UNIX and Linux (*nix) file system permissions specify owner, group, or world access along with read, write, execute a file, device, or resource. Read (r) has a value of 4, Write (w) has value of 2, eXecute (x) has a value of (1). Each category (owner, group, and world) has a value based on the access permission, for example, owner (rwx=7), group (rx=5), world (rx=5) has value 755 and appears as -rwxr-xr-xr.

As an example, the LINUX commands

chmod 755 -R /home/demo/tmp
chown greg:storageio -R /home/demo/tmp
ls /home/demo/tmp -al

will set files in all subdirectories under /home/demo/tmp to be rwx by owner, rx by group, and rx by world. Chown sets the ownership of the files to greg, who is part of group storageio. The command *ls /home/demo/tmp.al* will show directories with files attributes including ownership, permissions, size, modification, and other metadata.

Figure 4.11 shows various data infrastructure security–related items from cloud to virtual, hardware and software, as well as network services. Also shown are mobile and edge devices as well as network connectivity between on-premise and remote cloud services. Cloud services include public, private, as well as hybrid and virtual private clouds (VPC). Access logs are also used to track who has accessed what and when, as well as success along with failed attempts.

Other security-related items shown in Figure 4.11 include Lightweight Direct Access Protocol (LDAP), Remote Authentication Dial-In User Service (RADIUS), active directory

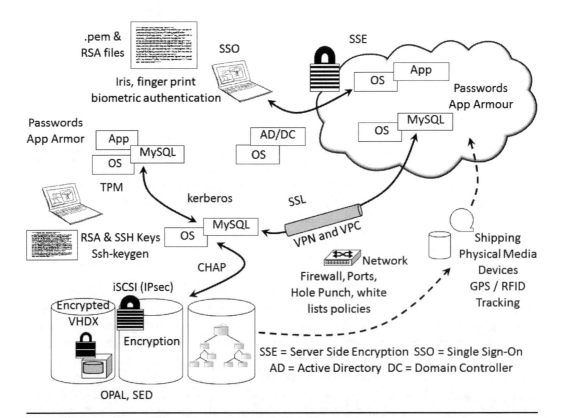

Figure 4.11   Various physical and logical security and access controls.

(AD), and Kerberos network authentication. Also shown are virtual private networks (VPN) along with Secure Socket Layer (SSL) network security, along with security and authentication keys, credentials for SSH remote access including Single Sign-On (SSO).

Encryption is shown in Figure 4.11 for data in-flight as well as while at rest on storage, along with server-side encryption. Server and storage I/O access includes port prohibits, port blocks, volume mapping and masking, along with other endpoint protection. Additional items include SSH and RSA key files, Linux App Armor, Challenge Handshake Authentication Protocol (CHAP), Internet Protocol Security (IPsec), and Trusted Platform Module (TPM).

4.13.4. Encryption Codes and Key Management

There are many different aspects to data infrastructure security. However, common services and functionalities include encryption of data at rest as well as while in-flight. Encryption can be done via applications, databases, file systems, operating systems and hypervisors, as well as network, storage system, and cloud services.

In addition to encryption, passwords, and access security certificates, hash, secure hash algorithms (SHA), and other codes are also used as checksums to enable data integrity checks of files, objects, folders, and buckets. Hash and SHA codes are also used to create index keys as well as in support of DFR de-dupe, among other uses. Keys, certificates, and other security certificates are created and managed in different locations with various tools for traditional, software-defined virtual, cloud, and container. Some tools include ssh-keygen, putty gen, and sigcheck, among many others built into various data infrastructure hardware, software, and services or as add-ons.

Tip: Note that there is a difference between FIPS certified and compliant: Ask the vendor whether they are in fact certified or simply compliant. Some vendors may be compliant and working or planning on becoming certified, as that is a longer process.

The key to encryption (pun intended) is key management. Keep in mind that these keys are not just for encryption, as there are also certificates and other access control items to be secured and managed. Similar to physical keys that might be attached to a key chain or ring, or placed in a safe, secure location, logical or cyber keys also need to be managed, organized, and secured. There are standards such as Key Management Interoperability Protocol (KMIP) along with its variations and implementations. Examples of enterprise key management (EKM) include SafeNet KeySecure, among others.

Encryption can be done on data at rest (i.e., once it is on disk, local or remote), while in-flight (i.e., moving over a network), on portable and mobile devices, as well as a combination of all the above. For data at rest, there are self-encrypting devices (SED) including HDD and SSD that secure the data on a drive internally via its firmware per OPAL standard. The advantages of SED drives is that if they are removed or unbound from their host server, laptop, or storage system, they are effectively shredded or encrypted. When the drives reattach or rebind to their known host, the data becomes usable again.

What this means is that, in addition to having secured encrypted devices, it is also possible to reduce the amount of time to secure erase for many general environments. Granted, depending on your environment, you may need to run additional secure erase patterns on the devices. The downside to drive-level encryption is that it needs the server, laptop, storage system, or appliance to support their key management.

Keys, certificates, and access control can be managed using data infrastructure resources such as Microsoft Active Directory and its companion resources, as well OpenStack Keystone among others. Encryption key management can be dedicated to a specific application or implementation, or span across different technologies. Features include the ability to import and export keys, and support for key certificates from different locations including self-generated.

Another approach is for storage systems, appliances, and software-defined storage software to implement the storage data at rest encryption (DARE) function. The downside to this is potential increased CPU processing to implement the compute-intensive encryption functions. The upside is tighter integration with the storage and management software.

Besides DARE, server-side encryption (SSE), as its name implies, is encryption for example on a service that is functioning as an application or data infrastructure node to ingest and store data. Data-in-flight encryption can be done in various places, including servers as well as network routers and other devices. Encryption can also be done in file systems, as well as in databases, email, and other locations as part of a layered security and protection defense strategy. Some examples of server software encryption include TruCrypt and Microsoft Bitlocker, among others.

4.13.5. Identity Access Management and Control

Beyond basic user passwords, group membership, resource ownership, and access control lists (ACLs), there are other aspects of identity access management (IAM) and control. These include assigning identifiers to resources (devices, applications, files, folders, services, metadata) such as a globally unique identifier (GUID) and other security identifiers (SID). The various granularities include access from the entire system, application, database, and file system to specific functions, files, or objects.

Access and control policies include group policy objects (GPO), not to be confused with cloud and object storage objects. Organizational Units (OU) define entities such computers, applications, or other data infrastructure resources that users or groups can be members of, as well as have different access roles and rights. For example, a user can be a member of an OU with the role to grant to other users various rights, as well as monitor, revoke, or suspend access.

Another functionality is the ability to grant subordinated or delegated management or rights authority to others. Subordinated management rights could be for a subset of full administrator capabilities, or to enable management of a particular resource such as a VM. Another variation of rights and access control is being able to grant full access to the system administrator, yet restrict access to particular applications and or their data.

Organizational Units are part of Microsoft Active Directory, but there are other variations for different environments such as OpenStack Keystone or those found in VMware, among others. In the case of AD, there are various forests (a group of domains) and trees (domains) that collectively describe, organize, and provide trusted access control for organizations. Microsoft AD can run on-premise on physical or virtual machines, as well as in the cloud, such as Azure AD. While being Microsoft-centric, many Linux and other environments, as well as clouds, also provide hooks (interfaces) into AD.

Tip: Another aspect of securing servers is having not only multi-tenancy with VM and containers, but also having shielded VM. For example, Microsoft Hyper-V can shield, isolate (quarantine) a misbehaving VM from impacting others, beyond normal multi-tenancy. Besides VM and cloud instance tenancy, there are also containers, among other options for isolating from noisy (loud) and nosey (snooping) neighbors in adjacent tenancies.

Tip: By "bleaching" a file, folder, or device, the data is removed by writing repeated patterns to make sure no traces of the data remain. In the case of object storage that is immutable, a delete operation, like a file system, may not remove the actual data right away. Instead, a "tombstone" is placed marking the "dead" data to be removed during later operations. Note that different cloud and object storage implementations vary in how they handle deletes, similar to file systems and databases.

4.13.6. General Data Infrastructure Security–Related Topics

There are many general security-related topics, tools, technologies, techniques, and data services for data infrastructure environments in addition to those mentioned. These range from definition, communication, and implementation of policies, terms, of service, or use, to digital forensics.

Tip: Context is important: There are digital fingerprints such as those used by biometric finger scanners to gain access to resources, and digital fingerprints in the context of an SHA or hash key, as well as nefarious digital fingerprints left behind (via access and audit logs) after doing things. Additional general topics include white and black lists for granting or restricting access to resources, as well as policies based on time, location, or other criteria for resource access.

Tip: Other activities and security data services include scans of media as well as data (applications and actual data along with metadata and settings) for integrity, as well as to proactively detect issues before they become problems. Scan media and data ranges from downloadable content from the web, or what is exchanged via USB, SD, and microSD cards, among other devices.

In addition to scans for virus, malware, ransomware, rootkits, or other nefarious items, integrity checks can be used or detect data (physical or logical) corruption or other inconsistencies. When infected or questionable items are detected, such as a file, folder, object, application, virtual machine, or other entity, it can be quarantined until properly handled.

Tip: Something else to keep in mind is whether the software, files, folders, or objects that you receive are signed with a valid digital signature. This includes data infrastructure software from hypervisors to operating systems, device drivers, tools, firmware, plug-ins, and other utilities. For example, make sure that VIB, ZIP, ISO, OVA/OVF, VMDK, VHDX, EXE, BIN, and IMG, among other items, are validated with trusted signatures for safe installation.

Reporting and alerts along with alarm notification are also features and data services. These range from simple access and activity event logs to more extensive analytics and machine learning features. For example, some software is capable of learning what is normal and abnormal and detecting that a particular device or user accesses resources from a set of known locations. However, when that user suddenly appears to access from another unknown location, an alert or precautionary notification can be sent similar to what you might receive from Facebook or some other social media sites, or your credit card company.

An additional capability is the ability of detection software to send an alert when you access a resource from, say, Minneapolis at 10 AM central time, then an hour later from Singapore (with no time zone adjustments). Somebody might be accessing the resource via different proxy servers, but for the typical person, for their normal known device to be used in two different locations half a world apart within only an hour should at least trigger an alarm!

Some additional security as well as audit-related certifications and accreditations include SSAE16 SOC1, ISO 27001 and 27002, CISSP and CISA, and AT101 SOC2 and SOC3. Additional security-related organizations, groups, topics, and accreditations include Authorization To Operate (ATO) for public cloud providers to support government agencies, Federal Information Security Management Act (FISMA), Federal Risk and Authorization Management Program (FedRAMP), Internet Assigned Number Authority (IANA), National Registration Authority (NRA), as well as Provisional Authority to Operate (P-ATO)

Considerations include:

- Dedicated Private Services (DPS) at managed and cloud service providers
- Local and private cloud, hybrid, and public cloud-enabled security
- Physical, virtual, container, cloud, and mobile-enabled
- Support for IoT, IoD, BYOD, and legacy devices as needed
- Should be an enabler instead of a barrier that results in security issues

4.14. Common Questions and Tips

What is the difference between FIPS 140-2 compliant and certified? Compliant means that the solution meets the specification (complies) with the standard for protecting and managing crypto and cipher (encryption) modules. Certification means that the technology, solution, software, or service has undergone formal certification by an accredited organization. Pay attention to whether your requirements are for certification or simply compliance, as well as what vendors offer when they say FIPS 140-2 (among other standards).

What is the best technology and location to do encryption? The best technology and approach is the one that works for you and your environment, which enables encryption without introducing complexity or barriers to productivity. Your environment may require different solutions for various applications or focus areas from a single or multiple vendors. Avoid being scared of encryption for fear of losing keys, performance impacts, or increased complexity. Instead, look at different solutions that complement and enable your environment.

Why would you want to do replication in a storage system vs. in an application, hypervisor, or software-defined storage? It depends on what your application PACE requirements are, along with SLO and technology capabilities. For example, your hypervisor, CI, HCI, software-defined storage, or storage system may only support asynchronous replication, whereas your database might support synchronous.

Why not use erasure codes everywhere, particularly with SSD? The simple answer is for performance: Erasure codes are good for inactive, or mainly read-based, data. A good strategy for many deployments is to use a mix of mirroring such as on SSD pools for update intensive including logs, journals, and databases, and then erasure code and parity protection for less frequent, higher-capacity storage pools.

What are some legal considerations regarding data protection, resiliency, and availability? There are governmental and industry regulations, which vary. For example, there are various laws that determine what data can be moved or stored outside of a country for privacy, among other concerns.

What are the legal requirements for where data can be protected to? There are many different industry, state, province, as well as federal government among other regulations that impact data protection. This includes where data can be protected to or stored, for example, whether it can be sent outside of a state or other jurisdictional area, or across country borders. In addition, there are industry-specific regulations such as for financials, among others, that determine how many copies as well as how far away they need to be located for safety. Besides the number of copies as well as versions in various locations, there are also requirements for being able to prove data integrity for a given level of a disaster to meet audit compliance requirements.

How do you know what type of data protection technique and technology to use and when? That is where tradecraft skills and experience come into play, including what you have learned (or refreshed) in this book. Keeping in mind that everything is not the same, there are similarities for different scenarios. Table 4.2 provides a general overview of different types of outages and incidents that can impact data infrastructures, applications, data, and organizations.

The impact of an outage such as those shown in Table 4.2 will depend on how your organization will function during or after an incident, as well as how your data infrastructure is configured to protect, preserve, secure, and serve applications along with their data. Will your organization try to conduct operations as best as possible, or shut down until applications and data, all or partially, can be restored? Similarly, the chance of something happening will vary by your location or proximity to danger.

In addition to what is shown in Table 4.2, Table 4.3 shows how to define your data infrastructure to protect, preserve, and secure applications and data against various threats. Note that this is not an exhaustive or definitive list, rather a guide, and your organization may have different mandates, laws, and regulations to follow.

How many failures do different types of protection and resiliency provide? Different configurations will tolerate various numbers of faults. Keep your focus on the solution, or a particular component or layer such as server, storage, network, hardware, or software. In Table 4.4, different numbers of servers are shown along with various storage configurations that provide varying FTTs. Focus beyond just server or storage or network, hardware or software, as availabity is the sum of the parts, plus accessibility, durability, and security.

Table 4.2. Disaster, Event, and Outage or Disruption Scenarios

Outage Result and Impact Reach	Impact to Data Infrastructure and Applications	Impact if Occurs	Chance of Occurring	How Organization Will Function During Outage
Local or regional impact: loss of site. Fire, flood, hurricane, tornado, earthquake, explosion, accidental, intentional act of man or nature.	Complete or severe damage to facilities and surroundings, data infrastructure components, applications, settings, and data.	High if no off-site (or cloud) copy, or no second site, or no BC/BR/DR plan.	Varies by location, region, as well as type of business.	Will the organization shut down for some time, or continue to function in a limited mode using manual processes?
Loss or damaged data or applications from virus, software bug, configuration error, accidental deletion.	Facilities and data infrastructure are intact, severe damage, loss of data has site useless.	High if PIT copies are not present and are not consistent.	Varies by industry and other factors.	Leverage strong security and data protection combined with change management testing.
Loss of power or communications. Power outage, power line or network cable severed.	Site and data infrastructure along with data intact, loss of primary power or network.	High if no standby power or network access.	Varies by location and system separation.	Leverage standby power, cooling, alternative networks, along with secondary sites and resilient DNS.
Failed component, server, storage, I/O network device.	Varies based on how much or what type of redundancy exists or is used.	High if no redundant devices configured.	Higher with lower-cost items.	Minimize disruption by implementing resiliency to isolate and contain faults.
File, object, or other data lost, deleted, or damaged	Varies based on your 4 3 2 1 rule implementation and ability to isolate and contain faults.	Varies, can be small and isolated or on a larger scale.	Relatively high and common occurrence.	Minimize impact with PIT copies for fast restore and recovery. If unattended, could lead to larger disaster.
Cloud or MSP failure. Loss of access due to network, DNS outage, or DDoS attacks. Loss of data due to bug in software or configuration error. Lack of DNS and cloud resiliency.	Varies depending on type of incident. Many cloud failures have been loss of access to data as opposed to actual loss of data. There have been data loss events as well.	Varies on how cloud is used and where your data as well as applications exist. Keep in mind the 4 3 2 1 rule.	Varies. Some cloud MSP are more resilient than others.	If all of your data and applications are in the affected cloud, impact can be very high. How you use and configure the cloud and MSP to be resilient can mean being available.

For additional resiliency, configurations similar or in addition to those in Table 4.4 can be combined with replication across servers, racks, data centers, geographies, or other fault domains.

Keep the 4 3 2 1 rule in mind: Four (or more) copies of data (including applications and settings), with at least three (or more) different versions (PIT copies, backups, snapshots) stored on (or in) at least two (or more) different systems (servers, storage systems, devices) with at least one (or more) of those versions and copies located off-site (cloud, MSP, bunker, vault, or other location). As we have discussed, 4 3 2 1 combines PIT copies such as backups, snapshots, and archives to meet specific recovery-point intervals, along with clustering, mirroring, replication, and other forms of resiliency to meet recovery-time objectives.

Table 4.3. How to Protect Against Various Threats

Outage	What to Do
Local or regional impact loss of site	DR, BC, and BR plan in place and up to date that implements 4 3 2 1 protection (or better). Secondary (or tertiary sites) that can be mix of active or standby to meet different RTO requirements. Data is protected to alternative locations per specific RPOs using replication, mirroring, and other forms of RAID as well as PIT copies with backups, snapshots, and archives. Balance protection to number and types of faults to tolerate along with needed speed of recovery and applicable regulations. Leverage DNS and network load balancer resiliency for local and cloud.
Loss or damaged data or applications	Have a DR, BC, and BR plan that can be used in pieces as needed to address various threats or incidents. Leverage various PIT copies as part of 4 3 2 1 protection for fast recovery. Have strong security and defenses along with change configuration management to prevent or minimize chance of something happening, while enabling rapid recovery.
Loss of power or communications	Standby power including generators as well as UPS batteries to carry load while switching from power sources. Look for and eliminate single points of failure (SPOF) and ensure proper battery, switch, and other facilities maintenance. Standby or alternative site to failover to, along with resilient DNS for network.
Failed component	Applications and data placed on resilient server, storage, and I/O paths. Leverage mirror, replicate, and other forms of RAID to meet specific application PACE and SLO. Align applicable fault tolerance mode (FTM) and technology to counter component faults for server, storage, network, hardware, and software. Isolate and contain fault with redundant components when needed to meet RTO, RPO, and other SLO as well as regulations.
File, object, or data damaged	Varies based on your 4 3 2 1 rule implementation and ability to leverage different consistency-point granularities.
Cloud or MSP failure	Implement 4 3 2 1 data protection along with other resiliency and availabity best practices in and across clouds. This means protecting critical data located in a cloud to another cloud or back to your primary site. Also leverage DNS and resilient network access.

Table 4.4. Numbers of Server and Storage Configurations and Faults to Tolerate

Server Nodes	Storage Protection	Storage Space Efficiency	Server FTT	Storage FTT	Characteristics
1	None	100%	0	0	No protection
1	Mirror N + N	50%	0	1	No server faults, one disk fault
1	Parity N + 1	Varies	0	1	No server faults, one disk fault Width, size, or number of disks varies
1	Parity N + 2	Varies	0	2	No server faults, two disk faults Width, size, or number of disks varies
2	Mirror N + N	50%	1	1	One server OR one disk, not both
3	Mirror N + N + N	33%	1+	2	Two faults, one (or more, depending on implementation) server, and two disk
4	Parity N + 1	50+%	2	1	Two (or more) server and disk faults Space varies depending on number of drives
4	Parity N + 2	Varies	2+	2	Multiple server and storage faults, varies by implementation and space overhead

4.15. Chapter Summary

Keep in mind that everything is not the same, so why protect, preserve, secure, and serve applications and data in the same way as your data infrastructure?

There are many aspects to availability for data infrastructures, including failures to tolerate (FTT), SLO, and application PACE to consider. RAID including parity and erasure code, mirroring, and replication are not a replacement for backup and need to be combined with recovery-point objective time-interval copy techniques.

General action items include:

- Any technology, hardware, software, or service can fail; be prepared.
- Backup, CDP, replication, and snapshots enable PIT and RPO protection.
- Balance rebuild performance impact and time vs. storage space overhead savings.
- Different tools, techniques, and technology support the 4 3 2 1 rule and FTT.
- Everything is not the same, thus there are different availability techniques.
- Protect applications and data at various levels, intervals, and granularities.
- RPO and RTO, along with other RAS capabilities, combine to enable availability.
- Use different approaches for various applications and environments.
- What is best for somebody else's environment may not be best for yours.

Keep in mind, if you cannot go back in time, how can you restore in the future?

Bottom line: Availability and data protection enable data as well as information to be accessible, consistency, safe, and secure to be served.

Chapter 5

Data Infrastructure Metrics and Management

Having insight and awareness avoids flying blind with data infrastructure management

What You Will Learn in This Chapter

- Putting together what we have covered so far
- The importance of metrics and insight to avoid flying blind
- Where to get and how to use various metrics that matter

The focus is on common data infrastructure (both legacy and software-defined) management and metric topics for insight. Key themes, buzzwords, and trends addressed in this chapter include analytics, metrics, server, storage, I/O network, hardware, software, services, CI, HCI, software-defined, cloud, virtual, container, and various applications, among others topics.

5.1. Getting Started

All applications have some performance, availability, capacity, and economic (PACE) attributes that vary by type of workload, environment, size, scale, and scope, among other considerations. Likewise, all data infrastructures, from on-prem legacy, bare metal to software-defined virtual and cloud, regardless of how packaged (converged, hyper-converged infrastructure, cloud in a box, systems or components) support application PACE needs.

Different environments, applications, sub-applications, or application component workloads also vary, having diverse PACE needs along with different service-level objectives (SLOs). Similarly, the applications, data, and metadata, along with the configuration of the data infrastructure resources they depend on, also need to be managed.

5.2. Avoid Flying Blind—Having Situational Awareness

Recall from Chapters 1 and 2 that all applications require some amount of performance, availability (durable, secure, protected), capacity (space, bandwidth), and economics (PACE) attributes. Different application PACE requirements depend on corresponding data infrastructure resource (servers, storage, I/O, hardware, software) needs that must be balanced.

Data infrastructure metrics provide insight into application PACE and their corresponding resource usage, service levels, and activity. Some metrics focus on activity usage and utilization, others on resource saturation or starvation, and others on errors and events. Other metrics involve metadata about systems, software, applications, and actual data.

Fast applications need fast data infrastructures, including servers, networks, and storage configured for optimal PACE. To enable optimization, do you have timely, accurate insight and awareness into your data infrastructure, or are you flying blind? Flying blind means that you lack proper instruments, impacting confidence and control to make decisions without situational awareness of your current or soon-to-be status. In other words, you could be headed for unplanned performance degradation problems or worse.

Do you have data infrastructure insight into how and where:

- Your application and resource bottlenecks currently exist, or where they may move to
- How NVM NAND flash SSD along with NVMe technologies can speed up applications
- Availability (or lack of it) impacts application productivity
- Performance degrades during recovery or failure modes and workload impact
- Role of PMEM, SCM, cache, CDN and application accelerators
- Application changes behave when deployed in production and productivity impact
- Additional resources needed (forecasting) and when
- Server, I/O and network bandwidth savings (or impacts)

Figure 5.1 is a reminder that all applications have some variation of PACE attributes. Some applications have and need more performance, while others focus on availability, capacity, or low-cost economics, and yet others use various combinations.

Figure 5.2 shows different layers of resources and focus areas for data infrastructures on the left, and aggregated views for analysis, cognitive AI/ML/DL, correlation, reporting, and management on the right. On the right can be a collection of standalone or integrated systems, depending on the size and scope of your organization. For example, smaller organizations might manage their environments with Excel spreadsheets, simple databases, or other

| Performance | Availability | Capacity | Economics |

Figure 5.1   All applications have some PACE attributes.

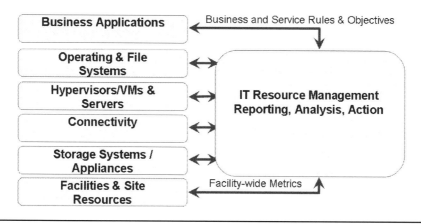

Figure 5.2   Various metrics that align with different data infrastructure layers.

solutions. Larger organizations may have IT service management (ITSM) platforms, configuration management database (CMDB), configuration repository, performance management database (PMDB), or various other DCIM-related systems.

Tip: Informed decision making spans from day-to-day operational and tactical administration to strategic architecture, engineering, planning, forecasting, and procurement, among other tasks. Informed, effective decision making, by humans or machines, requires timely, accurate, and relevant information. The lack of good information can result in garbage in, garbage out decision making. That is, garbage information (or lack of accurate insight) can result in garbage or poor decisions based on incomplete or inaccurate situational awareness.

Having timely, accurate, and actionable data infrastructure insight awareness facilitates:

- Avoiding flying blind, either without instruments or using bad data, to prevent bad decisions
- Informed problem resolution, proactive prevention, agile and smart decision making
- Establishment of performance QoS baselines to know what is normal and what is abnormal
- Maximized investment in data infrastructure resources
- Application productivity performance and availability
- Putting the customer instead of the vendor in control
- Addressing data infrastructure, application, and service questions

Figure 5.3 shows sources of information, insight, and awareness across data infrastructures layers accessed by and fed into different data infrastructure management tools. Depending on the size of your organization, your approach may be much simpler, or more involved.

DCIM and ITSM tools allow monitoring, reporting, tracking, and maintaining an inventory of resources including servers, storage, I/O, networking hardware along with software, and services. These assets can be tracked in CMDB and their activity monitored via PMDB. Some of the tools focus on lower-level DCIM facilities, while others are more end to end in focus, from higher-level business and information applications to how they use and consume data infrastructure resources and services.

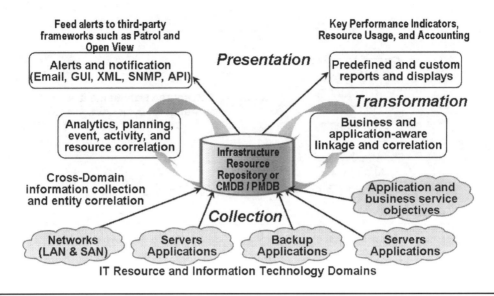

Figure 5.3　Various data infrastructure and IT information systems.

Performance depends on availability; availability relies on performance to support processing, movement, and storing of data along with associated applications. The cost of hardware continues to decrease. However, more of it is needed (servers, storage, networks) to support growth, new applications along with software-defined data infrastructures.

There is a tendency to focus on physical capital costs such as hardware, networking, and facilities. However, there are also opportunities to optimize operational expenses. Besides staffing, maintenance, and services fees, are you getting the maximum value and ROI out of your software? For example, are you getting the highest utilization and effective productivity out of your AWS subscriptions, Citrix, Cisco, Epic, Meditec, Dell EMC, Desix, EPIC, IBM, M1, Microsoft (Azure subscription, Azurestack, or other on-prem licenses), OpenStack, Oracle, SAP, SAS, and VMware, among other software investments?

Considerations, tips, and recommendations include:

- Leverage automation tools for the collection, analysis, and reporting of information.
- Organizations rely on applications to keep them informed about how they are running.
- Data infrastructures need applications to keep them informed about how they are running.
- The right metrics are the ones that have meaning in your environment.
- Avoid flying blind and making decisions based on guesses: Be informed.

5.2.1. Metrics That Matter (and Where to Get Them)

To address data infrastructure challenges, you need to be able to obtain applicable metrics promptly. This means metrics that are relevant, real-time, and do not require extensive manual effort to extract. There are many different tools and resources for obtaining metrics that matter.

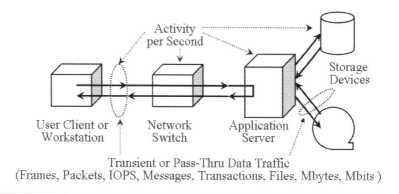

Figure 5.4   Data infrastructure metrics points of interest.

What is your area of focus, applications, database and file systems, management tools, operating systems, drivers, hypervisors, servers, I/O networking, and storage or cloud resources, among others? In addition to focusing on your area or technology domain, are you looking for metrics to troubleshoot and perform diagnostics for problem solving, service management, planning, or design? Are you looking for performance, availability, capacity, security, and cost information? For performance, are you looking for activity rates (transactions, gets, puts, frames per second, IOPs), or data movement (bandwidth, transfer rates), latency (response time), queue depth or resource consumption?

Figure 5.4 shows various data infrastructure points of interest as well as sources for metrics. These metrics can be used to support various data infrastructure management activities. In Figure 5.4, moving from left to right, there is the user (client, consumer of information services), there are devices including mobile, tablets, laptops, and workstations, access networks sending packets, frames, IOPs, gets, puts, messages, transactions, files, or other items. In the middle of Figure 5.4, there are networking devices including switches, routers, load balancers, and firewalls. On the right side of Figure 5.4 are servers supporting different applications that have various storage devices attached. Metrics can be collected at various points for different time intervals such as per second, and results can be correlated and reported for different purposes.

There are many different types of metrics that matter for data infrastructures. Metrics can be standalone, such as activity per time interval, e.g., I/O operations per second (IOPS), including block, file, and object gets or puts, transactions per second (TPS) or API calls, among others. There are also compound metrics with multiple items combined to provide a multidimensional (composite) view. For example, IOPS or TPS per watt of energy used, or cost per terabyte, among others.

Also recall that there are averages, peaks, standard deviation, and sustained metrics that are measured as well as derived or calculated. There are rates of activity and data movement along with ratios of change; some are server-based, others arise from the I/O network, storage, cloud, hypervisor, or component. Metrics also include availability, reliability, failures, and retries, as well as bandwidth, throughput, response time, and latency.

Another aspect of metrics is that they can be a higher-level summary or detailed for different time intervals. Figure 5.5 (left) shows an example of workload activity by month along with a response time threshold, response time, and activity. In the example, as activity increases,

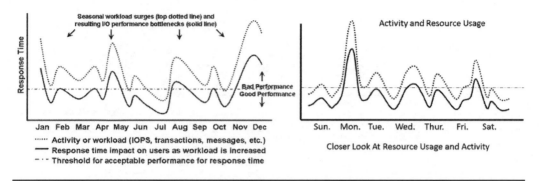

Figure 5.5   Server I/O activity: monthly view (left) and daily view (right).

response time also goes up (lower is better), with the threshold indicating an expected or required service-level objective.

Figure 5.5 (right) shows a drill-down or detail, looking closer at a specific week of a given month to see what is occurring on days of the week as well as an indication of the time of day. Further investigation into details of a specific day or hour time range can be seen in Figure 5.6, which shows workload across different physical or virtual servers.

Just as there are many different types of metrics for various purposes representing applications and data infrastructure, along with data center facilities, there are also multiple sources of metrics. These include different tools, some built into operating systems, hypervisors, drivers, file systems, networks, storage, and databases, among other points of interest. Some of the tools are available for a fee and are tied to a particular technology or focus area; others are free or open-source and community editions. Then there are neutral, independent tools and services for fees.

Server ID	1	2	3	4	5	6	7	8		Totals
	8	12	64	16	16	4	8	32	Avg. I/O Size (KB)	20KB
	50	550	250	1,100	500	1,500	800	250	Avg. I/O Rate	5,000
	0.4	6.4	15.6	17.2	7.8	5.9	6.3	7.8	Avg. Transfer Rate	67.4

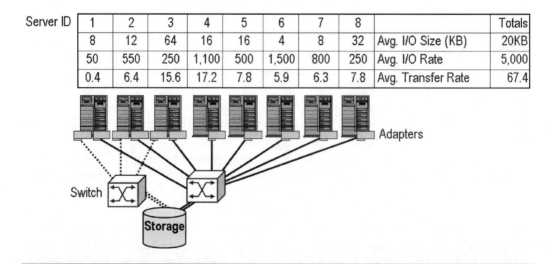

Figure 5.6   Server and storage I/O metrics.

Tip: In this age of digital, IoT, and IoD technology, a convenient, time-tested (pun intended) tool and technique to gauge the performance and response time of something is a stopwatch. This can be an analog or digital watch or wall clock, the clock on your computer display, or simply adding time stamps at the beginning and end of a script or command to see how long it ran.

Common to different sources of metrics is some focus on collecting telemetry and other activity or event data, either in real time or over time. Some specialize in analysis and correlation, while others concentrate on visualization, presentation, or export to other platforms. Then there are tools, solutions, and services that combine all of the above functions with different interoperabilities.

Tip: A metric-related term is test harness, associated with simulation, testing, and benchmark discussions. One context of test harness is a physical cable or connector for collecting electrical power or other telemetry data. Another context is a software wrapper, kit, shell, shim, or script package for a particular tool to make it easier to work with, as well as tailored for a given workload scenario. For example, there are several test harnesses that wrap around Vdbench to perform different tasks. These include the SNIA Emerald green and power tools, VMware HCIBench for testing standalone, CI and HCI including vSAN nodes, among others.

Additional examples of tools, scripts, services, and technologies for gaining metrics include those from or apart from AWS, Apple, Broadcom, Cisco, Dell EMC, Fujitsu, Google, HDS, HPE and Huawei, IBM and Intel, Juniper, Lenovo, Mellanox, Micron and Microsoft, NetApp and Nutanix, Oracle and OpenStack, Promise, Quantum, Rackspace and Redhat. Additional tools are available from Samsung, Seagate, Servicenow and Simplivity, Teamquest, Ubuntu, Veritas, VMware and WD, among others.

Some other examples of insight and reporting awareness tools as a source of metrics include solutions or services from Bocada, Caspa (network metrics), Cacti, Cloudkitty, Collectd, CPUID CPU-Z (server CPU metrics), Dashboard, Datadog (dashboard for various metrics from application to servers and cloud), Datagravity, Densify, and DPA (Dell EMC Data Protection Advisor).

Additional sources for metrics and insight include Firescope, Enmotus FuzeDrive (microtiering and server storage I/O metrics), ExtraHop, Freeboard, Graphviz (visualization), Hyper I/O (Diskranger and HiMon [windows server metrics]) and JAM Treesize (space usage). Some Linux tools include (blkdid, cat [/proc/cpuinfo], df, dstat, fdisk, iotop, hdparm, htop, lscpu, lspci, lshw. Other tools include Manageiq, Microsoft (MAP, Windows Admin Center, msinfo), Nagios, Ntopng, sar, sysmon, netstat MonitorDB as well as Nttcp (workload generator). Others include Openit, Opvizor, Quest, RRDtool, stashboard, Statsd, Solarwinds, Turbonomic, and Uila, among others.

Figure 5.7 shows using Linux *lspci* command to display PCIe LSI devices (adapters), along with performing a disk read performance test to device /dev/md0 (a software-defined RAID set). Refer to the Appendix for additional examples of workload simulation, benchmark, testing, and metrics.

More awareness tools include Perfmon (various Windows and related metrics), Ping (along with ipconfig, ifconfig, Ibping, Fcping among others), Jperf (visualization), Quest (Foglight, Spotlight along with other SQL and Oracle as well as AD tools), R (visualization), and RVtools (various VMware-related metrics and configuration information).

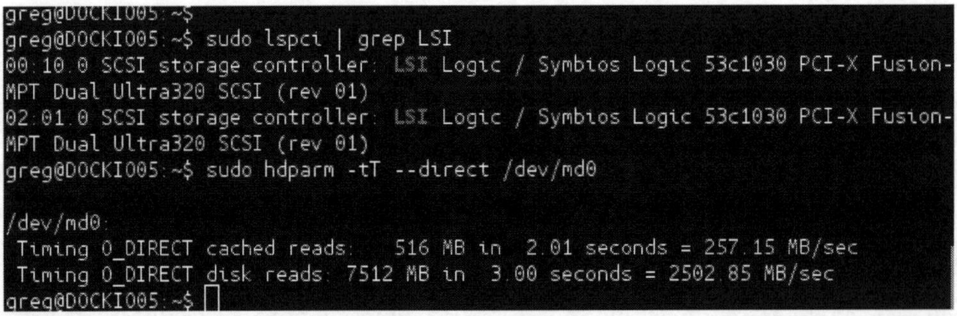

```
greg@DOCKI005:~$
greg@DOCKI005:~$ sudo lspci | grep LSI
00:10.0 SCSI storage controller: LSI Logic / Symbios Logic 53c1030 PCI-X Fusion-
MPT Dual Ultra320 SCSI (rev 01)
02:01.0 SCSI storage controller: LSI Logic / Symbios Logic 53c1030 PCI-X Fusion-
MPT Dual Ultra320 SCSI (rev 01)
greg@DOCKI005:~$ sudo hdparm -tT --direct /dev/md0

/dev/md0:
 Timing O_DIRECT cached reads:   516 MB in  2.01 seconds = 257.15 MB/sec
 Timing O_DIRECT disk reads: 7512 MB in  3.00 seconds = 2502.85 MB/sec
greg@DOCKI005:~$ []
```

Figure 5.7 Various Linux status commands.

Add to the previously mentioned tools, SAS (statistical analysis software) and Solarwinds (various metrics) along with Spiceworks as well as Splunk. Additional tools include Windows Task manager, Turbonomic (server, storage, I/O, and configuration metrics). Tools are also part of other operating system, hypervisor, server, storage, network, and cloud solutions. Other tools include Visual Studio (Microsoft) Web Performance and Load Tests, VMware Esxtop and Visualesxtop (VMware metrics), vSAN observer and Virtual Instruments (server, storage, I/O, and configuration metrics), among many others.

Needless to say, there are many additional tools for gaining insight and awareness for different layers or altitudes about data infrastructure. There are also tools for monitoring application workloads, as well as lower-level facilities as well as habitats for the technology. Among these are Atto tools (various workload and reporting tools), Benchmark Factory (database and other workload generator and reporting), Black magic for Apple platforms (storage and I/O workload generator), Cosbench (object storage workload generator), Crystal (various workload generator and reports) and dd (data copy tool that can be used to generate server storage I/O activity. Other workload generators, benchmark, and simulation tools include Dedisbench (storage workload generator with dedupe), DFSio (Hadoop and DFS), Diskspd (Microsoft open-source server and storage I/O workload generator) as well as DVDstore (mixed-application workload generator). For cognitive AI/ML/DL workload generation, simulation, test, validation there is the MLPERF tool set that includes vision recognition, language translate, commerce (recommendations), and general inference. MLPERF is a suite that includes model training.

Additional workload generation, simulation, and benchmark tools include ESRP (Microsoft Exchange workload generator), FIO.exe (storage workload generator), HammerDB (various TPCC workload generator), Silly Little Oracle Benchmark (SLOB), Hdparm (storage workload generator and configuration display), Iometer (storage workload generator), Iorate (storage workload generator), Ior (for HPC and Lustre large scale vs. general-purpose file systems), Iozone (storage workload generator), and Iperf (network workload generator).

Figure 5.8 shows VMware vSAN metrics with a series of thumbnail (small) performance and health indicators that can be clicked on to expand for further detail.

Besides those mentioned above, other workload, simulation, benchmark, and test tools include Jetstress (Exchange Email workload generator), Loadgen, LoginVSI (VDI and workspace workload generator), Mongoose (various object workload generators), PCmark (various

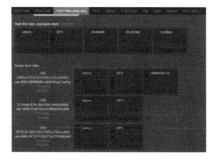 

Figure 5.8 VMware vSAN Observer dashboard.

server and I/O workloads), and Ptest (processor performance test. Additional tools include Quest Benchmark Factory (various TPCC and other workload generator, trace, replay and extensive reporting with automation), SharePoint Performance Tests, MOSS and WSS (various workload generator), STAC (workload generator for financial trading), Storage Performance Council (SPC) workload generator, SLOB, Swingbench (Oracle database workload generator and reporting), and Sysbench (Simulation and workload generator including database).

Then there are MLPERF for AI/ML/DL, Teragen/Terasort (Hadoop and DFS), TPCC (various database transactional, decision support and analytics workload simulation tests), Vdbench (simulation workloads, file and block I/O, various wrappers and test harness including VMware HCIBench, SNIA Emerald among others), Virtual Instruments (Simulation and Analytics), VMmark (Simulation, mixed workload based on DVDstore), Xbench (Apple-focused benchmarks) along with YCSB (Yahoo Cloud Serving Benchmark workload generator), among many others. Some of the tools can be found at download sites such as Git Hub.

Following is an example of a YCSB workload (update heavy, 50% reads, 50% writes) against a local MongoDB database. Other YCSB workloads include B (95% reads, 5% writes), C (100% reads), D (read latest inserts), E (short ranges of queries), and F (read modify writes or updates to existing records).

./bin/ycsb run mongodb -s -P workloads/workloada -p recordcount=10000000 -threads 2 -p measurementtype=timeseries -p timeseries.granularity=2000 >> results.txt

In addition to the above, there also various vendor solutions that are part of servers, storage, network, and cloud services, including examples in the Appendix.

Considerations, tips, and recommendations include:

- The most important metric and benchmark are the ones that matter for your environment.
- What is your objective for measuring and metrics, along with test and simulation?
- Some tools are for fee; others are free, open-source, or available as community editions.
- Focus and level (or altitude) for monitoring, measuring, test, or simulation.
- Application, database, API, object, file system, or block, among other focuses.
- Keep context of object in mind, as some tools focus on S3 or Swift objects vs. others.

5.3. Data Infrastructure Decision Making

Keep in mind that there is what you need (your must-have requirements and criteria) and then there are what you would like (your wants or nice-to-have items). Also keep in mind that there are what you need and must have, and there are what vendors, solution, service providers, and consultants or advisors might want (or need you to have).

Watch out for the wants and needs of others becoming your wants and needs if they are not applicable. Likewise, look for opportunities to leverage the different things people are suggesting or recommending, as they may become something of value. Table 5.1 shows requests for information, proposals, and tenders. These include bids that form the basis for tenders, which are formal bid-and-proposal processes.

RFI, RFP, RFQ, RFT, and SOW, among other processes, can vary in detail and scope. Generally, they include a due date for the submission, rules, processes, and procedures, as well as whom to contact, or whom not to contact. Details can include what the requirements are, compatibility, interoperability and other technical as well as business considerations.

Business or commercial considerations include costs and fee schedules for up-front as well as recurring maintenance, licensing, and subscriptions as applicable. Vendor or supplier background information, including technical, product, marketing, sales, service, and support, as well as financials, are other items. There may be questions to be addressed by the respondent, which may be simple yes, no, or more detailed. Responses may be specified to be general or very strict, with non-marketing-type answers.

Questions might also be ranked both regarding their weight of importance as well as encouraging the respondent to put a rank or weight on their solution. There might also be

Table 5.1. Request for Information and Proposals

What	Meaning	When and Why
RFI	Request For Information	Early in a decision-making process to assess the market, vendor, and technology offerings that might be applicable now or in the future. This is part of a learning and discovery process. Can be generic or specific to a set of requirements. Use as a means to meet with and learn about vendors, technology, and solution offerings in advance of a formal RFQ or RFP process. Information from RFI can be used to help prepare formal RFQ and RFP. RFI can be more general and may include broad or rough "for planning purposes" pricing costs.
RFP	Request For Proposal	Similar to an RFQ. You may have more general criteria requirements, leaving the actual solution up to a vendor, solution, or service provider to respond how they would address cost and terms. Both RFQ and RFP can be common for government-related projects, but also for commercial and private activities, large and small.
RFQ	Request For Quote	Similar to an RFP. However, you may know what you want in general terms, provide vendors or solution providers with your criteria for them to respond with a solution quote including pricing. Both RFQ and RFP are typically more formal activities with rules, processes, and guidelines along with timing specified on how the winner will be chosen. Likewise, there are usually criteria on how disputes will be addressed.
RFT	Request For Tender	Similar to an RFP or RFQ, vendors are invited or offered to respond to a formal tender (set of requirements and process) as to how they would provide a solution, along with costs.
SOW	Statement of Work	Summary (or expanded) description of what the work is to be done, by whom, when, what the general as well as specific expectations are. The SOW can include project milestones, goals, and objectives.

sections for competitive perspective from the respondents. Other items include terms for delivery, installation, and configuration and acceptance criteria. Acceptance criteria might include specific performance results validated with a benchmark or other proof of validation, as well as functionality and interoperability demonstration as proposed. Warranties, service, and support, including who will do what and when, may be included, along with other contractual terms. For example, what are the vendor or service providers remedies to make things right if the solution does meet its contractual and SLA terms?

What are your constraints regarding budget (CapEx and OpEx) now and into the future? What are your power, cooling, primary, and standby electrical power, as well as floor space, floor weight loading, and other data center (habitat for technology) constraints? What are your networking capabilities, local and remote, including for cloud access. Do you have any legal, regulatory, or other requirements to address? What compatibility and interoperability do you need with current hardware, software, networks, and services, as well as tools, staff skills, and procedures? What is your timeline for decision making, installation, acceptance, and deployment?

Understand what you currently have, how it works (or not) to meet your workload, as well as growth expectations. Also, what do you like or dislike about what you have, what do you need and want, as well as current strengths and weakness? What will be the cost to migrate to new technology, including applications along with data movement (and migration). Also, understand if there are any new technologies to learn, new processes as well as procedures to adopt. What will you do with old or existing technology and solutions; is there any residual value in some other role within your data infrastructure, or do the costs favor disposing of the item?

Tip: Look for consistency in what others recommend to you to use. Do they have a good history of being consistent in their advice and recommendations, or do they simply push whatever is new or whomever they are currently working for. Trust, yet verify.

A good salesperson's job is to remove barriers for his or her employer and to look out for the customer's long-term interest so that he or she can come back and sell you something again in the future. On the other hand, some salespeople are just looking for, or being told what to sell, at the current time and moment and may also set barriers for other vendors. Make sure that the salesperson and his or her organization are looking to partner and bring value, so you both win.

Tip: When you ask questions, be specific with context and follow-up detail as needed to avoid simple answers. For example, a question such as "Do you support snapshots?" might be answered with a yes, but does that tell you how extensive the snapshot features are.

If you have a concern or problem with a vendor or their solution, ask them to be candid, even if you have to go under a non-disclosure agreement (NDA) to get the information. It is better to know that something is broken or not working properly or supported so you can work around it than not to know what the issues are. Likewise, if you go under an NDA, honor it.

Watch out for apples-to-oranges (apples-to-pears) comparisons, where different things are compared that are not the same, fair, or relevant. Not everything will be apples to apples or the same. However, there are similarities, and different criteria can be used as needed. Also look for context, as that can help normalize the differences between apples-to-oranges comparisons.

Tip: Balance the pros and cons, feature benefits and caveats of open vs. closed, vendor propriety or commodity solutions, technology as well as how they work for you, your environment, and achieve what you need to do. Are you making a change or selection because it is what everybody is talking about, or will it bring actual benefit to your environment? Can you run a proof of concept (POC) or extended test to see how the solution works for your needs and requirements?

Some solutions are touted as having no single point of failure, being totally resilient, even with Internet and YouTube videos of people shooting with a gun or blowing something up while it continues to work. What happens if somebody misconfigures, sets the wrong switch setting (button, dial, knob, parameter), or applies software or firmware the wrong way, or simply unplugs the device. If something wrong can happen, it will, and usually it involves human error.

You might want or somebody needs you to spend a large amount of cash on a massive cache (SSD, SCM, or PMEM) for your server, storage, or network. However, upon investigation, you know or determine that yours is a random environment where a lot of cache is not needed, rather, a smaller amount in one or more locations that is also more effective and cash-friendly. Likewise, you might discover that while SSDs and SCMs can boost performance, the real benefit for your environment can be to reduce or eliminate time spent responding to user calls, then searching for and fixing various problems. In other words, SSDs and SCMs can be a form of IT and data infrastructure aspirin or ibuprofen pain relief.

A solution might look expensive up front as a capital expenditure, but it may have low recurring operating or OpEx costs including licenses, renewals, and maintenance. Likewise, something that looks low-cost up front may end up costing more with annual fees as well as usage and activity costs. Do your homework: Look for value near-term as well as longer-term.

Tip: Leverage vendors' hardware (and software) compatibility lists (HCL) to confirm as well as support remediation for devices, device drivers, patches, versions, and other updates. Also look into and leverage vendors' tools for managing updates, including automated, manual, or scheduled downloads and implementation. Vendors also have lab resources along with knowledge base, wiki, forums, and other resources to assistant with testing, troubleshooting, diagnostics, comparison, and remediation activities.

Considerations, tips, and recommendations include:

- Do you need multiple vendors? Are you comfortable with single or sole-sourced?
- Ask what might seem like obvious questions, as sometimes you can get unexpected answers.
- Likewise, ask about assumptions, dependencies, interoperability, and other requirements.
- If something is too good to be true, it might be. Do your homework.
- Find a balance between analysis paralysis (stuck in evaluations) and quick decisions.
- Trust yet verify when it comes to decision making, bids, proposals, and tenders.
- Keep in mind your needs and requirements vs. the wants (or needs) of somebody else.
- Manage your vendors, service, and solution providers while enabling them to do their jobs.

5.3.1. Comparing Data Infrastructure Components and Services

There are many different aspects and considerations when it comes to comparing data infrastructure components for legacy and software-defined environments. This includes looking at, comparing, evaluating, making decisions on what to buy, rent, lease, subscribe to, as well as how to configure for use. The chapters in this book lay out the various characteristics, attributes, and considerations in comparing different hardware, software, services, tools, techniques, and technologies for data infrastructures.

Tip: People often look for something with the lowest cost, and smart vendors or providers know this. Vendors may offer to price "as low as" or "from" or "starting at" along with additional fees for optional services and features. On the other hand, vendors and providers also offer premium services or products at premium fees all-inclusive.

There are also value offerings, which often get confused with cheap or low cost. Rather, for a higher fee, you get more services or capabilities. The value offering might be more expensive than the "starting" price of a basic product or service. However, when you add up the extra cost of the optional items vs. what's included in a value offering, the bundled solution may have a better overall cost. This is where comparing costs on apples-to-oranges basis comes into play.

For example, one server might be priced at $499.99 USD while another is at $2,999.99, causing somebody to ask why spend the extra $2,599.99? If all you need are the capabilities of the lower-cost server, that might be sufficient and the better deal. However, if the more expensive server has more processing performance, storage, memory, network ports, redundant power supplies and cooling, operating systems, and other bundled software that fits your needs vs. that might be the better value vs. a lower-cost model that you have to spend to upgrade.

Keep in mind that economics, while often focused on actual costs, also includes the cost of people's times to do things. While the above example is for servers, there also examples for storage, I/O, and networking, cloud, and data protection, among other things that we look at in each of the respective chapters. Also remember to account for taxes, shipping, installation, insurance, training, and other up-front, as well as recurring expense costs.

For some environments and applications, focus is on performance, for others it is on capacity, for others availability, including data protection, while for others it is all about cost. On the other hand, many environments have different PACE needs even within a given application.

Some use a mixed approach of different dedicated storage solutions or media assigned to an application, task, or role, while others use hybrid technologies. So what is the best type of storage device, component, or media and medium? It depends! What are your application PACE needs and requirements?

Some environments, applications, or sub-application pieces have the need for more performance with less storage capacity, which would probably lean you toward more SSD. However, what if most of those applications requests are reads of data with a high degree of locality, which means adding some local cache? The local cache can be a mix or DRAM for reads as well as SCM or PNEM, or other NVM on the server, as well as some shared DRAM and NVM on a storage system, appliance, or converted and virtual device that also could include some traditional spinning-media HDD for hybrid, an all-Flash array (AFA) or all-SSD array (ASA), or an all-NVM array solution. For performance environments, instead of comparing just cost per capacity, which does not reflect the functionality of fast storage, instead compare cost per activity such as cost per IOP, transaction, TPS, file, video, page, or object processed.

Watch out for comparing on a cost per capacity basis vs. cost per performance or productivity basis, or comparing cost vs. availability, accessibility, and durability. In other words, don't just buy capacity at the lowest cost without considering performance, availability, reliability, and cost to replace on a more frequent basis. For example, comparing a 1-TB NVM SSD to 1 TB of low-cost, high-capacity desktop or client-class HDD vs. low-cost, low-performance cloud storage is at best comparing apples to oranges, as they do not reflect the various characteristics and the ability of the different storage to meet different application PACE needs. Remember, everything is not the same, for workloads as well as technologies.

Keep in mind that some technology is older and has known capabilities as well as limits or issues. Likewise, some technology is newer with known features, but issues or limits may not be known yet. How to balance the old vs. the new is also how you can innovate by using old things in new ways, new things in new ways, sometimes even as companions in hybrid ways. Also, understand your options and alternatives, even if they are not your preference, so that you can articulate why you chose a solution.

Vendor lock-in may not be a bad thing if you get a benefit from it. On the other hand, if you do not get a benefit, then vendor lock-in can be bad. Also keep in mind that the responsibility for managing vendor lock-in is on the customer, although some vendors may help to facilitate the lock-in. Also keep in mind that the golden rule of virtualization and software-defined anything is that whoever controls the management tools and interfaces controls the gold (that is, controls the gold or budget).

Some solutions are low-cost to enter, starting small, but they do not scale without adding complexity and increasing overhead as well as costs. This can apply to smaller servers, storage, network switches, and CI and HCI solutions vs. larger variants that can scale with less cost and complexity. You might pay more up-front for that scaling, but keep in mind what your growth plans are.

Tip: Ask vendors (politely, of course, and with respect) "So What?" So What does something mean, or So What does something do for you or your environment? So What does something work with or require to work. As part of making decisions, do a SWOT (Strength, Weakness, Opportunities, and Threats) analysis of subjective as well as quantitative comparisons.

Beware of focusing on hardware and software solutions that promise near-term cost savings, yet lack the tools to manage and leverage those solutions effectively without added costs. Worse is that the solutions intended to reduce your costs are not used effectively and end up increasing your long-term costs.

If you have a capacity plan and forecast that includes server, storage, I/O and networking, hardware, software, and tools as well as PACE attributes, you can use that to leverage various end-of-the-month, end-of-the-quarter, or year-end deals. Likewise, sometimes vendors have excess product or inventory and offer promotions; if you know about them and can use the resources, you might have a good opportunity.

Tip: Look at how a solution initially deploys and how it can be expanded over time: how disruptive those upgrades and enhancements are. Disruptive means downtime, as well as any other hardware, software, or service and tools dependencies. Disruptive also means to your budget. Are you paying more up-front for lower-cost later expansion, or are you paying less up front and then paying more later.

Watch out for solutions that play to lower cost per capacity based on a given data protection, data footprint reduction (i.e., effective capacity), RAID level including parity and erasure codes to reduce costs. However, that also reduces your performance and productivity for primary workloads. These types of solutions, however, might be a good fit for other scenarios.

Tip: Speaking of cost, while it is important to look at NVM NAND flash, PMEM, and SCM SSDs on a cost-per-IOP or productivity and activity basis, which is where they perform well, an opportunity can be missed by focusing just on performance. For example, while an environment or application may not have strong performance needs for SSD, by implementing as much SSD as possible, even at a higher cost per capacity, if those devices magically clear up other application, troubleshooting, and support problems that in turn free up staff to do other things, not to mention making customers happy, then SSD can be a better value even if it is not being measured on a performance basis.

Considerations, tips, and recommendations include:

- Look beyond lowest cost per component: What's the effective enabling benefit value?
- How proven is a technology, solution, service or provider: Who else is using it?
- Understand your total cost of acquisition, install, training, migration, conversion.
- How will technologies work for you today, vs. you having to work for the solution?
- Does the solution require additional hardware, software, services, tools, staff and support?
- Vendor lock-in may not be a bad thing if you get a benefit from it.
- When in doubt, ask others for input or advice (my contact information is at the back of the book); however, do respect other people's time.

5.3.2. Analysis, Benchmark, Comparison, Simulation, and Tests

Analysis, benchmarks, comparisons, tests, and simulations can be used for assessing and validating new or planned technology as part of acquisition decision making. Testing and analysis can be used for problem solving, planning, engineering, validation, and verification of new application or data infrastructure software, hardware, services, and their configuration, as well as whether they function as intended. Other uses of a simulation (aka workload modeling) are to understand how new or changing applications and workloads impact performance as well as availability.

Another use for simulations is to troubleshoot, forecast, and perform what-if analysis to prevent problems. Workload simulation, test, and benchmark can determine what a particular hardware/software combination can do, or can be used to support some number of users, activities, or functions as part of a solution, as either a vendor, solution provider, or customer.

Will you be testing from the perspective of a user of applications (i.e., end to end or E2E), or as a consumer of data infrastructure services or data infrastructure components (server, storage, network, hardware, software or services)? What are the metrics (or insight) you are looking to obtain, what parameters for test configuration (duration, number of workers, workload mix)?

Where and what is your focus and objective?

- Stressing a system, solution, storage, software, or service under test (SUT)
- What will drive, generate, and act as a system test initiator (STI)
- Are you testing to saturation to see when and what breaks (failure scenarios)?
- Is your focus on utilization or at what point response time and usefulness degrade?
- Compare different technologies, tools, and techniques under various conditions.

How will you be testing, with recorded traces replayed against a given data infrastructure layer such as vs. an application, database or file system, operating system, hypervisor, server, storage, network or service? Instead of a trace replay, will you be running a random workload generator or script that runs a known workload that can be repeated with accuracy and consistency?

Will you be using a do-it-yourself (DIY) approach with your own or different scripts and tools, leveraging open-source and freeware, vendor-supplied or services? What workload will you be running—your own, somebody else's, something you found on the web, what a vendor, consultant or solution provider said to use? The biggest issue with benchmarks, tests, and simulations is using the wrong tool for the given scenario, along with the wrong configuration settings. Use the tool and settings that are relevant to your environment and application workloads, unless you can use your actual application. When in doubt, ask somebody for input and advice as well as understand what your application's workloads are.

Tip: Look for data infrastructure performance analytics solutions that not only automate and take care of things for you in an auto-pilot mode but also provide insight and a learning experience. For example, with the continued growth, scale and interdependence, automation helps to manage those complexities.

Does the tool or solution provide the ability to learn, enable analysis, and gain insight into why things are behaving as they are? In other words, can the automated solution help you manage while expanding your tradecraft experience and skill sets, while also applying those to your data infrastructure optimization needs?

Table 5.2 shows a basic five-phase process for conducting a simulation, test, or benchmark study project. With Table 5.2, keep in mind that everything is not the same in the data center, or information factory, as well as across different data infrastructures, and test and simulations will also vary. This means that not only are there different tools and technologies for simulating various workloads; the process steps can vary along with setup and parameter configuration.

You can increase or decrease the number of phases and steps to meet your particular environment needs, scope, and complexity. The basics are the plan, define, set up including practice, execute and analyze results, repeat as needed. This approach can be used for end-to-end exercise of the entire data infrastructure stack along with applications workloads or can be component-focused (i.e., on the server, storage, I/O network, or some other area).

Table 5.2. General Testing, Benchmark, Simulation Phases and Tasks

Phase	Action	Description, Characteristics, Tips, and Recommendations
1	Plan Learn Pretest Identify Schedule Obtain Tools Skills	The objective of what will be tested, when, how, where, for how long, by whom, using what tools and parameters. Identify candidate workloads that can be run in the given amount of time applicable to your environment or needs. Planning can also involve running some simple tests to learn how or what a tool is capable of to gain insight as well as see types of metrics or reporting available. Part of the planning involves determining an end-to-end or component (layer) focus testing, saturation, or responsiveness and productivity. Determine time schedules and resource availability, and create a project plan. Resources include people along with applicable tradecraft skills (experience) as well as tools and testing. In addition to planning the tests, what workloads, tools, configuration, and settings, also plan for how to analyze, interpret, and use the results.
2	Define Configure Validate Practice Pretest	Leveraging objectives, focus, and requirements for testing along with items from the planning phase, start to refine and define the test. Who is going to do what, when, preparations. This can also involve doing some additional pretest test runs to determine optimal configuration to establish the best foot forward for the actual test. After all, practice makes perfect, plus it is easier and can be more cost-effective to find bugs, issues, or problems with configuration early, before the actual test run.
3	Setup Test Validate Practice Review	Organize your test environment including applicable servers, storage, I/O and networking hardware, software, and tools, along with any cloud or managed services needed. This also means obtaining and configuring simulation, test, trace replay, or other benchmark workload tools or scripts. Initial setup and configuration of hardware and software, installation of additional devices along with software configuration, troubleshooting, and learning as applicable. Conduct any other pretest or "dress rehearsal" for practice runs and fine tuning. This is also a good time to practice using the results and subsequent analysis. Not to mention verify that all of the telemetry data collection, logs, and reports are working. Another consideration is whether you see the same or similar repeatable results with your test runs, or are they varying, and if so, why?
4	Execute Monitor Initial Report Assess	Now is the time to reap the benefits of the work done in steps 1–3. Run or execute the tests per your plan. Verify results to validate they are what you expected, re-run as needed, maintain good notes about configurations, what was done, any other observations on the SUT, as well as on the STI. Perform initial analysis to catch and correct if needed.
5	Analyze Report Disclose	Using the results, review: Are they what was expected? Are there any issues or anomalies (besides not getting what you wanted)? Identify issues, re-run if needed. Analyze and report results, including context about what was done, how done, configuration, and other disclosure information.

Additional considerations include whether the workload trace, test, simulations (aka so-called benchmarks) accurately represent your specific production environment, or are they relevant to somebody else? Part of developing and expanding your data infrastructure performance, availability, capacity planning, tuning, optimization, and engineering tradecraft skillsets is gaining relevant knowledge to make informed decisions vs. guessing.

Figure 5.9 shows a sample system test initiator (STI) and SUT configuration for testing various storage devices with database and file serving workloads based on an actual simulation. Note that there can be multiple STIs as well as many SUTs as part of a simulation. You can view more detail on simulation configuration and results at www.storageio.com/reports.

In the example in Figure 5.9, the STI performed workload to test the SUT using Transaction Processing Council (TPC) TPC-C (OLTP transactional) workloads. These workloads

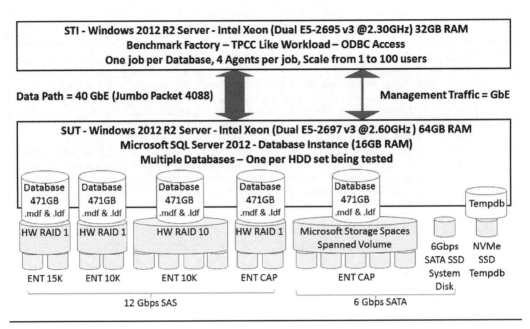

Figure 5.9   STI and SUT configuration examples.

simulated transactional, content management, metadata, and key-value processing. Microsoft SQL Server 2012 was configured and used with databases (each 470 GB, scale 6000) created and workload generated by virtual users via Quest Benchmark Factory (running on STI Windows 2012 R2).

General workload testing, simulation, and benchmark tips and recommendations include:

- Verify and validate what you are seeing.
- Format, Initialize, thin or thick, eager or full.
- Determine duration and reporting intervals.
- How much ramp-up and run-down time?
- What other workload running at same time?

Additional tips and recommendations as well as reminders include:

- What other features or data services are or need to be enabled?
- Is data compressed or de-duped? How does that impact testing?
- Number of threads and workers, local or remote (separate from STI and SUT)
- Data size and locality, cache friendly or not
- Reads, writes, random, sequential, large, small
- Long stride, short, bursty, skip sequences

Some context is that a long stride is not to be confused with long or short stroking, discussed in earlier chapters. Instead, a long-stride workload pattern is where many sequential reads (or writes) of various size are done, for example, a partial database table, file system, or another scan. Then a series of short, bursty random reads or writes are done. This could be for scanning an index or metadata to find a match, perform a sort or select, and then jump to another location to retrieve the actual data. Bursty workloads are just that: start, stop, pause, start, stop, and pause with various delays.

Tip: Some workload generation tools such as Quest Benchmark Factory allow you to specify various think and delay parameters as part of configuration to support different test scenarios. For example, to simulate user think time, add longer delays; to simulate a streaming server that sits behind a load balancer with hundreds or thousands of requests (i.e., no think time), the values can be set low or to zero, among other options.

Testing of CI, HCI, CiB, and other converged solutions may at first seem complex and difficult, particularly if you approach from a component or silo focus. However, if you approach from a different focus, that of multiple applications and workloads running on a "collective" or combined, aka converged, system, things might seem easier. For example, if you are used to running iometer, crystal, iperf, or nttcp, among others, you can still run those on different layers.

On the other hand, if you are used to running database simulations with Quest Benchmark Factory (BMF), Hammerdb, Sysbench, YCSB, Jetstress, Sharepoint (WSS, Moss, and others), VMmark or DVDstore, among others, you may be well on your way for running converged workloads.

If all you need to do is put a load on a CI, HCI, CiB, or other converged solution, you can use workload generators such as vdbench powered HCIBench for VMware (both vSAN and traditional vSphere) environments. For VMware environments, there is also VMmark, which is a collection of workloads (DVDstore). There are also tools for testing VDI and workspaces such as those from LoginVSI and Virtual Instruments, among others. For exchange, there is Jetstress (unless you can get your hands on a copy of ESRP). Likewise, there are various scripts for Microsoft Diskspd to exercise Windows and Azure environments among others on the companion site for this book (www.storageio.com/sddi).

You can even cobble together your own workloads using a combination of the above among others and then manually, or, doing some scripting, automate their staging, execution, and results processing. Keep in mind whether you are testing the storage, server, or networking performance, or what the user sees and experiences under a given workload scenario.

Also keep in mind that with converged solutions, the focus for some might be on just the storage, file system, server, hypervisor, or networking. For others the focus might be on the management interfaces, underlying data services functionality, and capabilities, among other points of interest. However, with converged, the focus should be looking at what the entire solution is capable of doing as a combined entity, all of the pieces and layers working together.

What this means is that while it is important and interesting to test or benchmark converged systems storage, or server, or networking capabilities as data infrastructure component layers, also test the entire solution end to end. This means that if your CI, HCI, CiB, or other converged solution is going to be supporting VDI and workspaces, then test and compare with applicable, relevant workloads (besides your own). If supporting SharePoint (Visual Studio test, WSS, and MOSS) or Exchange (Jet), then use other applicable tools.

Tip: If your converged solution is going to be doing transactional database (SQL or NoSQL), then use applicable workloads; if doing data warehouse, analytics, big data, video or other content-focused, again, use applicable workloads. There are different tools for testing general-purpose file systems; then there are others such as IOR for Lustre large-scale file systems. Use the right tool for the given scenario.

General considerations include:

- Keep accurate, good notes documenting initial configuration and parameter settings.
- Perform calibration of any hardware, software, and cloud services, as well as tools.
- Conduct any pretest tuning as part of practice runs before formal tests (best foot forward).
- Validate that test tools, scripts, and traces are working, data is being collected.
- Keep all telemetry (results), event, log, and configuration data along with screen shots.
- Verify that STI or network to SUT are not bottlenecks or barriers.

Considerations, tips, and recommendations include:

- The best benchmark, test, or simulation, is your actual application workload.
- Second best are those that accurately represent your workload.
- Workloads, tests, benchmarks, and simulations should be repeatable and verifiable.
- A successful test, benchmark, or simulation starts with a good plan and objective.
- Know what tools exist, and how to configure and use them for your environment.
- Peaks, averages, standard deviations, sustained and stabilized.

5.4. Data Infrastructure, Strategy, and Design Considerations

Data infrastructure design considerations include access, performance, availability, security and data protection, along with capacity optimization, economics, and management. Different environments and even portions of data infrastructures will have various design considerations to meet specific application PACE requirements and SLO. Also keep in mind that there are similarities across environments, so the following are some general considerations.

Your data infrastructure can be software-defined or legacy with software-defined management on-site, off-site, or in the cloud. Likewise, it can be private, public, or hybrid cloud and may leverage virtual, containers, and other technologies. The data infrastructure can exist on a single server, or CI, HCI, CiB, or cluster, as well as on a large scale to meet different needs.

While the technology components are important, keep the application focus and associated data in perspective. This means performance, availability, capacity, and economics (PACE) as well as applicable SLO, along with access and data services that enable some benefit. Also, design your data infrastructure with maintenance, service, support, and management in mind. Having a good inventory of your data infrastructure resources, hardware, software, services, cloud providers, management tools, policies, procedures, and applications can help in making informed decisions.

Common considerations include whether you will need dedicated resources for any application workloads (or data), or whether they can be shared with applicable tenancy, security, and performance. What applies to remote offices/branch offices (ROBO) and work groups might be similar for small–medium businesses (SMB), while larger enterprises may have different needs.

Performance considerations include:

- Application and data locality: Place active data as close to applications as possible.
- Keep storage allocation alignment in perspective for database and virtual environments.
- Fast applications need fast servers, software, and access to data on fast storage.
- Some applications will need support for smaller IOPs or transactions.
- Others will need large sequential streaming bandwidth or low-latency response time.
- Network bandwidth is important, as is latency and reliability.
- A little bit of SSD or cache in the right place can yield a big benefit.

Tip: Keep in mind that performance relies on availability, availability needs performance, and the two are related. Likewise, many configuration decisions have an impact on both performance and availability. For example, faults to tolerate (FTT) and resiliency to provide availability accessibility during failures can vary based on whether performance needs to remain consistent or can be allowed to degrade. Another consideration is the impact on applications during rebuild, repair, or reconstruction of servers, storage, or other data infrastructure resources during a recovery.

Clusters can be used to scale horizontally across multiple servers, storage, network, as well as CI and HCI solutions to increase available resources. Likewise, vertical scaling can be used to scale-up from smaller components, including those that are clustered. In addition to boosting performance and capacity, clustering can also be used to enhance availability with stability.

Availability, RAS, protection, and security considerations include:

- Hot spares, redundant components, failover to standby or active resources.
- Fault isolation and containment along with self-healing or repair capabilities.
- Leverage dual or multipath for server I/O to storage and general networking.
- Factor in data protection including versions, recovery points, and resiliency.
- Plan for rolling cluster upgrades and ability to have spare servers or storage.
- Will servers, storage, or network devices need to be removed from clusters for upgrades?
- Can you do in-place upgrades, or do clean installs have to be done?

Capacity considerations include:

- How much spare resources for servers, storage, and I/O do you need?
- Spare resources can be used for peak processing, support upgrades, and changes.
- What is your effective network bandwidth vs. advertised line rates?
- Are spare resources on-line, active or standby?

Considerations, tips, and recommendations include:

- Are your software licenses portable; can you move them across different servers?
- Can your software licenses be moved from physical to virtual to cloud, CI, or HCI?

- Leverage diverse network paths that do not have single points of failure.
- Note that you can have different network providers who have common paths.
- You can also have a single provider who has unique, diverse paths.

5.5. Common Questions and Tips

What does scale with stability mean? As you scale up and out to expand resources, this should occur without introducing performance bottlenecks, availability points of failure, or excessive resource overhead and management. In other words, as a result of scaling, your data infrastructure should not become unstable, but rather, more stable across PACE and SLO.

Are chargeback and orchestration required for cloud and software-defined environments? Different types of orchestration tools should be leveraged to help with automation of not only cloud but also other software-defined, virtual, and legacy environments. Depending on your environment needs, a chargeback may be applicable, or a showback as a means of conveying or educating users of those services what the associated costs, as well as benefits, are.

What level of audit trails and logging is needed? Maintain audit trails of who has accessed or made copies of data for event analysis. As important as is what you collect, it is also important how you use and preserve logs for analysis or forensic purposes. Leverage automation tools that can proactively monitor activities and events as well as distinguish normal from abnormal behaviors.

Who should be responsible for security? Some organizations have dedicated security groups that set policies, do some research, and do some forensics while leaving actual work to other groups. Some security organizations are more active, with their own budgets, servers, storage, and software. Security needs to be a part of activity early on in application and architecture decision making as well as across multiple technology domains (servers, storage, networking, hardware, and software) and not just via a policy maker in an ivory tower.

What tools exist that can help collect, assess, and plan for server, storage, and desktop among other migrations to virtual, cloud, or other software-defined data infrastructures? There are many different tools that can collect various data infrastructure and application resourced as well as activity information. Some of these tools focus on the operating system or hypervisor, some focus on enabling migration to different hardware, software, or cloud platforms. Tools can be used for performing inventory, collecting performance baselines, and other activities.

Figure 5.10 shows an example of the Microsoft Assessment Planning (MAP) tool that collects information on various servers, desktops, applications, and resource activity. The collected information can be used for making decisions to move to VDI workspace, virtual servers, or cloud, among others. Others tools are available from AWS, Citrix, Quest, Solarwinds, and VMware, among many others.

When should legacy vs. CI vs. HCI vs. software-defined cloud or virtual be used? That depends on what you are looking and needing to do. Different applications have various PACE attributes and SLO needs. Hopefully, you can leverage your expanded or refreshed tradecraft experiences from the various chapters in this book to determine what to use when, where, why, and how.

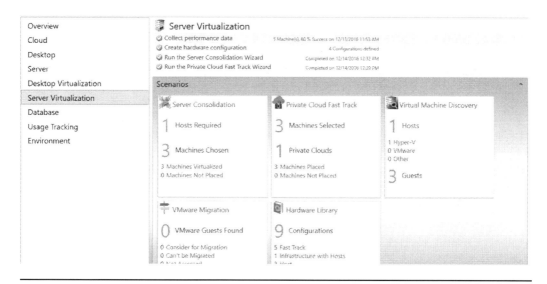

Figure 5.10   Microsoft Assessment Planning tool.

5.6. Chapter Summary

Having metrics and insight enables awareness to avoid flying blind with your data infrastructure, including decision making and other management tasks.

General action items include:

- Gain insight and awareness of your application workloads and data infrastructure.
- Leverage new and existing technology in new ways.
- Balance optimization for efficiency utilization vs. productivity effectiveness.
- Know your tools and how as well as when to use them in different ways.
- Decision making applies to acquisition, planning, configuration, and troubleshooting.

Bottom line: The best metrics are those that apply to your environment, applications, and data infrastructure to enable informed decision making (and avoid flying blind).

Part Three

Enabling Data Infrastructures

Part Three comprises Chapters 6 through 8, providing additional management insight and strategies for data infrastructure spanning on-site (on-prem), legacy, software-defined, public, private, and hybrid cloud across different application workloads.

Buzzword terms, trends, technologies, and techniques include application, big data and little data database, IoT, AI/ML/DL, among other applications, containers and serverless, cloud, converged, serverless, metrics, performance, availability, capacity, and economics (PACE) among others.

Chapter 6

Data Infrastructure Deployment Considerations: Part I

Where do you want to deploy vs. what your applications need.

What You Will Learn in This Chapter

- The roles of different techniques, technologies, and tools
- What to look for and consider in comparing features
- What approach to use for different scenarios
- Data movement and migration considerations

This chapter looks at various data infrastructure application workloads, including data deployment considerations. Topics include decision making and different strategies for on-prem, cloud, hybrid data infrastructure deployments, along with management considerations. The focus is on common data infrastructure (both legacy and software-defined) deployment topics. Key themes, buzzwords, and trends addressed in this chapter include server, storage, I/O network, hardware, software, services, converged infrastructure (CI), hyper-converged infrastructure (HCI), software-defined, cloud, virtual, container, migration, database, big data, and various applications, among other related topics.

6.1. Getting Started

In Chapters 3, 4, and 5 the focus was on managing data infrastructures including legacy, software-defined data centers (SDDC), software-defined data infrastructure (SDDI), and software-defined infrastructure (SDI). This included various application, technology, and SDDI life-cycle management (LCM) areas of focus. Now let's shift our focus to deployment considerations for various applications, as well as SDDI-enabling technology, tools, and techniques. Keep in mind that all applications have some type of performance, availability, capacity, and economic (PACE) attribute that vary by type of workload, environment, size, scale, and scope, among other considerations. Different environments, applications, or application component workloads also vary, having diverse PACE needs and service-level objectives (SLO).

6.2. Applications, Tips, and Learning Experiences

Many different application landscapes and workloads have been mentioned throughout this book. A few more buzzwords and buzz terms in addition to those already mentioned, include email; messaging and collaboration using AI/ML/DL, Axigen, IoT, Exchange, Exim, Google, O365, SharePoint, and others; big data and analytics, including Apache, Cloudera, Datameer, SAS, DataStax, Elastic search, Exasol, Hadoop and MapReduce, Hortonworks, Kafka, MapR, Pivotal, SAP HANA, Splunk and Tableau, among many others.

Additional applications, tools, and middleware include SITA, CDN, and CMS including Drupal, WordPress along with other Linux, Apache (HTTP) or Nginx, MySQL, PHP (web-focused), EPIC, Meditech, and Desix healthcare. Others middleware includes Tomcat, JBOSS, J2EE, IIS, and SAP, as well as Magneto and redis, among many others tools and applications.

While everything is not the same across environments and even the same applications, given the number of users and corresponding workload, as well as features or functions used, there are similarities. Likewise, all applications have some PACE attribute and SLOs. As has been discussed throughout this book, part of expanding or refreshing your essential data infrastructure tradecraft skills is gaining experience and understanding various applications that are part of the organization's business infrastructure and IT in general.

By having an understanding of the applications and their corresponding PACE attributes, you can avoid flying blind when it comes to making data infrastructures decisions. These decisions span from deciding what technology, architecture, and service trends and techniques to apply when and where to how to use different application workloads or environments.

Where applications can or should be deployed:

- On-site, off-site, or with another cloud service
- As physical (legacy, CI, HCI, CiB), virtual, container, or hosted
- On a single physical server with internal or external dedicated storage
- On multiple clustered physical servers, each with dedicated storage
- On multiple clustered physical servers with shared networked storage
- On aggregated servers, storage, and networks, or on disaggregated resources
- What type of I/O networks (local and remote) as well as storage to use

How applications, settings, metadata, and data are protected:

- Basic RAS and HA, FTT and FTM modes
- Mirroring, replication, and clusters for availability
- Point-in-time (PIT) copies, checkpoints, snapshots
- Logical and physical security, intrusion detection

Considerations, tips, and recommendations include:

- Turnkey service, buy solution, subscription, build DIY, some assembly required
- The application workload and PACE attributes along with SLO
- What are your design premises and priorities?
- Design for resiliency, performance or capacity, and cost savings
- Design for fault isolation, containment, or rapid failure-tolerant modes
- How resource failures are handled by applications including caches

6.3. Software-Defined, Virtual, Containers, and Clouds

Applications have different PACE attributes SLOs. Likewise, applications depend on servers (compute), local and remote I/O networking, and storage resources. These resources are managed as well as enabled and defined via software. Software defines hardware, other software, as well as various services to support different needs.

Figure 6.1 shows various software-defined and legacy data infrastructures supporting different application landscapes, services, and modes of consumption or use. These span from

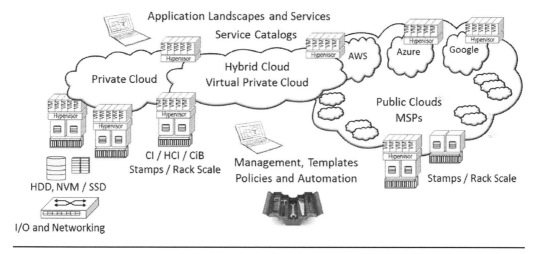

Figure 6.1   Software-defined and legacy data infrastructures.

legacy "brownfield" environments to "Greenfield," newly emerging, on-premise to all in the cloud. In addition to legacy, public and private, also shown are hybrid infrastructures adapting the best of available technologies, techniques, tools, and policies to different needs. Also shown are traditional compute servers, software-defined virtual and containers, CI, HCI, and rack-scale, along with hardware and software storage, networking, and management tools.

Benefits and attributes of SDDC, SDI, and SDDI environments include:

- Elastic to scale up, out, and "burst," or grow rapidly to meet application needs
- Growth including compute, storage, I/O networking, and PACE-related resources

- Flexible and scalable to meet different and changing needs
- Resilient, available, durable, depending on how configured or used
- Cost-effective, enabling you to pay for what you use, when you use it
- Multi-tenancy for privacy, security, and protection while sharing resources
- Track and provide accounting reporting, showback, chargeback, and insight
- Leverage new technology in new ways at a faster cadence (speed of doing things)

SDDC and SDDI utilize or are implemented using:

- Clouds—public, private, and hybrid
- Cloud stacks such as Microsoft Azure and OpenStack, among others
- Containers. Docker Linux and Windows
- Virtual machines (VM) on legacy as well as CI, HCI, and CiB solutions
- Workspace and virtual desktop infrastructures (VDI)
- Bare metal as a service (MaaS), such as dedicated private servers (DPS)
- Virtual private cloud and hybrid, spanning sites, locations, and services

General considerations include:

- How will you protect, preserve, and secure applications, settings, and data?
- Who are the users? Where do they access different applications?
- What are those applications' information services and data infrastructure dependencies?
- Balance lower costs with increased enablement, resiliency, and flexibility
- Large scale vs. medium size vs. remote office/branch office (ROBO) or small office needs
- Management tools, interfaces, and interoperability with what you already have

Considerations, tips, and recommendations include:

- "Greenfield" (brand new, from scratch) for your applications or data infrastructure
- "Brownfield" (existing applications or environment) to move, migrate, or re-host
- Who and how will resources and applications be managed as well as supported
- Where and what is your focus for convergence and management
- Control, security, privacy, data protection, and application resiliency
- What conversions of applications, data, virtual machines are needed
- What additional tools, migration, and conversion utilities are needed

6.3.1. Clouds: Public, Private, and Hybrid

Clouds have accounts with an owner, optional billing, and related information. Different clouds have various focuses, data services, feature functionalities, and service offerings. Activity and usage reporting can be tied to an account or users, as well as alerts, alarms, and health check status notifications. Billing and spend alerts can be set up to let you know when costs reach or exceed a particular point.

Tip: Pay attention to what region or location your applications and data are placed in, making sure they follow any applicable legal or regulatory privacy and compliance requirements.

Resources are assigned and owned by an account. These resources can be in different regions (geographical locations) with one or more sites. A site consists of one or more data centers that might be dedicated, or co-located in a multi-tenant secure facility. Note that different regions and sites can be used for enabling availability and resiliency.

Tip: Verify that cloud resources are disabled when you are done, or to turn off when you are not using them. With traditional resources, you might forget about them although they continue to be in use, without generating an invoice, chargeback, or showback report. With a public cloud, however, you might be surprised to see how those resources can run up an unexpected bill.

Management tools, capabilities, and interfaces vary, but they usually include, among others, REST/HTTP, HTML5-based GUIs, Wizards, templates and policies, XML and JSON formatted files. Other tools and capabilities include workflow managers, orchestration and service catalogs, dashboards, event, activity, resource, and cost use threshold alerts. Additional tools include import and migration along with conversion for moving applications, systems, and data to or from cloud environments.

Different cloud services have various management tools and interfaces including GUI, Wizards, and CLI, along with API. Also, there are various orchestration and dashboard tools as well as services that can span different cloud services as well as private and hybrid clouds.

Some of these tools also support on-site virtual, containers, and other software-defined data infrastructures along with legacy. Tools vary from simply monitoring, reporting, insight, and awareness to provisioning, workflow, and resource orchestration. Examples of tools include Ansible for orchestration, management, and automation, mesos, swarm, Kubernetes, Tectonic, cloudkitty, collectd, dashbuilder, Nagios, openit, rrdtool, Solarwinds, OpenStack, VMware, and Microsoft, among many others.

In the past, there has been time sharing along with service bureaus for supporting access to different resources and applications. Some of those were (or are) general, while others are application- or industry-specific. Likewise, some of today's clouds are general-purpose, while others are industry-, application-, or function-specific. For example, there are government-focused public clouds such as AWS GovCloud. However, there are also private government clouds (or services) providing services to financial security trading and airline reservations systems, among other businesses, institutions, and agencies.

Another approach for supporting applications and data infrastructures is outsourcing and managed services such as those supported by IBM and ASC, among others. In some cases the entire application along with support (and possibly developers) is transferred to the outsourced or managed service provider. In other words, they become employees of the service provider: The applications and associated resources are owned and operated on behalf of the customer to specific SLO, among other requirements. There are also scenarios where applications and data infrastructure resources remain physically where they are, but the service provider takes over the space and management of the various entities.

Table 6.1 shows various cloud, hosting, and co-location venues and characteristics.

Table 6.1. Cloud, Hosting and Co-location Venue Characteristics and Considerations

Venue	Characteristics	Considerations
Cloud service provider (CSP)	Provides various services and functionalities from application to resources, different granularities of computing, storage, network, development, and other tools. Features vary; some are very large, such as AWS, Azure, GCS, and Softlayer, among others. Some are small and regional. Similar to hosting firms who have expanded into the cloud, virtual private servers (VPS), and dedicated private servers (DPS), some traditional cloud providers have added DPS and hosting capabilities as well as other hybrid enabling capabilities.	Can be used to move your applications, production workloads, development, analytics, testing, or other types of processing for compute, storage, or network functions. Different levels of tenancy, as well as resources and cost along with SLO and SLA. Can also be used for a hybrid to co-exist with your legacy environment.
Hosting	Traditionally the web, email, DNS, domain hosting, WordPress blog, and related hosting services. Some offer cloud services and VPS or VM in addition to DPS, for example, Bluehost, and GoDaddy, among many others.	Can be used to offload specific functions and operations to free up resources for primary or core applications. Different levels of service, support, SLO, SLA, and feature functionality.
Co-location (co-lo)	Some supply servers, storage, and networking hardware or software. Others provide safe, secure, and optimally managed space for your technology. Context is needed for management, as it can mean simple monitoring or more extensive hands-on-support. You have control of your technology, how it is used, configured, managed, and maintained, along with troubleshooting. You are responsible for your technology, hardware, software, and its configuration. Understand the security (physical and logical), primary and standby power, as well as networking capabilities. Examples include Datapipe, Equinix, and Level 3, among others.	Use to supplement your existing data center or as an alternative to your own. Enable setup of new small sites where needed. Who has access to your technology and when? Space can range from a cabinet cage to a portion of a data center. Some have "direct connect" high-speed, low-latency connectivity into AWS or other clouds, bypassing normal front-end Internet-based access. Some are large; some are local.

In addition to public cloud services, hosting, co-lo, and managed service providers, you can also build and deploy your own private cloud. Likewise, you can connect your private cloud or legacy data infrastructure environment to public or other services for a hybrid environment. This also means configuring (defining) hybrid clouds that span different providers such as AWS, Google, and Azure, among others. Cloud stack software includes Cloud Stack, Microsoft Azure, OpenStack, and VMware, among others that you can build yourself (DIY).

Tip: On-board, or cloud instance, DAS, like traditional server DAS, can be useful as cache, scratch, or high-speed local storage, but pay attention to whether it is persistent or ephemeral.

DIY ranges from "some assembly required" to complete build-it-yourself from reference architectures, cookbooks, and other resources. There are tutorials and how-to guides from many different vendors as well as organizations, such as OpenStack, Ubuntu, RedHat, Suse, and others.

Tip: Similar to physical (or virtual) servers with dedicated DAS (HDD or SSD), cloud instances have similar feature in addition to persistent external storage. Pay attention to whether the instance is "on-instance" (i.e., DAS) and if that storage is persistent across reboots as well as system shutdown. Some services support persistent "on-instance" storage across reboots, while others do not. Likewise, some are persistent across reboots but ephemeral (your data gets deleted) across shutdown, stop, and restarts. Leverage some software to protect data across server shutdowns of ephemeral storage, including snapshots, backup/restore, and sync, when you need persistent data on cloud instances.

There are also turnkey solutions where you focus on the configuration, definitions of policies, templates, and other deployment tasks. An example of a prepackaged OpenStack solution software appliance is VMware Integrated OpenStack Appliance (VIOA). Another example is Microsoft Azure stack, and there are others. Which is best for your SDDC, SDI, and SDDI environment depends on what you are trying to accomplish or need to do.

Tip: With some services and stacks you can create an instance with attached volumes, build and define your environment with applicable software, and create configurations just as with traditional server images or builds. Once you have created your system, you can create snapshots for creating new volumes and systems. Likewise, you can also *detach* a volume and *attach* it to another instance, similar to removing a HDD or SSD from one server and moving it to another.

Volumes for cloud compute instances can be expanded in size for Windows and Linux systems similar to with physical and virtual deployments. Check with your particular cloud service or software stack solution provider as to what is supported and the steps involved, then leverage your tradecraft skills (or learn new ones) to do the operating system–specific expand steps.

Tip: Different public cloud services and private cloud software stacks have various features, data services and extent of functionality, as well as cost considerations. Some public and private cloud stacks provide tools, while others have open APIs along with SDKs to assist partners and developers with interfacing to those platforms. For example, leveraging various APIs, tools such as DataDog, RightScale, and many others can collect telemetry data to provide insight into activity, events, usage, and configuration information.

General considerations, tips, and recommendations include:

- There are similarities, including management and resources with different granularities.
- Cloud compute instances are similar to traditional servers (i.e., cores, memory, I/O).
- There are various types of storage for different tasks (i.e., block, file, object, tables, queues).
- Various networking options, from general Internet to high-speed direct connect.
- Leverage various tools for monitoring to gain insight and awareness.
- Monitor resource usage, activity, and events along with applicable costs.

Tip: Some cloud services and stacks allow you to launch an instance using preconfigured images on different types (tiers) of servers, storage, network, and security templates. Likewise, some allow you to set up customized instances including using your software images. In addition to providing instances with pre-licensed images, some allow you to bring your software licenses instead of using the service provider's.

Additional considerations, tips, and recommendations include:

- Pay attention to persistent and ephemeral storage along with instance settings.
- Verify that you have persistent settings for instance stop, shut down, and terminate.
- Leverage your tradecraft experience across physical, virtual, and cloud.
- Don't be afraid of clouds; be prepared and do your homework to learn about them.
- If you can list your cloud concerns, you can then classify, rank, and address them.

6.3.2. Public Cloud Services

Use public clouds when you need or want flexibility, agility, ability to pay as you go, and scale, along with leveraging off-site capabilities. Public clouds can also be used to move or relocate your IT and data infrastructure resources along with associated applications to, or, in a hybrid deployment, complement what you are doing on-site. There are many different types of public clouds along with managed service providers that have various areas of focus.

Tip: Public clouds can be used to replace on-premise or complement hybrid on-site data infrastructures. Other uses for public clouds include a place to do development, big-data and other analytics, high-performance computing, content rendering and aggregation, testing, and integration, among others.

Uses of public clouds include as a target or destination for copying, replicating, syncing, backing up, or archiving data in support of data protection activities (BC, DR, and BR). Public clouds can also be used as a place to tier data for applications that reside on-premise, as well as a place from which applications can be hosted.

Tip: Having concerns about clouds and public clouds, in particular, is not a bad thing in my opinion, as long as you can document what they are. If you can identify and list what your cloud concerns are, as well as why, then you can also indicate the severity or priority of those issues. From there you can work with others to identify how to resolve and address the concerns, find workarounds, or, in some cases, verify that cloud is not a good fit for a given scenario. However, if you cannot identify what your cloud concerns are, then how you cannot address them.

Various cloud services have different data services, management, features, functionalities, and personalities. Some clouds have personalities optimized for computing, others for specific applications, still others are general-purpose. Likewise, the extent of feature functionality also varies, so look beyond the basic checkbox of what is supported. Costs also vary, with some offering all-inclusive service, and others offering lower à la carte prices with various fees for different functionalities. Look into the service provider, the offerings, and the terms, including SLO, SLA, and fees as well as quotas and limits.

A sampling of public cloud and managed services providers includes Alibaba, Amazon Web Services (AWS), Apple, AT&T, Bluehost, Box, BT, Comcast, CoreSite, CSC, Datapipe, Dell EMC Virtustream, Dimension Data, Dreamhost, Dropbox, and DynDNS. Others include Equinix, Ericsson, FibreLight, Firehost, GoDaddy, Google Cloud Engine, IBM Softlayer, InterCloud, Joyent, Level3, Microsoft (Azure, Office 365, Xbox), NTT, Oracle, Orange, Peak, Rackspace, Salesforce, SMART, Tata, Telkom, Telstra, Telx, Verizon, Virtustream, Vodafone, VPS, VMware, Zayo, and many others. Table 6.2 shows a summary of some common service offerings from AWS, Azure, and Google.

Amazon Web Services (AWS) includes various applications, management, compute from instances (EC2) to Lambda micro services (containers), lightsail (VPS/DPS), block (EBS), file (EFS), and Simple Storage Service (S3) object. S3 includes policy-based standard, reduced redundancy (RR), infrequent access (IA), and glacier (cold for inactive archives) storage as well as relational database services (RDS) and table services, including RDS, Aurora, DynamoDB among others (SQL and NoSQL). Others include IoT hubs, management, SDK, and related

Table 6.2. Summary of Common AWS, Azure, and Google Features

	AWS	Azure	Google
Resource	aws.amazon.com/products/	azure.microsoft.com	cloud.google.com/products/
Compute	EC2 (instances), Lambda micro services (containers). Various size instances, types of images (Windows, Linux, applications), management options, LightSail private servers. Instance-based including SSD (i.e., DAS as part of the instance).	VM and container services. Various size instances, types of images (Linux, Windows, applications), management options. Instance-based including SSD (i.e., DAS as part of the instance).	Various compute engine granularities, sizes, and types (Windows, Linux) of instances and services. Instance-based including SSD (i.e., DAS as part of the instance).
Database	Various services from tables to SQL and NoSQL compatible. Database instance images also for EC2.	SQL databases, data warehouse, tables, DocumentDB, redistributed database on Azure VM..	Cloud SQL, Cloud Bigtable, NoSQL cloud datastore.
Block storage	EBS HDD and SSD	Disk (HDD and SSD)	Persistent (SSD)
Bulk Big data Object Content Archive Log and Snapshot Storage	S3 standard, RR (reduced redundancy, lower cost), IA (infrequent access, lower cost, slower access). Glacier (cold, very slow access [hours], low cost).	Blobs, various regional and geographical protection schemes. Various big data services, resources, and tools.	Object multiregional; regional, near-line, and cold are off-line. Various big data services, resources, and tools.
File storage	EFS (within AWS)	Azure File within Azure, external Windows SMB 3	
Networking	Route 53 DNS, load balancing, direct connect, VPC (virtual private cloud), Edge locations	Virtual networking, CDN, load balancer, gateways, VPN, DNS, ExpressRoute (direct connect), management	Networking, CDN, load balancing, virtual network, DNS, and interconnect

Figure 6.2   AWS EC2 instance and setting network access.

tools. General analytics, Route 53 networking, development tools, and much more. Different levels of services include performance, availability, durability, and capacity to meet various economic and SLO needs.

AWS has a large global presence in regions around the world, with multiple availability zones and data centers in each region. Figure 6.2 shows on the left an AWS EC2 cloud instance (VM) that has been provisioned and is being configured. On the right side of Figure 6.2, network security access for the EC2 instance is being configured for different ports, services, and IP addresses. AWS, like many other providers, has import/export capabilities, including where you can ship storage devices to compensate for slow networks, or where there is too much date to move in a short amount of time even on a fast network.

In addition to basic services, AWS also has services called Snowball (smaller appliance) and Snowmobile (semi-truck sized) that can scale from terabytes to petabytes of data moved via self-contained appliances. With these appliances, you simply plug them into your environment and copy data onto them (with encryption and other security). The appliances are then shipped back to AWS (or another provider of similar services), where the data is ingested into your account.

Figure 6.3 shows an AWS EC2 Windows instance on the left. Note that as part of the instance access, the password can be obtained with the proper security credentials and keys, along with an access script such as for RDP. The Windows Server instance desktop is accessed on the right of Figure 6.3. Note in the top right corner of Figure 6.3 that there

Figure 6.3   Connecting to AWS EC2 Windows instance.

are various AWS instance settings, including instance ID, type of processor, and instance, among other information.

Dell EMC Virtustream provides public, private, and hybrid cloud storage solutions. Google Cloud Services has large-scale compute, storage, and other capabilities in addition to their consumer-facing and email solutions, as well as collaboration and workspace applications. IBM Softlayer is another public cloud service with many different geographic locations.

Microsoft Azure is another large public cloud service that also supports interoperability with on-premises Azure Stack (Azure in a box at your site) as well as Windows Server environments. There are many different Azure data centers in various geographical areas, with new ones being added, along with increased functionality for compute, storage, networking, management, development, production, CDN, and analytics among others. Microsoft also has the Xbox as well as O365 clouds, and don't forget about LinkedIn, Skype, and others.

Rackspace is another cloud and managed service providers offering both traditional dedicated and shared hosting, DPS, VPS, and cloud instances. There are also many other small to medium-size local, regional, and international cloud and managed service providers; some are Telco's, some are hosting or co-lo, among others.

VMware is known as a supplier of SDDC and software-defined data infrastructure (SDDI) technology for organizations of various sizes (from small to large). However, it also supplies service providers. While OpenStack and other software are commonly thought of regarding the use of the cloud and managed service providers, some have found VMware (and Microsoft) to be cost-effective.

6.3.3. Private and Hybrid Cloud Solutions

Use private clouds when you need or want more control over your environment. These can be deployed on-premise at your location, or in a co-lo, or other managed service provider environment. Your choice of going private cloud may also be to establish a hybrid environment spanning your existing, new and software-defined, as well as public data infrastructure environments. Reasons to have more control include cost, performance, locations, availability, or security along as well as privacy among others.

Private cloud and cloud software includes Cloudian, Cloud Stack, Dell EMC Virtustream, Microsoft Azure Stack, OpenStack, Pivotal, Swiftstack, and VMware, among many others. Figure 6.4 shows an OpenStack dashboard display CPU compute (i.e., hypervisor). The image in Figure 6.4 is a multi-node OpenStack deployment I did using Ubuntu and available OpenStack deployment guides.

Tip: As part of protecting an OpenStack environment, make sure to have a backup or other copy of your various databases, as well as snapshots of critical servers or nodes. When something happens, being able to restore all or part of a configuration database with metadata, or configuration files or a point-in-time snapshot can mean the difference between availability and downtime.

OpenStack has emerged as a popular software-defined cloud stack for implementing SDDC, SDI, and SDDI (as well as cloud) environments on both large and small scales. It is used by large service providers who customize it as well as by smaller organizations in different

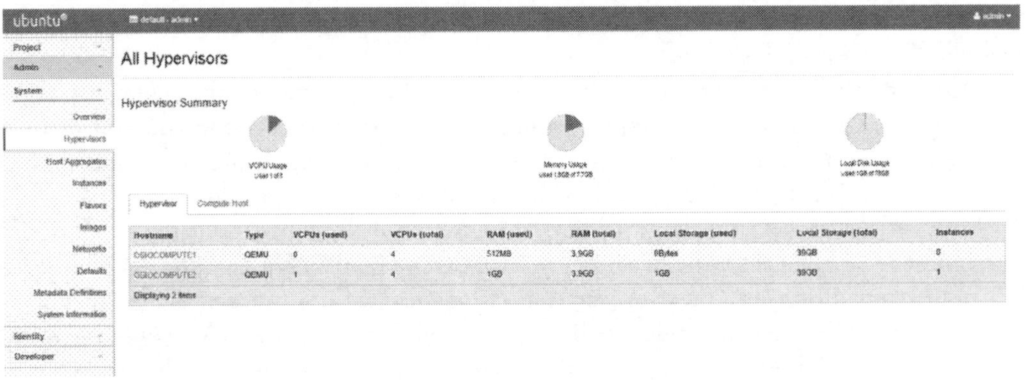

Figure 6.4   OpenStack Horizon dashboard showing compute resources.

ways. Keep in mind that OpenStack is a collection of data infrastructure components (aka projects) that address different functions and have different functionalities. These projects or components feature well-defined APIs and are highly customizable, from functionality to appearance. Core functionality components include Keystone (security and access), Horizon (management dashboard), Neutron (Networking), Nova (compute), Glance (image management), Cinder (block storage), and Swift (object storage), among many others. Note that you can run compute and dashboard (along with network and security) without Swift object storage, and Swift without compute capabilities.

OpenStack leverages databases such as MySQL or one of its various variant engines as a repository for configuration, security, users, roles, endpoints, access controls, and other metadata. Various configuration files define functionality, as well as support for plug-ins or tools to use, for example Rabbit vs. other messaging software.

Tip: The benefit of doing an install from scratch, such as with OpenStack is to gain insight into what the pieces and parts are, and how they work. Also, it will give you an appreciation for the customization and extensiveness of a solution, along with what will be involved to maintain a production environment vs. using bundled solutions.

Besides OpenStack install from scratch using various cookbooks and tutorials available from OpenStack and other venues, there are also automated build scripts you can find with a quick Google search. Some tutorials and scripts are for a single node, which might be good enough to get some "behind the wheel" or "stick time" with the technology.

There are also some appliances such as the VMware Integrated OpenStack Appliance (VIOA). You can download VIOA from VMware as an OVA and then deploy on a vSphere ESXi system. Likewise, you can download different pieces of OpenStack such as Swift for object storage from OpenStack, as well as others such as Swiftstack.

Figure 6.5 shows a generic OpenStack architecture with (top left) a Horizon dashboard having interfaces to various components. Various components include Keystone (security, identity assessment management), used by other OpenStack services. Other services include Nova

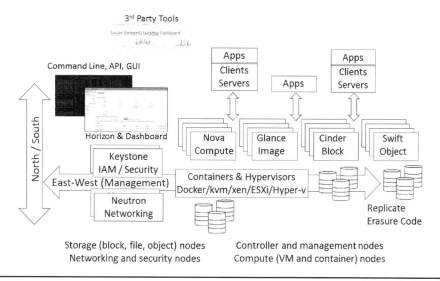

Figure 6.5   OpenStack generic architecture.

compute with various forms of hypervisor support (bare metal, Docker, ESXi, Hyper-V, libvirt [Xen and LXC], Qemu, and XenServer, among others) along with Glance image management.

Note that there is also Magnum (i.e., containers). Software-defined storage includes block provided via Cinder, with files via Manila and objects with Swift or using other plug-ins. Also shown is Neutron (SDN and NFV) networking, facilitating private east–west management or intrasystem communications, as well as intersystem communications with the outside world.

There is also north–south (aka northbound, southbound) access of resources shown, as well as other functionalities within networking. Other networking functionalities can include border gateways, DNS, and DHCP, among other network functions virtualized.

Depending on the size and scope of your OpenStack, deployment will involve a different number of nodes (servers) for the various services. For high availability (HA) and resiliency, set up two or more controller nodes, and distribute different functions across nodes depending on workload and performance. Smaller environments can consolidate to fewer nodes, or even containers, using persistent Docker storage (more on this later in the chapter).

Note that OpenStack can overlay VMware vSphere ESXi as well as Microsoft Hyper-V hypervisors (among others), which mean that it can be used as a point of management and orchestration convergence. On the other hand, for simplicity, OpenStack can be deployed with VMware or Microsoft, among others, as a management layer along with other hybrid approaches.

General implementation tips and considerations for private clouds include:

- Implement data protection, including basic as well as HA for resiliency.
- Implement recovery point objective (RPO) protection with snapshots and backup.
- Protect the various databases that contain configuration, authentication, and metadata.
- Deploy redundant nodes and configuration, replication, and other techniques.
- Compute can have local storage similar to a physical server with DAS.

Tip: Besides OpenStack, third-party tools, extensions, and plug-ins can be added to enhance management and orchestration. Some third-party (and open-source) tools for OpenStack include Ansible (policies, templates), Awnix, cacti, Chef, Cloud kitty (billing, invoicing), Collectd, Datadog, Dell EMCcode, Freezer, Kubernetes, Nagios (monitoring), RedHat, RRDtools, Swiftstack (object storage management), Storpool, Suse, Trilio and Ubuntu (metal as a service [MaaS]), and many others. Some other useful tools to have include Cloudberry, curl, Cyberduck, gsutil, S3 Browser, S3FS, S3motion, ssh, wget, and others.

Considerations, tips, and recommendations include:

- Protect your private cloud with resiliency and point-in-time data protection.
- Everything is not the same with cloud, hosting, and managed service providers.
- Some services and features work inside (intra-) a cloud, others are external (inter-).
- Balance the value of your time and budget with DIY vs. kit or turnkey solutions.
- Understand how you will customize and then manage those changes through new versions.
- Do proof of concept (POC), understanding what's involved with DIY for various solutions.
- Leverage POC to determine production considerations including support and maintenance.
- Utilize reporting to monitor resource usage, activity, and costs as well as alerts.

6.4. Docker, Containers, and Microservices

Compute containers are a form of computing that provides more tenancy (private isolation) for a process, task, or program instance than on a normal-running shared server environment, without the overhead of a virtual machine.

Tip: Some context is needed here to distinguish a standard intermodal shipping container (Figure 6.6), commonly seen on railcars, ships, and trucks, and a Docker (or other) compute server microservice. The reason context is important here is that some large-scale environments leverage variations of standard physical shipping containers to "stuff" with data infrastructure components, including servers, storage, networking, and other items.

Further context is needed in that while data infrastructure components are shipped in physical containers from factory to data centers or another habitat for technology, some are also configured as mini-data centers or data center modules. Here, "modules" means that the physical containers are preconfigured with data infrastructure components that "plug in" to data center power, HVAC, and networking, and then are defined with software to perform various functions.

The other context, which is the focus here, is that of a compute service that is a subset of a traditional server (i.e., a microservice). Thus context is important when it comes to containers.

Docker is a popular container management platform, along with tools including kubernetes, mesos, and warm, along with "back-end" engines that execute (i.e., host) as microservices running container instances (images).

Figure 6.6   An intermodal shipping container.

Tip: There are Linux-based engines as well as Windows. Key context here is that when you hear "container," and in particular "Docker," you need to know whether it is referring to the management or the engine. This context is important because containers built on and for Linux engines can only run on a Linux engine. However, they can be managed from Windows, Linux, or others. Likewise, a Windows-centric container only runs on a Windows-based engine although it can be managed from different platforms. In other words, like programs or applications, "binary" bits or executables built for a specific operating system or hardware architecture, containers have a similar affinity.

Containers are more lightweight, resulting in carrying less overhead baggage than a virtual machine or requiring an entire PM or BM. Containers essentially rely on certain libraries or tools being in place on the host engine, so they do not have to carry that extra baggage.

Think in terms of taking a trip and not having to pack items that you know will be at your destination, such as irons, ironing boards, blankets, pillows, and towels. The result is that you need fewer things in your suitcase, roll-aboard, or backpack, making it lighter, easier to travel with, and will adapt as well as a plug-in to where you are going.

Tip: There is a myth that containers are only ephemeral (e.g., stateless) and cannot be used with or for persistent (e.g., stateful) applications that need to maintain state with persistent storage, or backing store. This is true by default. However, it is also true you can configure containers to use persistent local (not a good idea, as it reduces portability), shared network, or volumes mapped to the networked shared cloud or other storage. Later in the database section of this chapter, there is an example showing MySQL running in a container as well as Dell EMC ECS (Elastic Cloud Storage) images.

Good deployment scenarios for using containers include when you do not need an entire PM or BM, nor the overhead of a VM or full cloud instance. This can be to run in production, development, test, research, operational support, DevOps, among others, or a specific application, program, module, process, stream, or thread.

Another deployment scenario is where you need to stand up or provision very quickly an environment that can be torn down just as quickly. This includes developers, testers, production support, and students, among others. Keep in mind that containers are stateless by default, so for persistent data, they need to be configured accordingly.

Another good use for containers is where you need to launch very quickly images that may have short life-cycle management durations. By being lighter weight, they start up (and shut down) faster, using fewer resources. For example, on public cloud sites, compute instances or VM are usually billed on an hourly basis of granularity. Container services, on the other hand, may be billed on a second, microsecond, or even smaller granularity. What this means is that if you are using only a fraction of a cloud instance, consider deploying into a container or container-based service. Likewise, if you find your monthly compute invoices are getting too large, that might be a sign you need a cloud instance, or a cloud instance configured with multiple containers.

Tip: Various management tools facilitate the creation and container build management, versioning, and other common tasks including scheduling. You can use various tools, settings, and templates to set the amount of CPU, memory, and other resources used, as well as track their consumption as a compute service. Your storage options include ephemeral nonpersistent, persistent local to host, shared network, and portable access using container volume management tools such as Dell EMC RexRay, among others.

Containers by default may be immutable (fixed) with ephemeral (nonpersistent) storage for stateless applications. This is useful for fixed or static applications that perform a given set of tasks, processes, or functions without being stateful. For those types of applications where statefullness is needed, they can connect to a database in another container, VM, cloud instance, or bare metal to store persistent data.

Tip: Display the last 15 Docker log entries for an instances using the `--tail` option in a command such as `Docker logs --tail 20 ecsstandalone`.

Those applications can also access persistent storage via Docker or container volumes, local host, or NAS shared storage. The caveat with using local host storage is that it negates the portability of the container, creating affinity to a given server. Using storage and volume plug-ins, containers can access different shared storage as a persistent backing store while maintaining portability. An example of a plug-in is the libstorage-based open-source RexRay.

Tip: An important value proposition of containers is light weight and portability. Just because you can launch a container to use local storage on a host for persistence does not mean that you should. By doing so, you create an affinity that restricts that container to running on that host. Instead, if you need the flexibility to move containers and run on different hosts, then use shared networked storage (block, file, and object) or a volume plug-in that provides similar functionality.

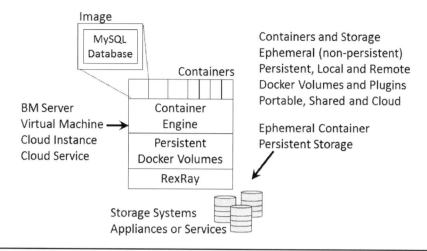

Figure 6.7   Containers using persistent shared storage.

Figure 6.7 shows a MySQL database container image using persistent storage via a container storage volume plug-in such as RexRay.

Note that Docker supports many different drivers, overlays, and plug-ins that have different characteristics. Which is best for you will depend on your workload PACE requirements and other preferences. Figure 6.8 shows container images running on various platforms including cloud-based services, cloud instances, virtual, and PM or BM. Also shown are repositories or hubs where containers are stored and accessed from, which can be public or private. Public services include Docker among many others.

Figure 6.9 shows a *Docker ps –a* command displaying running Docker container images with information including ID, name, and status, among other items.

Figure 6.10 shows an example of containers using persistent Docker volumes leveraging pluggable volumes with the persistent backing store. In this example, various container

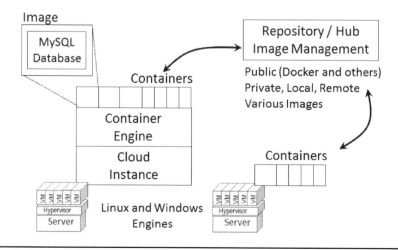

Figure 6.8   Containers live in repositories and run in various places.

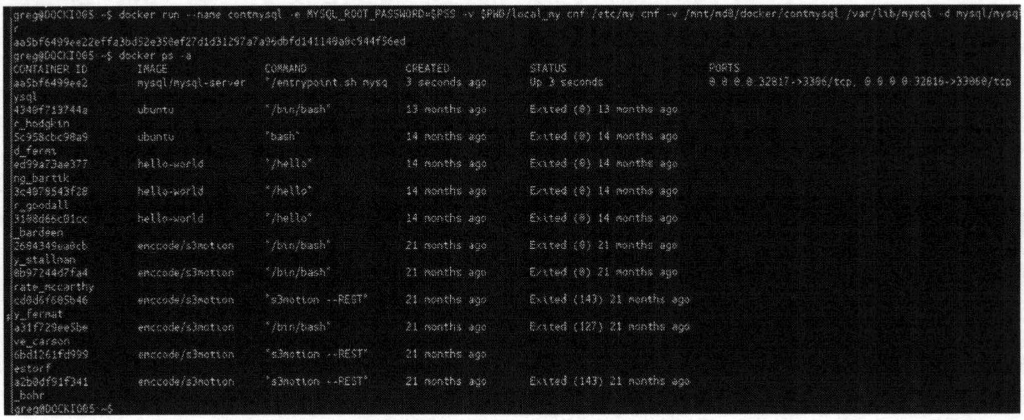

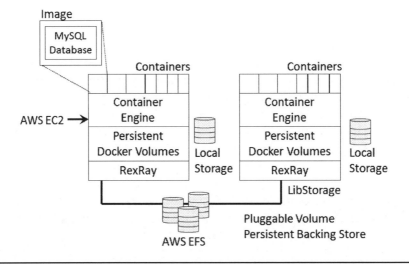

Figure 6.9   Displaying Docker container ID and image information.

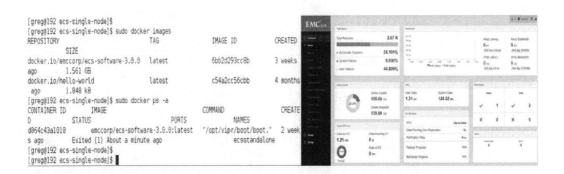

Figure 6.10   Docker containers with persistent storage.

Figure 6.11   Docker images and containers.

images are running on a cloud host (an instance such as AWS EC2 or Azure) that also has libstorage-based RexRay installed as a storage orchestration for volume-handling management. The Docker (another container) engine then uses the persistent storage managed by RexRay for accessing and storing data on shared storage as a backing store. Keep in mind that while many applications or software-defined storage can access object storage natively, or via gateways, some still need file access support. Thus, in this example, access to shared cloud file-based storage is shown.

Figure 6.11 shows, on the left, Docker images and containers, including one for Dell EMC ECS, whose dashboard is shown on the right. The point is to show that containers can be used to perform tasks often relegated to VM or even PM.

Tip: Watch out for container creep, which is similar to VM sprawl; that is, containers, like VM and other technology techniques, are good for some things, but just because you can use them for others, ask yourself if that is the only option, or only what you want to use.

Some vendors, services, solutions, and tools include Apache, Apcera, Atlantis, AWS (EC2, Lambda compute, EFS), Azure File Service, Ceph RBD, Convoy, and CoreOS. Others include Dell EMC (RexRay), Docker, Flocker, Github, Kubernetes, Libstorage, Linux (LXC/LXD), Mesos, Mesosphere, Microsoft Azure and Windows, NetApp, NFS, OpenStack Nova and Magnum, Panzura, Portwk, Storpool, Swarm, and VMware (VIC, Photon), among others.

Considerations, tips, and recommendations include:

- Place logs for active applications, containers, or other busy workloads on fast storage.
- Containers (or their contents) need to be made persistent (stateful) somewhere.
- While containers are immutable and can be ephemeral, protect the hubs they live in.
- Protect the storage or backing store where persistent container data volumes live.
- Just because you can do almost anything with a container, that may not mean you should.
- Leverage containers as another resource allocation tools similar to PM, BM, and VM.

6.5. Workspace and Virtual Desktop Infrastructure

Virtual desktop infrastructure (VDI), also known as virtual workplaces, complements virtual and physical servers and provides similar value propositions as VM. These value propositions include simplified management and reduced hardware, software, and support services on the desktop or workstation, shifting them to a central or consolidated server.

VDI or workspace benefits include simplified software management (installation, upgrades, repairs), data protection (backup/restore, HA, BC, DR), and security. Another benefit of VDI, similar to VM, is the ability to run various versions of a specific guest operating system at the same time, similar to server virtualization. In addition to different versions of Windows, other guests, such as Linux, can coexist.

Depending on how the VDI or workspace is deployed, for example, in display mode, less I/O traffic will go over the network, with activity other than during workstation boot mainly

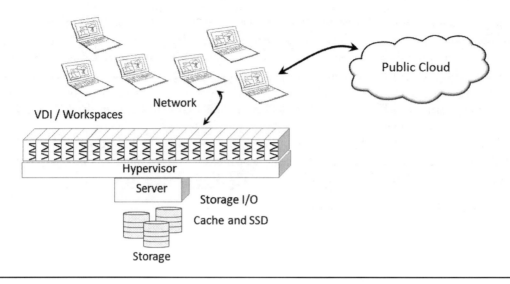

Figure 6.12   VDI and workspace environments.

being display images. On the other hand, if the client is running applications in its local memory and making data requests to a server, then those I/Os will be placed on the network.

Figure 6.12 a workspace or VDI environment being served via (lower left) private on-premises SDDC and SDDI environments. The top right shows workspaces being delivered via cloud services. On-premise options include traditional, CI, and HCI solutions for small and medium-size or ROBO environments. Scale-up and scale-out CI and HCI, as well as rack-scale systems, are options for larger-scale environments.

If many clients boot up at the same time, such as after a power failure, maintenance, or another event, a boot storm could occur and cause server storage I/O and network bottlenecks. For example, if a single client needs 30 IOPS per second either in a normal running state when it is busy or during boot, most servers and networks should support that activity.

Tip: Boot storms are a common focus for VDI, which tend to be read-intensive, and good candidates for linked clones as well as SSD-backed read-cache (as well as read-ahead). However, also keep shutdown activity in mind, where many users may need to save their data before going on break or leaving for lunch as well as wrapping up their work day. Shutdown storms result in more data being written, so plan accordingly, with write-back and write-through caches that provide persistence and data integrity as well as performance acceleration.

The above simple example does not factor in the benefit of caching and other optimization techniques. However, it does point to the importance of maintaining performance during abnormal situations (boot and start-up as well as shutdown storms). Note that storms are the flurry of activity resulting from everybody starting up their workstations (lots of reads), or shutting down (lots of writes to save data). This means that for performance-sensitive application workloads, there needs to be consistency within normal running periods and during disruptions or outages (planned and unplanned).

Table 6.3. 8K Four Corner (128 threads) IOPs vdbench Result (NVMe and HDD)

	(IOPs) i/o rate	MB/sec 1024**2	bytes i/o	read pct	resp time(ms)	read resp(ms)	write resp(ms)	resp max(ms)	resp stddev	queue depth	cpu% sys+u	cpu% sys
8K 100% Seq. 100% Write												
4TB 5.4K HDD	1570.07	12.27	8192	0.00	80.992	0.000	80.992	305.655	38.656	127.2	5.1	1.7
NVMe PCIe SSD	44069.48	344.29	8192	0.00	2.878	0.000	2.878	1205.039	11.187	126.8	41.8	24.4
8K 100% Seq. 100% Read												
4TB 5.4K HDD	59184.16	462.38	8192	100.00	2.156	2.156	0.000	1624.718	10.984	127.6	32.9	24.1
NVMe PCIe SSD	91562.29	715.33	8192	100.00	1.391	1.391	0.000	1369.334	8.392	127.4	58.8	43.1
8K 100% Random 100% Write												
4TB 5.4K HDD	56.17	0.44	8192	0.00	2240.453	0.000	2240.453	5912.785	1493.667	127.6	1.2	0.3
NVMe PCIe SSD	39462.39	308.30	8192	0.00	3.227	0.000	3.227	1464.869	17.303	127.3	42.3	25.5
8K 100% Random 100% Read												
4TB 5.4K HDD	653.25	5.10	8192	100.00	194.842	194.842	0.000	2016.777	256.913	127.6	1.8	0.6
NVMe PCIe SSD	94770.49	740.39	8192	100.00	1.339	1.339	0.000	1512.827	7.676	126.9	60.5	46.3

Tip: How many IOPs, gets, puts, reads, writes can an HDD or SSD do? That depends, although there are many old rules of thumbs and dated metrics floating around. Likewise, there are some dated methods that underestimate performance based on revolutions per minute (RPM) of drives that do not take into consideration read as well as write cache. Today's HDD and SSD vary in read and write performance across different types of media and capacities (refer to Chapters 5 and 7). Table 6.3 shows four corners (random, sequential, reads, writes) for 8K across a 5.4K 4TB HDD and an PCIe AiC NVMe SSD using vdbench with 128 threads.

Another consideration for VDI and workspace I/O performance is the size and type of I/O, for example, small 4K or 8K, larger 64K and 128K, or even larger 1MB-sized I/Os, which may be random or sequential reads and writes, cached or noncached. Note that during a typical operating system start-up sequence, there are different types of I/Os, some small random reads, some large sequential, as well as writes to logs to plan for.

Tip: For more server storage I/O performance, refer to www.storageio.com/performance, where there are links to various performance-related tools, results, and related information in addition to those shown elsewhere in this book.

Part of VDI assessment and planning should be to understand the typical storage I/O and networking characteristics for normal, boot, and peak processing periods to size the infrastructure appropriately. Solutions include those from Citrix (XenApp and XenDesktop), Microsoft, VMware Horizon, and View, among others, including those from cloud providers.

Considerations, tips, and recommendations include:

- Understand the different applications and workloads being hosted and your resource needs.
- Use GPUs and increased video RAM (real or virtual) for graphic-intensive applications.
- Leverage linked clones to optimize performance as well as capacity.
- Remember that aggregation or consolidation can cause aggravation (bottlenecks).
- Utilize read/write cache solutions to speed up performance and eliminate bottlenecks.
- Where will the workspace and VDI services be delivered from (on-site, via cloud)?

- What are the applications being used? Do they require extra compute, I/O resources?
- Do the applications require graphics acceleration or other special resources?

6.6. Data Infrastructure Migration

Context is important when it comes to discussing data infrastructure–related migration. Migrations can be one-off endeavors or recurring events involving many applications, either along with their data or isolated. Migration can be performing a physical to virtual (P2V) of a server along with its operating systems, applications, and data (e.g., lift and shift or rehost) or can involve some type of conversion. Another migration can be moving email, contacts, and calendar data from on-prem Exchange or different email to O365, or from Google to another service, among other variations.

Data infrastructure management includes migrations of various types. Examples of data infrastructure migrations include moving applications along with data between data centers or cloud availability zones, as well as moving between P2V, physical to cloud (P2C), virtual to virtual (V2V), virtual to cloud (V2C), cloud to cloud (C2C), and cloud or virtual to physical (V2P). Another P2V variation is creating a virtual hard disk (VHD) or VHDX—for example, of a running Windows system—that in turn can be used by Hypervisors such as Hyper-V, among other uses both on-prem and in clouds.

Another type of data infrastructure–related migration involves moving from old to new servers, storage systems, network hardware, and software. Other examples of data infrastructure software migration include a hypervisor, operating system, file system, database, backup, and data protection, among other tools. Other data infrastructure migration activities can be the conversion of storage from lower-level BIOS to UEFI and MBR to GPT in support of server operating system (and hypervisor) upgrades, as well as network enhancements.

Fundamental data movement and migration questions include:

- Frequency—is it one-time or recurring?
- If this is a recurring activity, what is the frequency?
- What are the constraints, barriers, and other dependencies?
- What is the reason for the conducting the migration?
- What is the scope and context of the data infrastructure migration?
- What is the timeline: is this a one-time or recurring activity?
- Where and what are the source and the destination?
- Will this be a data and/or application conversion, movement, or both?

Common data movement and migration activities include:

- Discovery and analysis of what will be moved, when, where, and how
- Determination of dependencies of various systems, applications, data, and resources
- Remediation, cleanup of any old data items, empty the trash
- Security and data privacy concerns including encryption and access control
- Planning for the move and migration, scheduling, and testing

- Actual data movement, log and error event analysis
- Problem resolution and data integrity verification
- Post–data migration optimization

Additional data movement and migration considerations include:

- How will the data be moved: online or offline, all at once or in phases?
- Will data be moved electronically via networks or via bulk physical transfer?
- What software, hardware, and other tools, along with services, will be needed?
- Will data be converted from one format to another?
- How will offline data movement be resynchronized with online changes?
- Will data be kept in its stored format or exported and re-imported?

Cloud service providers, as well as other vendors and professional services organizations, have various migration and movement offerings. Some of the cloud providers have services that include hardware, software, cloud management portals, among other tools for both online and off-line movement. Also, cloud and other providers have various conversion and data transformation tools, ranging from data format to application conversion.

Some examples of cloud service provider offerings include bulk data movement appliances from AWS (Snowball Edge and Snowmobile), Google Transfer Appliance, and Microsoft Azure Data Box offerings. Some of these appliances, besides having storage capacity, also have optional compute capabilities to support data transformation, data conversion, and data preprocessing before sending it to a cloud storage resource. Additional examples include various AWS, Azure, Google, and other cloud service provider migration tools, along with those from Microsoft (including storage migration service), Oracle, VMware, and many others.

6.7. Common Questions and Tips

How do you decide between buy, rent, subscribe, or DIY (build) solutions? That comes down to your environment and available resources including staffing, amount of time, and budget. If you have more staff and time than budget, that might push you toward DIY, build, or some assembly required, using open-source or other technologies. On the other hand, if time is money, you might be able to buy time via leveraging technology acquisition either turnkey or with some assembly required. Likewise, for different sizes and types of environments, things will vary.

What are the most important factors when deciding where to site an application, workload, or data (cost, performance, security, scalability, ease of control)? Understanding the application and organizational objectives, requirements, and PACE characteristics all come into play. Also, where are the users of the services of the applications that will be hosted by the data Infrastructure? Do those applications need to be close to the users, and data close to the applications? What applicable threat risks need to be protected against, and what are the cost considerations?

Where do server and applications focus (or domain) start and stop vs. storage, I/O, and networking activities? That depends on your environment, area of focus, and perspective, among other factors. For a heavily siloed or compartmentalized perspective, the lines of demarcation between server, storage, I/O, networking, hardware, software, hypervisors, operating systems, file systems, databases, middleware, applications, and data protection, among others, is well established. However, from other, more converged perspectives, the lines are blurred from technology, task, activity, technology, and management perspectives. If you are a server person, it is time to know more about storage, I/O networking, hardware, software, virtual, cloud, and containers. If you are a storage person, expand or refresh your tradecraft on servers, applications, cloud, virtual, containers, and other related data infrastructure topics. The same applies to networking, applications, database, facilities, and other focus areas.

Keep in mind that servers need storage, storage needs servers, servers and storage need I/O and networking, networking and I/O exist to provide communications, hardware needs software, software needs hardware—they all are used to create and support data infrastructures.

6.8. Chapter Summary

Everything is not the same across different environments, applications, data infrastructures, and resources. However, there are similarities in how data infrastructure resources can be aligned to meet different application PACE and SLO needs. Use new and old tools, techniques, and tips in modern as well as hybrid ways to adapt to your needs and environmental requirements. Different solutions, services, hardware, software, and tools have various attributes beyond simple cost per resource.

General action items include:

- Keep context and scope in perspective when planning and making decisions.
- How will you define hardware, software, and services to meet your PACE and SLO needs?
- Balance PACE efficiency (utilization) with effectiveness (productivity).

Chapter 7

Data Infrastructure Deployment Considerations: Part II

What You Will Learn in This Chapter

- What approach to use for different scenarios
- How to apply your data infrastructure essential tradecraft skills

This chapter converges various themes and topics from the previous chapters combined with some additional tradecraft, insight, and experiences. The focus is on common data infrastructure (both legacy and software-defined) deployment topics. Key themes, buzzwords, and trends addressed in this chapter include server, storage, I/O network, hardware, software, services, converged infrastructure (CI), hyper-converged infrastructure (HCI), software-defined, cloud, virtual, container, database, big data, scale-out, grid, cluster, and various applications, among other related topics.

7.1. Getting Started

Let's continue our discussion about data infrastructure deployment considerations keeping in mind that all applications have some type of performance, availability, capacity, and economic (PACE) attribute that vary by type of workload, environment, size, scale, and scope, among other considerations.

7.2. Microsoft Azure, Hyper-V, Windows, and Other Tools

Microsoft SDDC, SDI, and SDDI capabilities include traditional workstation, desktop, laptop, tablet, and mobile solutions. In addition to the desktop and workspaces along with various

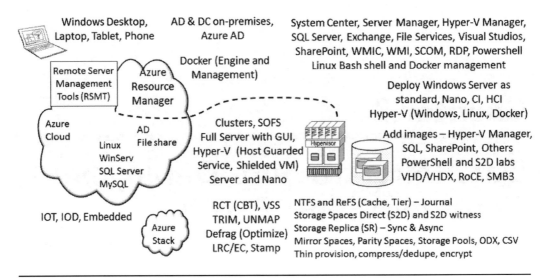

Figure 7.1   Microsoft topics including Azure and Windows.

applications such as Exchange, SQL Server, SharePoint, and Visual Studio, and development tools, among others, there is also Windows Server. Windows Server can be deployed with a desktop GUI user interface or in non-GUI mode, on bare-metal physical, virtual, and cloud compute server instances. Note that there are 32- and 64-bit versions of Windows.

Windows Server, along with some newer versions/editions of Windows desktop, supports Hyper-V virtual machines. As a hypervisor, Hyper-V naturally supports Windows-based operating systems, as well as various Linux solutions including Windows Subsystem for Linux (WSL). There is also Hyper-V server as well as Storage server, among other offerings.

Figure 7.1 shows various Microsoft data infrastructure–related tools and technologies from Azure cloud services on the left, Azure stack (a private on-premise version of Azure you can run on your hardware), Windows Server, Hyper-V, and other tools. Also shown in Figure 7.1 are Microsoft management tools including System Center, Active Directory (AD), Server Manager, Hyper-V Manager, SQL Server, Visual Studio, SharePoint, and Exchange, among others. Additional Azure tools and services include those to support IoT, including hubs, gateways, tables, queues, databases, IAM, and management.

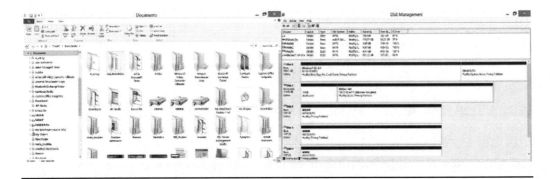

Figure 7.2   Accessing Windows storage without using drive letters.

In Figure 7.1, Storage Spaces Direct (S2D) is Microsoft's software-defined storage (SDS) solution, which can be used to create aggregated (HCI) and disaggregated (CI) scale-out clusters. Besides being on Windows Servers, Microsoft has also made SQL Server along with associated management studio and tools available on Linux (and containers). Microsoft Windows (and Azure) supports virtual hard disks (VHD) and extended (VHDX) for VM and physical machines.

Figure 7.2 shows a Windows folder (left) with various subfolders. Also shown in the center of the left-hand image are three disk or storage-shaped images which are VHDX virtual disks. These are mounted in an existing folder path as opposed to being given drive letters. On the right-hand side of Figure 7.2 is the VHDX, shown mounted in the lower portion of the display. Instead of accessing contents of a storage device with a drive letter path, an existing folder path is used. The storage contents simply become part of the folder tree.

The default file system for Windows servers (and workstations) for several years has been NT File System (NTFS), and File Allocation Table (FAT) for portable devices. With Windows Server 2016, the default file system is now Microsoft's Resilient File System (ReFS), which is a journaling solution including integrated data integrity checks. NTFS will continue to be supported for many years, as will FAT for interoperability.

In addition to traditional local storage, Windows Server 2019 builds on Windows Server 2012 and 2016 Storage Spaces by adding new software-defined storage functionality with Storage Spaces Direct (S2D). Besides local and direct attached storage, Windows servers also support access to storage via block iSCSI and Fibre Channel, among other interfaces and protocols. SMB file sharing along with NFS are also supported among other options, including clustered shared volumes (CSV) and SMB3 direct.

Windows servers can be deployed as standalone or clustered, as disaggregated CI and aggregated HCI using S2D and clustering. Likewise, Windows Server and Workstation support Hyper-V and guest Windows and Linux systems, as well as being a guest itself on VMware and other hypervisors as well as cloud instances.

Other tools include *Disk2vhd* (for migrating from physical disk to VHDX), *Diskmgr, Diskpart* (for managing disk partitions and volumes), and *Diskspd* (benchmarking, test, and simulation). Additional tools and utilities include *fsutil* to create large empty files for testing, *Manage-bde* (BitLocker command line), Netsh (for network-setting configuration), and PowerShell for local and remote, SQL Studio, and SQL configuration utility. Windows Admin Center (WAC), formerly known as Honolulu, is another Windows management tool.

Other tools include Task Manager (enables disk status via the command line with *diskperf –y*), Virtual Machine Migrate (for converting from physical to virtual, including VMware to Hyper-V), and WMIC (displays various configuration and device information).

Figure 7.3 shows, on the left, a Microsoft Azure dashboard provisioning and accessing a cloud instance (virtual machine) instance on the right, which is a Windows Server 2016 instance. Microsoft has been working on enhancing the management and user experience of working with and across traditional Windows platforms as well as Azure. This means that Azure and Windows are compatible and work together, yet can also be used independently.

Microsoft Azure cloud service exists in several different geographical regions, with more being added similar to how AWS is growing. Services which continue to evolve include compute instances such as virtual machines, naturally Windows as well as many different Linux flavors along with containers. Besides compute, Azure also supports development environments and

Figure 7.3   Azure compute access (left) and Windows instance (right).

tools, analytics for big data, media, and CDN. Other components include identity and access management (IAM) and security, SQL and NoSQL databases and table services, a data warehouse, queues, and Redis cache and storage. Besides table and database storage (and services), Azure also supports file access including via remote Windows servers, as well as blobs (object storage) and non-blob blocks.

In addition to the Azure public cloud, Azure Stack, Windows Server, and traditional desktop workspace applications including Microsoft Office, Microsoft also has the Office 365

Table 7.1. Microsoft Compute Server and Storage Platforms

Resources	Characteristics, Attributes, Tips, and Recommendations
Azure public cloud	Public cloud services including applications, resources, compute instances and containers, analytics, big data, little data, bulk storage and CDN, off-site distributed resources, block, file, and object storage, tables, queues, database, development, and testing. Leverage different geographical locations. Use as a replacement for on-site, on-premise resources or as a complement including for HA, BC, DR, and elasticity.
Docker and Windows container	Docker management of Linux-based containers hosted on Hyper-V as well as Windows-based containers. Use for micro services, threads, and processes that do not need an entire VM to perform specific tasks.
Azure Stack private or hybrid cloud	On-premise version of Azure public service that allows you to select different hardware options for deployment. Leverage as a private cloud to move beyond what you might do with traditional Windows servers, as well as for deploying hybrid clouds. Complement or alternative to OpenStack.
Hyper-V virtualization	For hosting guest virtual machines including various versions of Windows as well as Linux as servers, desktop, workspace, VDI, database, or other applications. Supports consolidation of resources and management or as part of deploying SDDC, SDI, and SDDI environments.
Windows Nano	Streamlined Windows operating system for Hyper-V or bare metal. Workloads where a user interface is not needed; uses less CPU and memory.
Windows Server	For traditional bare metal as well as on virtual servers and cloud instances as the operating system for various applications including Active Directory (AD), Domain Controllers (DC), networking, storage, SQL Server, Exchange, SharePoint, and many others. Nano version for lightweight non-UI–based management, full GUI desktop for user interface–based management, Hyper-V for hosting guest virtual machines.
Workstation desktop	Where a server version is not needed on laptops, physical workstations, tablets, or mobile devices. Note that, depending on version edition, there are common management tools across server and desktop. Some editions also support Hyper-V virtual machines as well as management access.

(O365) cloud-based service. This capability allows you to decide on using hosted (cloud) subscription-based desktop productivity tools such as Excell, Word, PowerPoint, and email, among others, as well as traditional on-site hosted (physical or virtual) tools.

Table 7.1 shows suggestions on when and where to use different Microsoft SDDC, SDI, and SDDI solutions to address different needs.

Considerations include:

- Where and how will your IoT devices be managed?
- Will you use the same services for general event management as well as IoT?
- What are the applications? Where are users accessing resources from?
- Do you have an all-Windows, all-Linux, or mixed environment?
- Do you need legacy storage support of Fibre Channel, iSCSI, or NAS using storage spaces?
- Software-defined storage with Storage Spaces Direct (S2D) and replication.
- Local and remote networking needs and requirements.
- Licensing models including enterprise license agreements (ELA).
- Different environments from SOHO to ROBO to SMB to enterprise.
- Consider context of SMB vs. CIFS/SAMBA file sharing.
- SMB3 can mean direct connect low latency deterministic, or general file and storage sharing.

7.3. VMware vSphere, vSAN, NSX, and Cloud Foundation

VMware SDDC, SDI, and SDDI capabilities range from virtual server infrastructure (VSI) hypervisors such as vSphere ESXi to Horizon virtual desktop infrastructure (VDI) and desktop workspace client (View). Other pieces of the VMware software-defined portfolio include virtual storage (vSAN) integrated with vSphere, along with NSX software-defined networking (SDN), many management tools, and solution suites.

In addition to having solutions that can be purchased for a fee along with annual maintenance and licenses, there are also subscription models and enterprise license agreements. VMware also has free software such as basic vSphere ESXi, which provides hypervisor functionality without additional management tools such as vCenter, vRealize, and others.

Figure 7.4 shows a software-defined data infrastructure (SDDI) implementation in the form of VMware Software-Defined Data Center architecture, solutions, and suites. VMware supports virtual desktop infrastructure (VDI) and workspace with Horizon (virtual server) as well as View (clients). Various management tools and suites are available as well as virtualized compute (VM and containers), storage, and networking.

The various VMware components can run on-premise on BM and PM (hosts), nested (on virtualized servers), as well as on some cloud platforms such as AWS. VMware vSphere ESXi hypervisor can also be managed and used by other stacks or frameworks such as OpenStack. Likewise, there is a VMware Integrated OpenStack Appliance that runs on the VMware software-defined data infrastructure. Another capability is VMware vSphere including VSAN and NSX deployed on AWS EC2 dedicated servers.

VMware management tools such as vCenter are packaged as an appliance, meaning they can run on top of and leverage underlying tools while enabling simplicity of deployment. In

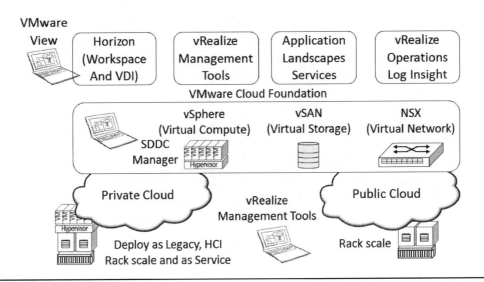

Figure 7.4   VMware Software-Defined Data Center.

addition to vCenter, other VMware tools are also available as preconfigured virtual appliances, as well as close hypervisor kernel integration, for example, with vSAN.

The different VMware technologies can run standalone or in conjunction with other components leveraging different packaging. Different packaging and deployment include legacy server, CI, HCI, and rack scale, as well as the cloud.

Table 7.2 shows the three primary VMware data infrastructure software-defined building blocks converging virtual server compute (vSphere ESXi hypervisor), storage (vSAN), and software-defined networking (NSX). Management is via vRealize suite, among other tools.

Table 7.2. Core VMware Software-Defined Building Blocks

Component	Characteristics, Attributes, Tips, and Recommendations
vSphere ESXI compute	Server virtualization hypervisor that runs on physical servers, and can also be nested installed on top of itself. Supports various physical hardware devices as well as guest operation systems including Windows and Linux. Virtualized CPU, memory, I/O storage, and networking devices along with video among other key resources. VMware File System (VMFS) file system overlays underlying storage resources; VMDK is virtual disks. Also, virtual volumes (VVOL) are supported. Can be deployed standalone without vCenter or other tools as well as clustered. Dynamic Resource Scheduler (DRS) facilitates optimization across clustered hosts, policy and automation along with storage QoS. Data at rest encryption (DARE) support for virtual machines.
vSAN storage	Virtual storage integrated with underlying vSphere hypervisor for HCI deployments scaling from 2 to 64 nodes with various FTM options to meet different FTT needs. Hybrid and all-Flash configurations, support for RAID mirroring, replication, and parity erasure codes along with encryption, compression, de-dupe and thin provisioning. Tools include vSAN Observer and vSAN Console along with vSAN Health Check, among others.
NSX network	Software-defined networking (SDN) including micro-services and segmentation enabling finer granularity as well as enhanced scalability of virtual resources.

APIs include VAAI (VMware API for Array Integration) and VASA (VMware API for Storage Awareness). VASA enables providers (storage systems, appliances, and software) to convey insight up the stack to VMware vSphere, so it has insight into capabilities and configuration of storage resources. Also, VASA combined with VVOL enables vSphere to have finer granular access and insight for optimizing snapshots and other functions.

Another vSphere API is VAAI, offloading some functions from the VM to a compatible storage system that supports specific features. VAAI functionality includes granular SCSI lock management on shared storage volumes or LUN, hardware-assisted VM cloning or copy, and data migration for VM movement—for example, offloading some copy and resource initializes, among other tasks. For storage systems that do not support VAAI, those functionalities (zero copy move, SCSI enhanced locking) are performed by the hypervisor server.

Another vSphere functionality to help address scaling of multiple busy VM on a common PM is Storage I/O Control (SIOC), which enables a proprietary scheme for load balancing. With SIOC, those VM that need I/O performance can be tuned accordingly to prevent bottlenecks from occurring. In addition to VASA and VAAI, other VMware APIs include those for data protection (formerly known as VADP), which facilitates optimization for various data infrastructure tasks. VAIO (vSphere API for IO filtering) supports third-party data services.

Table 7.3 shows various VMware tools and technologies along with deployment as well as consumption models spanning server, storage, networking, software-defined virtual and cloud as well as VDI workspace along with management tools.

Other tools include vSphere web client, VMware converter (supports P2V migration), as well as a workstation and desktop variants of vSphere such as Workstation for Windows, and Fusion for Apple-based systems. Workstation and Fusion enable a vSphere-type environment to be run on a desktop for training, support, development, and testing, among other activities. Workspace ONE is for mobile application management, SSO, and identity access control.

Tip: Leverage 10 GbE (or faster) network interfaces for east–west management traffic including monitoring, cluster heartbeat, logging, server and storage vMotion, as well as vSAN activity.

Proper configuration of virtual video RAM may seem intuitive for graphics and VDI types of application workloads. However, in some scenarios, where the database or other applications appear to be running slow, increasing the video RAM might help if the bottleneck is not the database, but rather the buffering and display of results.

Virtual machine optimization considerations include specific hardware support such as Intel VT assist and 64-bit capabilities. Management tools include metrics and measurements for accounting, tracking, capacity planning, service management, and chargeback. Hypervisors also support APIs and management plug-in tools such as Hyper-V working with VSS writers with application or guest integration. Keep in mind that virtual resources and functionality need memory to hold their software-defined data structures as well as programs and data.

Tip: Standard built-in drivers such as those for networking and storage I/O (HBA), among others, work well out of the box. However, VMware supports optimized "para-virtualized" drivers for networking and storage I/O, among others. These drivers along with VMtools can boost effective performance and in some cases also reduce CPU or other overhead.

Table 7.3. Sampling of VMware Tools and Technologies

Resources	Characteristics, Attributes, Tips, and Recommendations
VMware Cloud Foundation	Unified SDDC platform for hybrid cloud leveraging vSphere, vSAN, NSX, and SDDC manager for automation of data infrastructure operations. Use for turnkey scenarios where faster deployment is needed, leveraging various VMware partner hardware solutions deployed on-site. Integrated with other VMware tools. Replaces EVO as a converged deployment solution.
AWS Management Portal for vCenter	vCenter plug-in that enables migration and conversion of VM from VMware environments to AWS EC2 instances. In addition to migration of VM, the plug-in also provides management integration with EC2 for coordinating AW resources from vCenter. This includes Active Directory (AD) and other identity tools also enabling role-based access controls (RBAC).
VMware Cloud on AWS	VMware tools such as vSphere, vSAN, NSX, and associated management tools running on AWS private servers. Note that these are not normal EC2 instances, rather the equivalent of dedicated private servers. This service enables VMware environments to leverage AWS to seamlessly move or migrate (vMotion) servers, storage, and other resources in a hybrid manner across different software-defined data infrastructures.
vCenter Appliance	vCenter is a central platform, place, and tool for managing, orchestrating, and performing common VMware SDDC and SDDI tasks with various plug-ins. Configure multiple vCenters for scaling performance, availability, or capacity.
Horizon View	Horizon is a set of tools and servers for configuring, orchestrating, composing, and delivery of VDI and workspaces to View clients.
OVA OVF	Open Virtual Appliance (OVA) and DMTF Open Virtualization Format (OVF). These are standards and protocols for packaging for deployment virtual appliances and simplifying virtual application deployment instead of building from scratch using ISO or other image builds.
vMotion	Tools for moving server VM and storage, either inactive or while in use.
vCloud Air	VMware public cloud offering to use as an off-site companion to your private cloud or another VMware deployment, or for compatibility migrate VMware-based software-defined data infrastructure, VM, and applications too.
VIC	VMware Integrated Containers with Photon lightweight Linux kernel. Speeds time of deploy with integrated VMware management for containers hosts.
HCIBench	Test harness tool leveraging vdbench for driving various workloads and reporting metric results on traditional vSphere servers as well as vSAN.
VIOA	VMware Integrated OpenStack Appliance is a self-contained, easy-to-deploy and easy-to-use method of doing a quick proof of concept, support development, and other experiences without having to build from scratch.
vApp	A collection of one or more VM, resources, and policies aligned and grouped for ease of management—for example, start-up/shutdown of all VM together as part of an application system collection of resources.

Storage I/O Controls (SIOC) functionality enables performance QoS and other automation including resource allocation with policies. Combined with DRS, policies, and other VMware functionality allocation of data infrastructure resources including server, memory, I/O, storage and networking can be orchestrated and automated in an efficient as well as effective manner.

Tip: In addition to officially released and supported software products, tools, and drivers, VMware, like other vendors, has a collection of tools called "flings." These flings are released via VMware Labs and are a collection of tools and add-on software to enhance, extend, and facilitate management of VMware products and solutions. For example, HCIBench, among others, can be found at labs. vmware.com/flings/hcibench.

Considerations, tips, and recommendations include:

- Align applicable FTM mode and durability (copies) to meet FTT needs.
- Establish performance baselines using HCIBench or other tools for future reference.
- Implement enterprise-class SSDs for write-intensive cache functions and applications.
- Leverage VMware "fling" optional tools to assist with data infrastructure management.
- Refer to the VMware Hardware Compatibility List (HCL) for support configurations.
- Utilize SIOC and another server, storage, and network policy automation.
- Verify that devices and drivers along with other software tool plug-ins are up to date.
- VMware supports 4K page allocations, but make sure applications are page-aligned.

7.4. Data Databases: Little Data SQL and NoSQL

Databases and key-value stores or repositories can be used and optimized to handle transactional analytics, also known as data mining. Transactional databases tend to be read-write-update, whereas analytics, references, and data mining, along with decision support, tends to have fewer updates but more reads. Transactional data can be moved into reference and analytics databases or data warehouses at different intervals or frequencies. Databases are also used for supporting websites, blogs, and other applications as well as for handling metadata. Databases can be open-source or proprietary, as well as Structured Query Language (SQL)–based access or NoSQL (non-SQL)–based.

In addition to how databases get used (activity), they also support various types of data, including columnar tabular, text, video, and other entities. Databases and key-value stores can be in-memory, as well as on disk (HDD or SSD) on-premises (PM, VM, containers), or in clouds as a service or instance.

As the name implies, in-memory databases leverage large-memory servers where all or major portions of the database are kept in memory for speed. For availability and durability, some form of high-speed persistent memory or storage is used to load data rapidly, as well as provide consistency of journals and redo logs. The benefit of in-memory is a faster query and processing of certain functions.

Tip: Look into details of your database or key-value repository to see vendor suggestions and best practices for in-memory processing. Some solutions are optimized for queries and others for transactions. Note that some systems may have higher overhead handling transactions even if they are in-memory, due to data consistency, vs. those handling cached queries and reads.

Besides in-memory databases and applications such as MemSQL, Oracle, Redis, SAP, and SQL Server among others, most databases also support various forms of caching with memory, as well as NVM. NVM including storage-class memories (SCM) and persistent memory (PMEM) along with SSD can also be used for journals, transaction and redo logs, checkpoints, metadata and system configuration, system and temporary tables, and scratch space, as well as indices and main data tables.

Tip: Historically, DBAs and others working with databases have been taught the importance of having as many "spindles" or disk drives as possible to spread data out for performance. Using SSD and other forms of SCM and NVM, in some scenarios fewer devices can be used to deliver a higher level of performance than many drives. However, make sure to have enough SSD or SCM to enable availability using a mirror or, when needed, parity-based erasure code RAID. For larger workloads, multiple SSD can be used to further spread out the workload.

Components include a logical database server instance (the database server software), which is installed on a physical, virtual, cloud, or container instance. Note the context that a database server can be the actual server system that runs the database software. However, the database software running on a server can also be called the database server. Keep context in mind. Other components include the server processors (CPU), memory, and I/O network along with storage performance and capacity configured for some level of availability.

Figure 7.5 shows a database server (software) such as Cassandra, IBM, Kudu, MongoDB, MySQL, Oracle, or SQL Server, among many others. Local and remote users, applications, processes, services, and devices access the database, adding, updating, or reading data.

Depending on the particular database solution, there can be one or more instances of the database server, each with one or more databases. For example, on a given PM, BM, VM, container, or cloud instance, there can be a SQL Server database server instance called TESTIO,

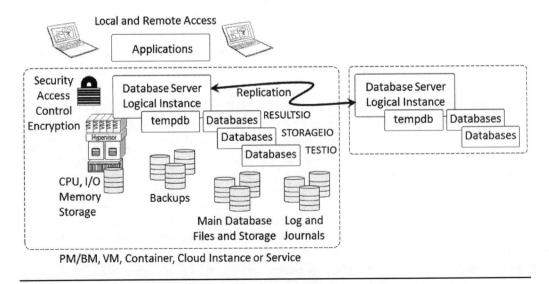

Figure 7.5   Database server instance and database items.

another called RESULTSIO, and another called STORAGEIO. TESTIO might be used for running various test workloads with different databases. Results such as Benchmark Factory, among others, may be stored in databases served by the separate instance RESULTSIO. The general activity might exist in other databases in STORAGEIO.

Also shown in Figure 7.5 are different databases along with a temporary database (tempdb) used for sorting and other temporary functions. The various databases have one or more data repositories (usually a file on or in a file system) that exist on one or more backing stores (storage volumes). Also shown are how databases can be backed up, replicated, as well as unloaded (export or dump) and loaded (import or restore). Resources including CPU, memory, I/O, and storage space capacity. Also shown are security including encryption and access controls to databases, tables, and other resources.

While it is possible to put all databases into a single instance, having different ones enables those instance servers to be tuned and optimized differently. Also, those database instances can be stopped, maintenance performed, and started independently of the others. Work with your DBAs or others responsible for database administration to determine what type of configuration is needed to meet different needs. How and when to protect the databases along with their configuration settings will vary based on PACE and SLO needs.

Additional components include system configuration and metadata for the databases such as a master or system database, and temporary databases for sorting and other functions, also known as tempdb. Then there are specific database instances (databases) that have collections of database entities stored in primary objects along with log and journal files.

Different database systems and their implementations will have various names and locations for these items. Note context here is that a database object is an item or entity and database object storage does not mean S3 or Swift object storage (although for some implementations it might).

Remember that databases store entities and their data structure object items in files as repositories—examples include .ora, .dbf (among others for Oracle), and .mdf for Microsoft SQL Server, among others. For MySQL, MongoDB, and others on Linux systems, you may find the default database files in a location such as /var/lib/MySQL or /var/lib/MongoDB unless they have been moved.

Tip: There may be a temptation to use lower-cost, higher-capacity Flash SSD for databases, which might be ok for mainly read application workloads. However, for update, write-intensive, and cache use, enterprise-class SSD tend to have better wear or durability endurance measured in TB written per day (TBWD), lasting longer and can also be faster on writes. Keep in mind that Flash SSD will wear out over time, so use the applicable type of NVM aligned to your specific workload and PACE needs. Some database and key-value repositories also support Direct Access Extension (DAX) leveraging underlying NVM and SCM.

General management activities include:

- Allocate and provision space, expand space
- Compress, compact, and optimize (reorganize)
- Import, load, and export, unload
- Log and journal file shipping or copies

- Tune resource parameters, buffers, threads, and sessions
- Protection with consistency points and checkpoints

Tip: There are different tools for performing database unload (export) and load (import) in support of data protection, maintenance, and optimization or data migration. Some tools process data in a serial fashion, while others create multiple parallel data streams to move more data in a shorter amount of time. In addition to using tools that support different data import and export methods, also make sure to have enough temporary or scratch space for data being moved.

Additional database and repository management function include:

- Move and migrate, detach, attach
- Performance tuning and troubleshooting
- Relocated backing stores files and storage
- Clean-up, purge, compression, and reorganization
- Protection, backup, clone, replication, checkpoint
- Data load (import) and unload (export)

Tip: Gain insight into data performance activity and resource usage using vendor-supplied as well as third-party tools, for example, Oracle automatic workload repository and performance status, as well as those from IBM, Microsoft, Quest, Solarwinds, and many others. Having insight into resource use, bottlenecks, and constraints can enable smart decision making such as when and where to use SSD along with how much for cache or storing data.

Availability and protection includes:

- Access (local and remote) control and encryption
- Checkpoint and consistency point frequency and retention
- Backup, snapshots, and point-in-time copies
- Replication and mirroring (local and remote)
- Storage placement and configuration
- Redo logs and journals

Tip: Belt-and-suspenders data protection includes using database replication for higher-level strong transactional consistency, along with checkpoints, snapshots, and other point-in-time copies to meet RPO requirements. Lower-level hypervisor, operating system, or storage-based replication can also be used with different frequency and granularity, along with redundant cluster nodes and components with failover capability.

A hybrid approach leverages server or database replication for long-distance synchronous and lower-level storage asynchronous replication. Some local databases can also be replicated not only to other physical or virtual database system servers, but also to some cloud services.

Optimize and allocate resources:

- CPU (cores and threads) along with speed
- Memory (lots and fast) for buffers, cache, applications, and data
- I/O for storage and network access and connectivity
- Storage space (primary, indices, scratch, logs, journals, protection)
- Vary the number of threads and sessions supported per database instance

---

Tip: To ensure performance and availability, proper database maintenance should be done, including purging, archiving, optimization, or reorganization, even if deployed on SSD. Also make sure to have adequate free space on scratch, work, and primary backing store or storage devices, and that proper security authentication is in place for local and remote access. Also, make sure that your system tempdb or equivalent space used for sorting and other functions has enough space to avoid job termination or other errors.

Troubleshooting tips include verifying that the database physical and logical server instance are on-line and functioning. Verify that the database server has adequate storage space for specific databases and there are main as well as log files. Also check to see whether there is adequate system temporary space for sorting, work, and other tasks and that proper permissions or quotas are in place. Double-check network connectivity, firewalls, and network security as well as whether associated tasks are running. Check your various error logs to see whether resources such as memory, CPU, storage, or threads and sessions have been exhausted or there is some other problem.

Figure 7.6 shows (1) a standalone server with DAS that can be a hybrid mix of HDD and SSD, or all-Flash, or all-NVM. Also shown in (1) are local backups made to disk, tape, or cloud along with checkpoints and other protection techniques. Storage in (1) can be protected for availability using RAID 1 mirroring or other variations including RAID 10 as well as various erasure and parity code checks. The example shown as (1) is good for smaller environments or those with specialized needs.

At the top center in Figure 7.6, (2) shows a standalone system with additional dedicated or shared DAS. The top right (3) shows a standalone server with the hypervisor and VMs supporting database workloads. This scenario can be used for application and server consolidation. To increase resiliency or scale resources, additional hosts can be added.

Tip: Keep in mind that there is a difference between virtualizing a database system or application and consolidating. Databases can be virtualized, but keep performance in perspective using different QoS and policy parameters vs. simply consolidating as many servers as possible. To meet performance needs, some databases may need their host for most of the time, but you can leverage virtualization for agility, maintenance, availability, load-balancing, and other data infrastructure operations. When the database does not need all the performance, additional VM or containers can be load-balanced on the host.

In Figure 7.6 in the middle on the left (4) are multiple host servers (non-virtualized or virtualized) sharing direct attached storage such as for a simple small availability cluster. In

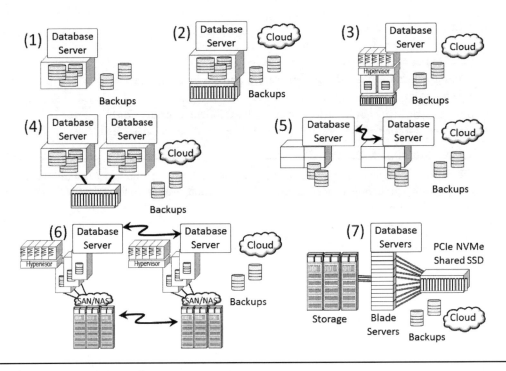

Figure 7.6   Various database deployment scenarios.

the middle of Figure 7.6 on the right (5) are CI and HCI clusters that are replicating to other CI and HCI systems. Replication can be done via the database, server, or CI and HCI data services. An approach such as shown in (5) is useful for larger SMB or larger ROBO and work-groups that need resiliency across locations.

In Figure 7.6, (6) shows an example of rack-scale and scale-out disaggregated compute servers with SAN, NAS, or other software-defined storage configured for availability and performance for larger-scale or larger-size environments.

The lower right of Figure 7.6 (7) shows a hybrid approach using shared direct attached SSD or SCM attached via low-latency PCIe and NVMe, along with general-purpose storage (HDD or SSD). The shared SSD is used for tempdb, scratch, indices, commonly accessed tables, or other items. Locking and consistency are provided by database software such as Oracle, among others. General-purpose storage is used for less frequently accessed data, checkpoints, import/export, and other scratch space.

Tip: There might be a temptation to use erasure code and some parity-based protection approaches to boost storage space capacity (efficiency), but keep performance in mind. Erasure codes have a higher overhead in terms of CPU usage and longer latency (time required for software to think about how to optimize) to store data and thus should not be used for active-update data. On the other hand, backing stores for backups or archives can be an option for using erasure codes.

Data protection for the scenarios above is a combination of mirror and replication for residency, as well as point-in-time copies for recovery and consistency point protection. Also shown

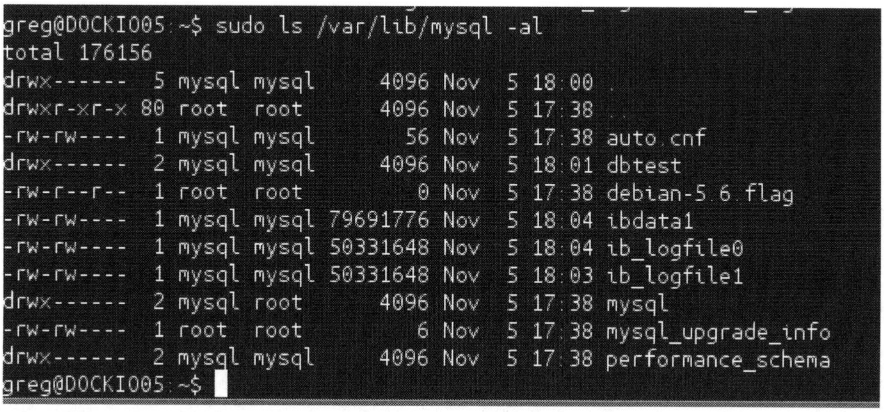

```
greg@DOCKIO05:~$ sudo ls /var/lib/mysql -al
total 176156
drwx------   5 mysql mysql     4096 Nov  5 18:00 .
drwxr-xr-x  80 root  root      4096 Nov  5 17:38 ..
-rw-rw----   1 mysql mysql       56 Nov  5 17:38 auto.cnf
drwx------   2 mysql mysql     4096 Nov  5 18:01 dbtest
-rw-r--r--   1 root  root         0 Nov  5 17:38 debian-5.6.flag
-rw-rw----   1 mysql mysql 79691776 Nov  5 18:04 ibdata1
-rw-rw----   1 mysql mysql 50331648 Nov  5 18:04 ib_logfile0
-rw-rw----   1 mysql mysql 50331648 Nov  5 18:03 ib_logfile1
drwx------   2 mysql root      4096 Nov  5 17:38 mysql
-rw-rw----   1 root  root         6 Nov  5 17:38 mysql_upgrade_info
drwx------   2 mysql mysql     4096 Nov  5 17:38 performance_schema
greg@DOCKIO05:~$ █
```

Figure 7.7   Default MySQL data file locations.

are protecting data locally as well as to clouds, as well as having databases in the cloud. Which is best depends on your environment, applications PACE, and workload, where applications are located (with data close to them), along with size, scale, SLO, and other considerations.

Tip: Configuration files can usually be found in (or in a subdirectory) of */etc* such as */etc/mongod.conf.* These configuration files specify where database files are located and other parameters that can include some sessions, memory for buffers, and other items. Likewise, logs can usually be found in */var/log.*

Figure 7.7 shows an example of default MySQL data file locations.

Figure 7.8 shows a MySQL database installed on a Docker container on an Ubuntu Linux system using default, ephemeral (nonpersistent) storage. In the example, a container named contmysql is started and a MySQL *show databases* command executed to display databases in the database server instance. Next, a MySQL *create database gregs* command is executed, followed by a *show databases* that displays databases. To accommodate the nonephemeral storage (by default for containers), the container is stopped and removed, then restarted using

```
Docker run --name contmysql -e MYSQL_ROOT_PASSWORD=$PSS \
-v /home/user/local_my.cnf:/etc/my.cnf \
-d mysql/mysql-server
```

Next, a MySQL *show databases* command displays known databases, and *gregs* no longer exists.

Note that the MySQL configuration file in the container is overridden by an external (local to the host server) configuration file.

Figure 7.9 shows an example of how persistent storage can be used for containers with applications such as databases that need stateful data. The difference between Figures 7.8 and 7.9 is that the container has persistent storage.

When the container is started, in addition to using an external configuration file, the container default storage path for MySQL *(/var/lib/mysql)* is mapped to an external persistent storage location *(/mnt/md0/Docker/contmysql).*

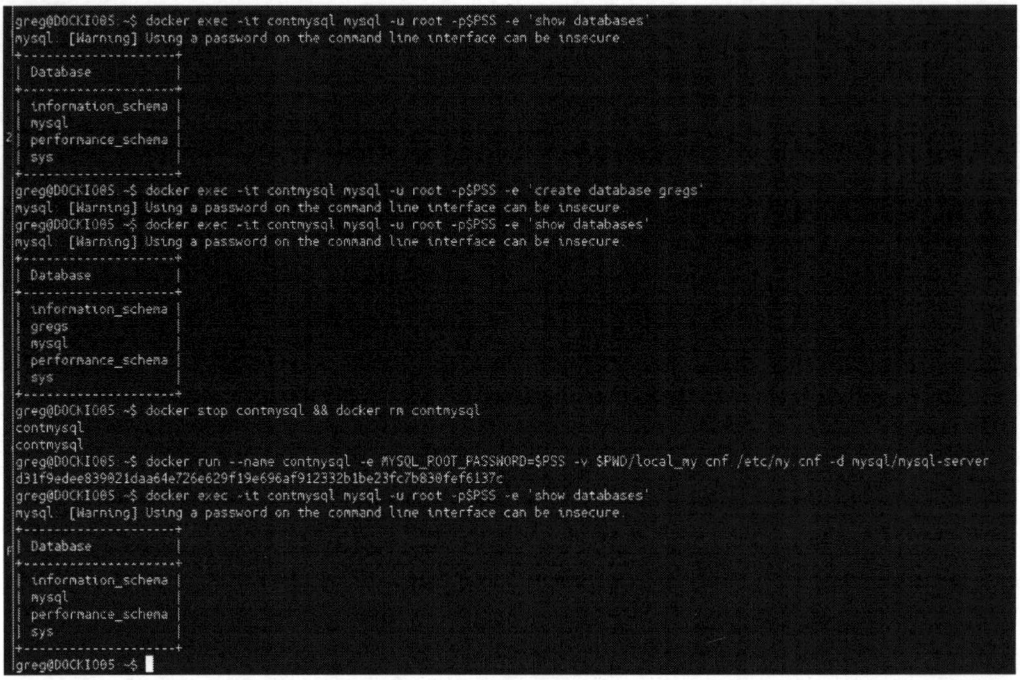

Figure 7.8 MySQL database nonpersistent storage example.

```
Docker run --name contmysql \
-e MYSQL_ROOT_PASSWORD=$PSS
-v /home/user/local_my.cnf:/etc/my.cnf \
-v /mnt/md0/Docker/contmysql:/var/lib/mysql \
-d mysql/mysql-server
```

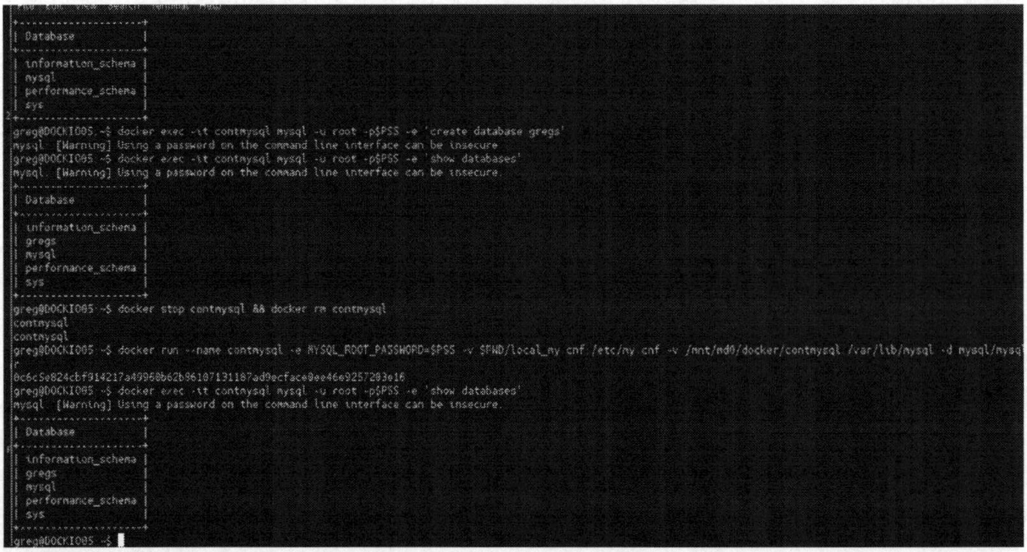

Figure 7.9 MySQL persistent container database storage.

Tip: In Figure 7.9 the persistent storage points to a local storage volume that also ties to or creates affinity with the container to a specific host. Other options include mapping the backing store (the storage location) to a network file share, iSCSI volume, or Docker volume, using plug-ins such as RexRay to map to various persistent storage.

In Figure 7.9, similar to Figure 7.8, the databases are shown, then a database *gregs* is created, the container is shut down and removed, then restored. Unlike in Figure 7.8, however, in Figure 7.9 the container database storage is now persistent, as the database *gregs* exists across reboots.

Tip: If you stop a database server (software) and then copy the associated data files from one location to another (make sure you have a good backup, just in case), make sure you have the security and authentication parameters correct. This includes ownership, access, and other permissions on the files, folders, directories, and other items. For example, if your database does not start after moving it, check your logs to see whether there are permission errors, then check that your destination directory from the root on down to see what is different from the source.

Databases (SQL and NoSQL) and key-value data warehouses and other repositories include Aerospike, AWS (RDS, Aurora, and others), Blue Medora, Basho/Riak, Cachè, Cassandra, ClearDB, Couchbase, Greenplum, and HBase. Ohters include IBM (DB2/UDB and Netezza), Impala, Inodb MySQL engine, Kudo, MariaDB MySQL engine, Memcache, MemSQL, Microsoft (SQL Server [Windows and Linux], various on Azure), and MongoDB. Additional databases and key-value stores include MySQL, OpenStack Trove, Oracle, Parquet, Postgress, Redis, SAP, Spark, Splunk, Sybase, Teradata, TokuDB, and Unisys, among others.

Tip: Use DBA tools such as those that are part of databases and repositories along with third-party and open sources to assess, analyze, report, and gain insight into resource needs, usage, bottlenecks, and optimization opportunities. Tools include those from Microsoft, Oracle such as AWR, MySQL workbench, Quest DBAtools, and many others.

Tools include various studios and workbenches, mysqldump and mysqldumper, among others. Database-related transactions and workload generators such as TPC as well as other workloads include Hammerdb, Quest Benchmark Factory, Loadgen, Sysbench, Virtual Instruments, and YCSB, among others. Analytic, processing, and visualization tools include Hadoop and Kafka, MapReduce, MapR, M1, Pivotal, R, SAP, and SAS, among many others.

Tip: Establish a performance baseline with queries and test data that you can run when problems occur, to compare with known results to verify as well as isolate problems.

Considerations, tips, and recommendations include:

- Databases and repositories are also used in support of big data, including for metadata.
- Everything is not the same, such as applications and their databases or key-value repositories.

- Know your applications, their workload, and PACE requirements, as well as database needs.
- Place data as close to the applications as possible for performance.
- Leverage enterprise-class NVM, Flash, SCM, and SSD for write-intensive applications.
- A little bit of cache in the right place can have a big benefit impact.
- A lot of cache or Flash or NVM SSD and SCM can also have a big benefit.
- Fast applications and fast databases need fast data infrastructure resources.

7.5. Big Data, Data Ponds, Pools, and Bulk-Content Data Stores

In addition to those already mentioned in this chapter other applications and workloads in various industries or organizations are also resource intensive. These include those that are CPU compute, memory, I/O, networking, and or storage space capacity intensive. Some of these application and workload characteristics include large amounts of compute using multiple server instances (PM, VM, cloud instance, or container); others are memory focused.

For some of these applications, many lower-performing, lower-cost processors in a grid, cluster, or redundant array of independent nodes (RAIN) scale-out topology are used; others leverage general-purpose multi-socket and multi-core systems. Other applications leverage GPUs for graphics and other compute-intensive activities, including analytics, along with graphics or their rendering. For applications such as genomic sequencing, specialized processors, or cards with GPU, ASIC, and FPGA such as Dragen, can reduce the time required to process large amounts of data.

Figure 7.10 shows various data repositories including (top left) database, (top middle) data warehouse, (top right) data lake, (bottom center) bulk, and other shared storage or data

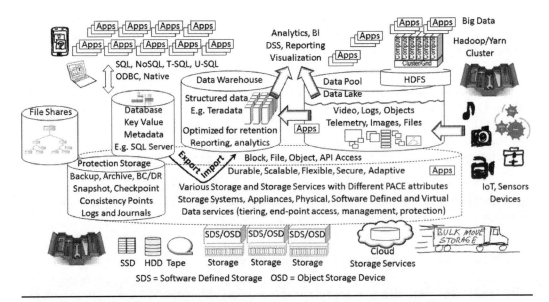

Figure 7.10   Various data infrastructure data repositories.

services. at the top left are SQL and NoSQL databases as well as key-value repositories used for operational, transactional, look-up, metadata, and related functions. Characteristics are highly-structured (software-defined data structures), with applications defined to use a schema of how data is stored. Other attributes include strong consistency, protected, secure, governance, and large and small items accessed by various applications or devices. Examples include Cassandra, MongoDB, MySQL, Oracle, SQL Server, and many others.

At the top middle in Figure 7.10 is data warehouses used for various purposes. Whereas the databases on the left are used for operational or frequent updates or read activity, the data warehouse, as its name implies, is larger, with more structured data for reporting, look-up, and storing other back-end data. Examples include Teradata, SAP, and others.

At the top right in Figure 7.10 is data lakes, with various analytics and applications supporting unstructured, semistructured, structured, and raw data. Different data flows along with data protection and management are shown in Figure 7.10. Keep in mind that everything is not the same, and different environments use databases, data warehouses, and data lakes in various ways. Some environments may not have a data warehouse, instead focusing on data lakes, or vice versa, which in turn are used in different ways to meet their various application and business needs.

At the bottom center in Figure 7.10 is storage that could be one or more systems, solutions, or services including cloud or other repositories that are hardware- and software-defined. Also shown across the bottom of Figure 7.10 are various devices (HDD, SSD, and tape), clusters of converged servers and storage, along with other resources to support the data infrastructure layers.

Other characteristics, as discussed in Chapter 2, include the velocity (how fast—the speed of data arrival) of small or large data items. There are also high volumes of small and large data along with different characteristics, reads, writes, and corresponding metadata. Recall that different applications have diverse PACE needs.

Also recall that there are variations in performance (small or large I/O, IOP or bandwidth, latency, read, write, random, sequential stream, queues) that apply for block, file, object, and APIs. Examples of various applications and workloads that are resource-intensive include big data, big fast data, and bulk data, data warehouse and business intelligence (BI). Additional examples include enterprise data hubs (EDH), click, stream, and other analytics (real-time, postprocessing) along with data transformation and tagging, IoT management and orchestration, log filtering, machine learning, and artificial intelligence.

Tip: Big data means many different things to different people, with diverse application usage scenarios and views. Some focus is for data scientists or other researchers, some for business analysts and business intelligence, some for modern-day executive information systems (EIS) and decision support, an extension of a traditional data warehouse or data marts.

Additional examples include preventive, predictive, and planned maintenance of fleets and other devices, places, and things. Remote monitoring, management of things and places, utilities and other SCADA, also now more commonly referred to as IoT, as well as active archives, libraries, and reference data repositories, factory and process automation including CNC, robotics, and sensors, among other devices, stream and telemetry processing, and visualization, among other activities.

Tip: Context with the acronym BD is important, as it can mean big data, backup device, backing device (where data is stored, or stored in), as well as business development aka BizDev (i.e., sales or creating sales). Another context item is EMR, which can mean Elastic Map Reduce, an AWS big data analytics Hadoop cluster service. However, EMR can also refer to electronic medical records.

In addition to the workloads above, applications that are resource-intensive (compute, I/O, and storage) include those for advertising and actuary, energy and mineral exploration, engineering, financial, trading and insurance, as well as forecasting; gaming, government, healthcare, life science, medical, pharmaceutical, and genomics; HPC, IoD, and IoT; logistics, AI, machine learning, manufacturing, media and entertainment (audio, video, photos, and images); seismic, scientific and research, security and surveillance, simulation and modeling, social media, supercomputing, travel and transport, as well as the web, etail, and shopping.

Common to the applications mentioned above are a need for large amounts of:

- Server compute for processing algorithms, programs, threads, tasks, analytics
- Network and storage I/O to move, read, write data, and communicate with devices
- Ephemeral storage and memory during processing of data and data streams
- Bulk persistent storage for storing large amounts of data and metadata
- Scalable, elastic, flexible access, various tenancies, durable, cost-effective resources
- Resiliency leveraging multiple lower-cost components and data copies

The above applications and landscapes workloads and data infrastructure needs have in common large amounts of unstructured and semistructured as well as some structured data needs. Some of this resulting data is large (big actual files, objects, images), others are small in size but with large quantities (many small files or objects). Another variation is telemetry and log files or streams, where the event, activity, status, and other data whose records, fields, lines, or other data structures are relatively small, yet there are very large numbers of them.

Tip: Fast content applications need fast software, multi-core processors (compute), vast memory (DRAM, NAND Flash, SSD, and HDDs) along with fast server storage I/O network connectivity. Content-based applications benefit from having frequently accessed data as close as possible to the application (locality of reference). Also, to prevent bottlenecks, place frequently accessed (read or write) logs and other data onto fast storage repositories, services, and devices.

The resulting log file may be very large and being appended to, or consist of many smaller files or objects. Some applications such as web click analysis or other stream processing can monitor telemetry and other log activity data in real time to spot trends and patterns and enable machine or software-enabled learning. For example, clock analysis running in real time can detect what the user is looking at, and present relevant ads based on predictive analysis and machine learning about the user's browsing behavior. The result is that it might seem like magic when a website starts to display ads or content that might be of interest to you, which in turn causes you to pursue it to learn more.

Tip: Keep locality of reference in mind; that is, place applications and their compute resources near the data they use, or place the data close to where the servers process the date. This can include placing some processing capability at or near where data is ingested for stream and other processing, as well as elsewhere for subsequent postprocessing or analysis, among other tasks.

Besides performance, availability varies from basic RAS to HA, different SLO, and FTT determining FTM configuration or durability, resiliency, RPO and PIT protection, along with logical as well as physical security. The applications among others need large amounts of resource capacity (server, storage, I/O, and network) that is cost-effective. Table 7.4 shows various resources and attributes.

Table 7.4. Data Infrastructure Resources and Considerations

Resource	Attributes and Considerations
Compute memory	Servers physical and software-defined cloud and virtual as well as containers for running code, algorithms, programs, threads, tasks, and analytics. Analytics and other algorithms for processing data can be done during ingest, including tagging, transformation, and filtering, as well as sending copies to different downstream applications and/or data stores and services or tasks. Scale-out compute nodes and instances combined into grids, clusters, RAIN. Specialized cards, ASIC, and FPGA off-load graphics and other task-specific functions. Security using role-based access control (RBAC) defined via different software at various layers.
I/O	Some of the applications and workloads mentioned in this section are sequential streaming (parallel or high concurrency) of data (reads or writes), large or small I/Os. However, there are also random small I/O (IOPS, gets, puts, reads, and writes) of metadata, key values, and related look-up–type activities. Unstructured data including logs and videos, among others, is written sequentially to some backing store, data lake, bulk, object, file system, or another repository. Metadata is added to various SQL, NoSQL, key-value, and other repositories for subsequent processing and use. Applications and services on servers as well as data on storage is accessed via endpoints, protocols, and interfaces.
Network	Various network resources, local and remote, are used for device to servers, servers to servers, servers to storage, storage to storage, and site to site. The networks rely on various underlying mediums, interfaces, and topologies, legacy and software-defined, as well as network function virtualization. Data services include encryption, rights and access control, VPN, firewalls, VPC and VLAN, and micro-segmentation as well as IPv6, among others.
Storage	Bulk (large capacity, low cost, durable), scalable, elastic and flexible, cost-effective, local on-premise, cloud-accessed from on-site, and cloud-accessed from within the cloud. Various access, including block, file, object, API, queues, and tables, among other storage services. Various PACE needs and storage service personalities. Different endpoints, protocols, and interfaces for accessing of storage, storage applications, and data services.

Various solution approaches include:

- Turnkey solutions, services, subscription, DIY, or some assembly required
- On-site, cloud, hybrid cloud accessed from on-site
- Scale-out clusters, grids, RAIN, and software-defined scale-out
- Compute and storage clusters, aggregated or disaggregated
- Various application platforms, middleware, processing software
- Different repositories, databases, SQL (T-SQL, SQL-H, U-SQL), NoSQL, key value

Applicable data infrastructure technologies, tools, and services include databases (SQL and NoSQL) for metadata and other management of data, clusters, grids, rain, tightly and loosely coupled Blue Medora, Cassandra, ClearDB, Couchbase, HBASE, Kafka, Kudu, MemSQL, MongoDB, MySQL, Oracle, Redis, Riak, SAP, and SQL Server (Windows and Linux); AWS RDS, Azure, Google, OpenStack, Oracle, Softlayer, Virtustream, and VMware; Cloudfoundry, Cloudera, Hadoop and YARN, Hive, Hortonworks, Map Reduce, MapR, Morpheus, Pentaho, Pivotal, R, SAS, SAP HANA, Spark, Splunk, and TIBCO, along with various log insight and analysis tools; Docker, Kubernetes, Mesos, and RexRay, among others.

Other technologies, tools, services, providers, and solutions include Blockbridge, Alluxio, Adobe, Apple, Atto, Avere, Avid, Axis, Broadcom, Ceph software-defined storage, Cisco, Cloudian, and Cray; DataStax, DDN, Dell EMC ECS and Isilon, HDS HCP, HPE, IBM Cleversafe, Informatica, Intel, and Inerplay; LTFS (Linear Tape File System) and LTFS EE+, LSF, and Lustre clustered file system; Maxon, Mellanox, Microsoft, NAS and file access (NFS, pNFS, SMB3, HDFS), Nasuni, NetApp StorageGrid, Nexenta, and NooBaa; OpenStack Swift and SwiftStack, Panzura, Quantum, Supermicro, Stornext, Storpool, Seagate Clusterstor, Sony, Spectralogic, Teradata, Tiger, Vmware, and WD, among others.

Tip: Internet-of-things topics touch many different aspects of data infrastructures. While the IoT devices may be outside the data center and data infrastructures, they have various dependencies and impact. Similar to how users of information services have (and continue) to interact with applications supported by data infrastructures, so to do IoT devices. In some cases, the IoT devices are consuming information or simply being monitored as well as managed via applications supported by data infrastructures.

IoT devices are supported by data infrastructures including on-site, on-premise, as well as cloud and hosted. Another group of IoT devices, in addition to being monitored or managed, also create data along with log, event, and other telemetry data streams. For example, a video camera, in addition to capturing video, also logs time, location, and other metadata. The net result is a need for data infrastructure compute, I/O, and network along with storage resources. IoT data infrastructure resources and components include management service hubs (not to be confused with a physical or virtual network device) and application security authentication and authorization. Additional IoT data infrastructure topics include Protocol gateways, device registry, and rules engines along with end-point management. Other resources and components include developer tools, rules engines, and SDKs. There are various providers that have different IoT-related data infrastructure services, including AWS, Azure, B-SCADA, Google, and Softlayer, among others.

Some IoT protocols, standards, and tradecraft topics include Advanced Message Queueing Protocol (AMQP), Bluetooth and Bluetooth Low-Energy (BLE), Cellular (GSM, 3G, LTE, 4G), Constrained Application Protocol (CoAP), and Device twin or shadow (virtual device with current device state even if turned off). Device to cloud, cloud to device, command, control, communication (C3), LPWAN, NFC, WiFi, WebSocket, PPP, Ethernet, IP, TCP and UDP, JSON, HTTP, and REST. Other IoT topics and terms include MQ Telemetry Transport (MQTT), SCADA and telemetry, along with X.509 public key certificates.

Bulk storage repositories are large, scalable, elastic cost-effective places where structured and semistructured data is stored. This includes a file, object, and other techniques along with various storage mediums (SSD, HDD, tape), locally and in the cloud. Another marketing name for bulk storage is data pools, data ponds that have streams of data flowing into them.

Various applications work with and process data that can then be added to the repository. Metadata about the data can be stored in various SQL and NoSQL databases and key-value stores. Bulk repositories and data lakes can be accessed with flexibility using file, object, APIs, and other means. Security and regulatory data services functionality vary by implementation, solution, or service, including WORM and immutable, litigation hold, multi-tenancy, and subordinated management along with logging, secure digital destruction, and encryption, among others.

Data lakes are storage repositories for storing large amounts of unstructured and semistructured data with durability. A data lake is an implementation of a bulk storage pool or repository and can be a single system, cluster, grid, or federation collection of multiple systems, as well as cloud resources. Some solutions and implementations also provide tiering across different endpoints and namespaces, enabling global namespaces spanning local and cloud, object, and file systems. Different solutions can be optimized for ingest of streaming data, playback of large streams, or processing many small files, among other personality characteristics.

Considerations, tips, and recommendations include:

- Workload simulation tools include Cosbench, vdbench, Mongoose, STAC, and YCSB.
- What availability and data protection, including security, needs to be enabled?
- How will you migrate large amounts of data to clouds (bulk moves)?
- Different bulk and object storage have different performance personalities.
- Do your application workloads need or benefit from GPUs or special devices?
- What data services and functionalities are required for security and regulatory needs?
- Are there geographical location and regulatory concerns for where data is placed?
- Audit, reporting, logging, and access controls.

7.6. Legacy vs. Converged vs. Hyper-Converged vs. Cloud and Containers

What is the best platform, deployment architecture, solution, technology, or technique approach for your data infrastructure, or a specific set of applications or functionality? The "converged" folks will generally say that it is CI, HCI fans will say hyper-converged, legacy lovers will say—surprise—legacy, the cloud and container crowds usually say containers and clouds.

Likewise, there are the aggregate vs. disaggregated, open source vs. proprietary, software-defined and less hardware, turnkey, DIY, or some assembly required. In some scenarios, for different applications, workloads, and environments as well as preferences, any of the above can be applicable. However, just as everything is not the same, there are similarities, and while legacy, CI, HCI, cloud, container, and other approaches can be used for many different scenarios, they may not be the right fit for everything.

Of course, if you are a solution provider, or focused on a particular approach, that will often be the focus of what is needed. When I get asked what's the best, my short answer is "It depends." It depends on the application, workload, PACE requirements, SLO, and other needs, environment, constraints, existing technology and tools, as well as preferences, tradecraft

Table 7.5. General Considerations of What to Use When and Where

Approach	Characteristics, Considerations, When and Where to Use
Standalone BM, PM, host specialized server	Small environment, SOHO, ROBO, workgroup, department, lab, or specialized role or function. Standalone or part of the network, BM host operating system or hypervisor with VM. Many different applications. If BM, consider installing a hypervisor and/or containers to increase flexibility and granularity along with multi-tenancy (security) for applications as the first step to an SDDI, SDDC, and virtual environment. Pay attention to special device needs as well as software licenses as well as data protection.
Networked	Multiple data infrastructure resources (servers, workstations, desktops, routers, storage) networked for communication, application access, storage and data sharing, cloud as well as mobile access. Local, remote, and cloud access. Protect with redundant components, firewalls, access controls.
Cloud	Hybrid. Best of both worlds (public and private), adapt to your needs. Provide elasticity, flexibility, agility, pay for what you use as you consume it, different access modes and granularity of service. Public for pay-as-you-go and off-site, leverage economies of scale and size. Complement your on-site and legacy with hybrid, or go all in, moving everything to the cloud. Private cloud for when more control or large-scale costs preclude using public.
Containers	BM, VM, or cloud hosted provides more isolation of workloads vs. standard non-virtual machine. Less overhead than a virtual machine or of a full cloud instance. Good for small applications, tasks, or components of a larger application that can be compartmentalized. Keep data persistence and ephemeral containers and volumes in mind, as well as portability.
Converged CI, disaggregated,	Scale compute and storage independent converged, hybrid with legacy, SAN, NAS, object, and servers. CI for ease of deployment and management.
Data lake	Unstructured and semistructured bulk data, big data, large-scale file serving
Hyper-converged, HCI aggregated	Small scale, SMB, ROBO, SME, workgroup, a special application for converged management, resources, scaling resources together, ease and speed of deployment. Large enterprise, cloud, and service providers leverage rack-scale CI on a hyper-scale for converging management and deployment. Dedicated to workloads such as VDI/workspace, general VSI, the web, and general applications including databases, among others.
Cluster, grid (small, large)	Big data, little data, and databases, VM, compute, the web, and others where larger scale-out is needed to meet various application PACE resource needs.
Rack-scale	Legacy, CI, HCI, and software-defined at scale with various software.
Software-defined virtual	Flexibility, extensibility, on-premise or cloud, various applications, different architectures and functionalities for the server, storage, and network. From small to large scale, SOHO and ROBO, to enterprise and cloud scale.
Small cluster *Tip:* Combine with PIT data protection.	Two or more nodes, basic HA removing the single point of failure with one device(s), active/active or active/passive based on applications and data infrastructure software capabilities. Applicable for databases, file and content serving, the web, virtual machines, and many other uses.
Protection	Enable availability, reliability, resiliency, and PIT protection for the above. Leverage various software, services tools, and above approaches.

skillsets, and experience, among others considerations. Leveraging your tradecraft skillset and experience helps to determine what is applicable, or how to compare/contrast on an informed decision basis, or justify a decision.

Let's start wrapping up with Table 7.5. Table 7.5 provides general characteristics and recommendations of various data infrastructure options. Table 7.5 is not the definitive cheat sheet for decision making; it is a guide to combining with your software-defined data infrastructure essential tradecraft to define your data infrastructure to meet application needs.

Keep application PACE resource needs and SLO requirements in mind. This includes knowing who the users are and where they access the applications, as well as what the resource needs are and the availability (data protection, security, RAS) requirements. Applications should be located on a data infrastructure close to where users access it, or via fast, resilient networks to enable productivity. Data should also be located close to where applications use it (locality of reference) for good productivity.

Data infrastructure management, decision making, and deployment considerations include:

- Abstraction and integration layer software along with middleware.
- Aggregate (HCI) and disaggregated (CI or legacy) resources.
- Acquisitions and selection of technologies or services.
- Are you able to bulk unload (export) and load (import) data, metadata and policies?
- AI, analytics, and automation leveraging policies and templates.
- Can you bring your hardware, software, licenses, and policies?
- Data protection, including availabilities, durability, PIT protection, and security.

Additional considerations include:

- Health check, troubleshooting, diagnostic, and automated remediation
- Monitoring, notification, reporting, and analytics
- Orchestration of service delivery and resource deployment
- Performance, availability capacity planning, chargeback, show back
- Manual, self- and automated provisioning of resources and services
- Special devices such as GPU, video and other cards, FPGA or ASIC
- System, application, metadata, and data migration or conversation

General data infrastructure considerations include:

- What tools do you have, or will you need to assess and analyze your environment?
- What, if any, geographical regulations apply to where your applications and data can be?
- Will applications be kept available, including for updates, during migrations?
- Does your inventory of resources include applications, databases, middleware, and tools?
- Do you have insight into what device drivers or software update dependencies exist?
- Can you bring your license to cloud or software-defined environments?
- What are your contingency plans for applications, data, data infrastructure, and organization?

There are many different tools that support performance along with capacity and availability planning, optimization, reporting, assessment, inventory, and migration. Some of these tools are focused on particular destinations (cloud, container, virtual server, or desktop workspaces), others are more generic. Tools from various vendors and service providers include AWS, Citrix Project Accelerator, among others, Google, Liquidware Labs VDI Assessment, LoginVSI, Microsoft Assessment Planning (MAP) toolkit along with Azure, among others tools, OpenStack, Quest (various), Solarwinds (various), Turbonomic, Virtual Instruments (insight, assessment, simulation), and VMware (various), among others.

Note that in addition to the above tools and those mentioned elsewhere, many cloud service providers have tools and calculators to estimate your costs for services. However, the key to using those tools, along with those for on-premise, is having good insight and awareness of your environment, applications, and data infrastructure resources, as well as configurations, policies, and your tradecraft experiences.

7.7. Common Questions and Tips

Is a data lake required for big data? Big data does not require a data lake per se, but some repository or place to store large amounts of data is needed. Likewise, data lakes, ponds, pools, and repositories including data warehouses are not exclusive to big data. Of course, that will also vary depending on what your view or belief of what is or is not big data.

Is big data only for a data scientist? There are some big data–centric solutions, approaches, tools, technologies, and techniques that are aligned as well as focused on data scientists. However, big data, in general, is not exclusive to data scientists and is inclusive of everybody from business intelligence (BI) to decision support systems (DSS), AI, business analysis, and many others. Just as there are different types of big data, applications, and tools, so too are there many different types of users and focus areas.

Explain the role and relationships of service catalogs, chargeback, show-back, and how to determine costs of services. Often a picture is worth a hundred or more words, and Figure 7.11 shows various data infrastructure items. Top center is a service catalog of offerings; this can also be accompanied by costs, different types and levels of services, as well as PACE and SLO attributes. Top right is users or consumers of services who subscribe to services, if a public cloud; they get invoices for activity or what is used. For nonpublic clouds, there can be informational or show-back accounting to indicate resource usage and costs. Those costs are tied to the services offerings, left center, which are defined using policies, templates, and bills of materials (what resources are needed) to meet different PACE and SLO.

In the center of Figure 7.11 are how resources are packaged and presented as services defined on the left. Bottom center is various resources that also have costs. Those costs include physical (or cloud) facilities, electrical power, cooling, floor space, staffing, insurance, hardware (servers, storage, network, power distribution, desktops), software, and management tools, among others. The collective costs (dotted box around resources) of a given service is the proportion of resources (and their costs) needed to support a given service offering and its subsequent consumption.

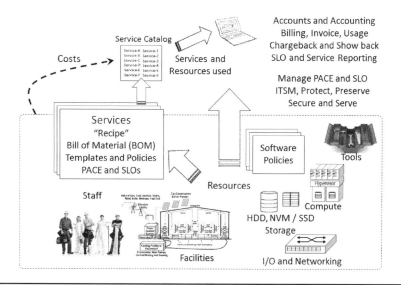

Figure 7.11   Service catalog offerings and costs.

Clarify service catalog and orchestration. Like its name implies, a service catalog (top center of Figure 7.11) is a list or menu of service offerings, starting from the lower level, raw or virtual infrastructure as a service (IaaS) such as compute, storage, network, or other resources. Service offerings can be higher level for platform and development such as PaaS, along with even higher-altitude applications along with software as a service (AaaS and SaaS). Those offerings can vary in granularity, scope, and scale as well as cost and SLO. The orchestration is the management tools, processes, policies, templates, and automation that all come together to enable service delivery.

7.8. Chapter Summary

Everything is not the same across different environments, applications, data Infrastructures, and resources. However, there are similarities in how data infrastructure resources can be aligned to meet different application PACE as well as SLO needs. Use new and old tools, techniques, and tips in new as well as hybrid ways to adapt to your needs and environment requirements. Different solutions, services, hardware, software, and tools have various attributes beyond simple cost per resource. Likewise, different applications workloads or services need various approaches to support them: One size does not fit all scenarios.

General action items include:

- Understand your business application focus to determine data infrastructure needs.
- Avoid flying blind by having accurate insight awareness into applications and resources.
- How will you define hardware, software, and services to meet your PACE and SLO needs?
- Balance PACE efficiency (utilization) with effectiveness (productivity).

Bottom line: Evolve and scale today with stability for tomorrow.

Chapter 8

Data Infrastructure Futures, Wrap-up, and Summary

What You Will Learn in This Chapter

- Review and recap of what has been discussed in the various chapters
- Emerging techniques, technologies, tools, topics, and trends
- What to do next, where to learn more

This chapter converges various themes and topics from the different chapters along with some additional context, insight, and experiences. Key themes, buzzwords, and trends addressed in this chapter include data infrastructure, trends, tradecraft, and software-defined, among other topics.

8.1. Getting Started on the Wrap-up

As we wrap-up, here are a few more context matters to keep in mind.

Your data infrastructure management tradecraft is (or should be)

- Essential skills and experiences spanning different technologies and focus areas
- In addition to knowing the trends, tools, and technologies, is also aware of techniques
- Knowing various techniques to use new and old things in new as well as hybrid ways
- Expanding awareness into adjacent areas around your current focus or interest areas
- Leveraging comprehension, understanding application of what you know
- Evolving with new knowledge, experiences, and insight about tools and techniques
- Hardware, software, services, processes, practices, and management
- From legacy to software-defined, cloud, virtual, and containers

Some reminders and additional context include the fact that *client* can have different meanings, including software or applications that communicate with a server or service, local or in the cloud. Another variation of *client* is a type of device, such as a tablet, laptop, mobile device or phone, as well as a workstation with varying software for accessing different data infrastructure as well as applications. Another context for *client* is the user, person, or thing such as IoT that accesses and interacts with client software or server and services of application or data resources. Yet another context for *client* is a consumer of lower-level data infrastructure resources or higher-level applications services.

Developers can refer to those who create lower-level (low-altitude) data infrastructure and resource-centric applications, drivers, shims, plugins, utilities, operating systems, hypervisors, SCM, PMEM, ARM, GPU, ASIC, FPGA, BIOS/UEFI, and firmware, among other forms of software (and their packaging). At a higher altitude up the data infrastructure and IT stack is developers who create, implement, customize, or support business-focused applications. Those applications can be developed in-house, customized from a third party, or using various tools and platforms including cloud to implement as well as deploy. Context matters as to what type of developers are being referred to.

Another context topic is *DevOps*, which can refer to developers and operations converged, or to developers who are working on software for operations and infrastructures. The latter has ties to what in the past were known as systems programmers (aka sys progs), technical services developers, among others, working on applications that support or enable data infrastructure as well as upper-level applications (and developers).

Another context matter is *software engineer*, which can refer to a system programmer or DevOps specialist or developer, which in turn can mean higher-level applications, or lower data infrastructure, or working for a vendor on one of their solutions. Context is also needed for the term *applications*, including lower-level data infrastructure–related, or higher-level business-focused.

Fabric can also have different context and meaning. It can refer to a network of switches, directors, and routers tying together servers, storage, bridges, gateways, and other devices, but it can also be associated with higher-level application functions, or a cluster of servers or services, as well as data. Keep context in mind regarding *fabric*: whether it is referring to lower-level physical and logical networks, or applications and data, among others.

Roles have different context meaning, including what the role or function a person does with data infrastructure, for example, as an architect, engineering, administrator, operations, or other function. Software applications and utilities also have different *roles* in terms of what they do or pertain to. This includes adding roles or feature functionalities including data services for different hypervisors, operating systems, or data infrastructure software. Context is needed when discussing the roles of people and software, as well as access authentication of people and things to use resources.

A couple more context items are *greenfield*, referring to a new environment, applications, data infrastructure, or facilities, with *brownfield* indicating that something is existing. The platform can refer to a physical or software-defined server, as well as data infrastructure applications such as hypervisors, operating systems, or databases.

Also, *platform* can refer to different development tools and environments, among others. In general, platform 1 refers to legacy mainframe-type processing environments and platform 2 indicates a client server, 2.5 being a hybrid between current client service and next-generation platform 3. Platform 3 refers to the cloud and web-based among other software-defined services, including container tools, technologies, and techniques, while platform 4 is still to be defined (at least as of this writing).

Scale with stability means not introducing complexity or loss of performance and availability. *Scale-up* (vertical) means using larger-capacity, faster resources to scale PACE attributes. *Scale-out* (horizontal) combines multiple resources to support scaling. *Scale-up and -out* uses larger-capacity, faster resources and more of them. *Scale-down* is the inverse of scale-up. *Scale to tomorrow* means future-proofing, enabling your environment to scale with stability for today and tomorrow to meet various needs, without increasing complexity (and costs).

Tip: Keep in mind the software-defined anything fundamental is that applications (lower-level data infrastructure and higher-level business, among others) are software programs. Application software programs can be packaged and delivered in different ways (download, cloud, plugin, tin-wrapped appliance, embedded, ASIC or FPGA, BIOS among others. This means that the algorithms are the software that act upon data structures (and data) that define and enable SDDC, SDI, SDDI, SDS, SDN, NFV, IoT, data protection, and other data infrastructure–related management topics.

Remember that *tradecraft* is skills, experiences, tricks, and techniques along with knowing what as well as how to use various related tools as part of what it is that you are doing. At the beginning of this book, I gave the example of an automobile technician who, after years of experience, might become a master mechanic. Another example is engineers and architects (non-IT) who have basic design along with engineering discipline tradecraft, as well as specialties such as mechanical, electrical, HVAC, or environmental, among others. They can leverage their basic tradecraft while extending and enhancing it by gaining insight as well as experience in adajcent areas of focus.

There are many other examples, including salespeople who have the tradecraft of selling, including account as well as relationship building along with the ability to learn new tradecraft related to the trade or items they are or will be selling. And then there are pre-sales and systems engineers, technical marketing, product and program management, test and development, R&D engineering, IT and technology architects, among many others.

8.2. People, Process, and Best Practices

Become familiar with the business or what your organization does, and the information that it depends on via applications along with the underlying data infrastructures. This means understanding what the organization does, how it works, why it uses various applications, and data infrastructure needs.

When I worked at a railroad that was easy, as I liked trains and related topics, so learning more about the business was fun; plus, it helped to be able to speak the language of the business, such as waybills, lifts, moves, and other functions. That, in turn, enabled translating those business functions into data infrastructure resources needs and vice versa. While working at an electrical power generation and transmission company, going out into the power plant helped me to understand what needed to be done when writing preventative maintenance systems, among other business applications.

Tip: If people, processes, politics, or organizational practices are barriers to convergence and productivity, then address those instead of using new technology in old ways. Also keep in mind that while software defines other software, hardware, and services, people define software via programming, configuration, policies, and related activities.

Some general tips, considerations, and recommendations include:

- Ask for and provide context to help clarify what is meant during discussions.
- Pay and play it forward; help others learn; be a student and teacher.
- Give credit where credit is due, including attribution of sites and sources.
- Be respectful of others' time when you ask them for help or how to do something.
- Leverage reference architectures, templates, designs, and tutorials.
- Learn the tricks of the trade that may not be spelled out in tutorials or other materials.

Tip: Get some hands-on, behind-the-wheel time with various technologies to gain insight, perspective, and appreciation of what others are doing, as well as what is needed to make informed decisions about other areas. This also means learning from looking at demos, trying out software, tools, services, or using other means to understand the solution.

Additional tips and considerations include:

- Expand your social and technical network into adjacent areas.
- Get involved in user groups, forums, and other venues to learn and give back.
- Listen, learn, and comprehend vs. simply memorizing to pass a test.
- Find a mentor to help guide you, and become a mentor to help others.
- Collaborate, share, respect and be respected; the accolades will follow.
- Evolve from focus on certificates or credentials to expansion of experiences.
- Connect with me and others via LinkedIn, Twitter, Google+, and other venues.

8.2.1. Skills Development

Learn some programming, including languages and tools as well as how to use them. Once you learn the fundamentals of programming, requirements, analysis, design, and test and trouble-shooting, you should be able to transfer those tradecraft skills to using different languages and tools on various platforms.

If you focus on just the tool or technology, that could become your point of lock in or single tradecraft domain experience. While becoming a master, expert, ninja, or unicorn in a particular tool or technology area opens opportunity doors for that domain focus, it can also become an inhibitor. Instead, look to expand your tradecraft skill into other related and adjacent tools, technologies, and domain focus areas. For example, if all you know is .net, Java, C+, Cobol, and Python, then learn another programming (software defining) language. However, also move beyond the language to expand on what can be done with those tools, such as the language or programming environments (e.g., the tools) and expand what you can do with them in new ways (e.g., increase your tradecraft) and what you might become tied to. If your focus is servers, then expand your tradecraft learning about storage, I/O network, hardware, software, and related topics. If your focus is on business applications, learn about the business as well as the underlying technology. And vice versa, if your tradecraft domain focus is lower-level data infrastructure, such as hypervisors, devices, and cloud, among others, learn about the business side of things.

Tip: Some tools and technologies have long-lasting lifecycles, particularly when used in new and different ways. Likewise, fundamental tradecraft skills, techniques, tricks, and experiences can span different generations of technologies and environments. This means knowing how to learn new technologies and apply your tradecraft to use them effectively, without making old mistakes.

Project planning, along with project as well as program management, is another skillset to add to your tradecraft. This can be as simple as understanding how to put together a simple project plan on the back of a napkin together with a statement of work (SOW) involved. Take a class or tutorial, watch a video, read a book, or talk with somebody who has project and program management experience to learn more.

Assessments are done in various layers (altitudes) across data infrastructures, from high-level to low-level. The assessments can be done to discover what applications and associated resources are needed, or data protection including backup coverage, among others. Examples of assessments include gaining requirements and fact finding for design or configuration, along with decision making of new technology, or changes; and health and status checks of applications, services, and other resources during normal operations, as well as part of troubleshooting. Other activities involving assessments and gaining insight about data infrastructures include forecast, planning, design (or decision) validation, tendering (RFP, RFI, RFQ), and assets inventory, among others.

Tasks related to development, design, analysis, planning, and project and program management, among others, are job task analysis (JTA). A JTA is an assessment of what jobs, tasks, steps, or procedures are done, or need to be done, to support something, or complete a given piece of work in support of something. In the case of data infrastructures, JTAs can involve understanding what is being done, as well as what needs to be done to improve service, remove complexity, or reduce costs, among other initiatives.

Keep in mind:

- Your tradecraft is evolving, expanding, and perhaps even refreshing over time.
- How to apply experiences, reasoning, and comprehend different scenarios.
- Moving beyond the tools and technologies to techniques for various situations.
- Track and manage your tradecraft skills with a résumé as well as online venues.
- What you know and don't know, and learn how to learn.

8.3. Emerging Topics, Trends, and Predictions

Before we wrap up, let's take a few moments to look at some emerging topics, trends, perspectives, and predictions about software-defined data infrastructures and related technologies, techniques, and topics.

Some environments will evolve quickly to all-software-defined cloud, converged, container, or virtual. Other environments will evolve more slowly in hybrid ways to support past, present, and future applications workloads, software, tools, and other technologies. Likewise, some environments will move quickly to all-Flash or other form of NVM technology including various SCM and PMEM, while most will continue to increase the use of SSD in various ways. Note that there are different categories (tiers) of NVM and SSDs, similar to HDDs.

Servers, storage, and I/O networking devices will continue to do more work in a smaller physical footprint; there is also more work to be done, data to move and store, applications to run needing additional resources. Some servers will become physically smaller. Likewise, higher-density modular and fat or thick blades continue to be popular, as well as fat twins and quads.

Safe (perennial favorite) predictions and perspectives include:

- Data infrastructures continue to evolve in hybrid ways to support different environments.
- Data's value will change over time; some will find new value, some will lose value.
- Hardware will need software, software will need hardware, both need to be defined.
- More data will find its way into unknown value for longer periods of time.
- Applications and data infrastructures will enable data with unknown value to have value.
- There is no such thing as a data recession, as more information is created and used.
- Business, IT, application, and data infrastructure transformation will continue.

NVM and persistent memory, including NAND Flash among other SSD, PMEM, and SCM, have become popular, affordable, and cost-effective storage for use internal as well as external to servers. With the continued decrease in cost and increase in capacity and durability of NVM, SCM, and SSD, HDD also continue to follow similar improvement curves. The amount of data being generated and stored for longer periods of time, along with protection copies, will increase demand for cost-effective storage.

This is where, at least until early in the next decade, HDD will continue to be a viable and cost-effective option for storing infrequently accessed, bulk, cold, and secondary or tertiary protection copies. Granted, SSD will continue to increase in deployment and handle more workloads, with faster adoption in some environments. For other environments, budget and capacity constraints, including for cloud service providers, will lead to a hybrid mix of resources. Hybrid resources include a mix of HDD and SSD (tiered storage). Other tiered resources include different types of servers allocated as containers, VM, and cloud instances, as well as Metal as a Service (MaaS), PM, BM, and dedicated cloud instances as well as DPS. Also, to compute servers and storage, tiered networking resources that are also hardware, as well as software-defined, will be leveraged. Another industry trend is that data infrastructure resources will continue to be enhanced with more capability into physically smaller footprints.

Some other emerging enhancements include new I/O and memory access as new applications are developed. Meanwhile, existing memory and I/O models continue to adopt object while also using file, block, composable, and other API-based storage services. Part of I/O and memory enhancements includes leveraging storage-class memories (SCM) along with Persistent Memory (PMEM) for persistence along with new application libraries. These libraries, such as DAX among others, allow programs to leverage SCM and other persistent memories without having to use traditional object, file, or block I/O protocols. Part of enabling SCM and other persistent memories is the media themselves, as well as processors, chipsets, and motherboards along with associated software to leverage them.

In addition to server, storage, and I/O enhancements, network function virtualization (NFV) along with software-defined networks (SDN) will continue to evolve. Similar to how server micro-services such as Docker (mesos or kubernetes) and other containers enable finer grain to compute resource allocation, micro-segmentation for networks will also continue to gain awareness, adoption, and deployment. An example of micro-segmentation–enabled solutions includes VMware NSX among others. Another server I/O topic for accessing memory, storage, networks, and other servers is protocols including PCIe Gen 4, NVMe along with various NVMe over Fabrics (NVMeoF), as well as Gen-Z for enabling composable data infrastructures.

There is also renewed re-awareness of ASIC and FPGA along with GPUs including those from NVIDIA, among others, and other specialized processors that are software-defined to offload general-purpose CPUs. Keep in mind that FPGA are Field Programmable Gate Arrays, meaning that they can be redefined with new software, similar to BIOS, firmware, or other packaging and implementations.

Even though the industry trend remains toward using general-purpose, off-the-shelf commercially available servers (both x86/x64/IA, ARM, and RISC among others), solutions from small scale to web scale are leveraging ASIC and FPGA to wrap software that define those devices' functionality.

For example, Microsoft leverages servers with custom FPGA in their Azure and other clouds that enable them to implement new algorithms via a software update vs. physically replacing servers. The FPGA enable Microsoft to offload certain functions including networking from the general processor, which is then able to handle other work. Google is using custom ASIC in its servers which enable offloads as well as some performance advantage, but without the flexibility of re-programming. Which is better, GPU, ASIC, or FPGA, general processor? That depends on your needs and PACE among other criteria, since everything is not the same.

Keep in mind that there are different timelines for technology that vary by domain focus area. Researchers are on a different timeline than IT organizations that eventually deploy new technologies. For example, you might hear of a breakthrough announcement of new technology and technique in the research and development labs. However, it might take months, years, or more before it can work its way through production labs to commercially viable to mass production in a cost-effective way. From there the technology moves into customer labs for initial testing.

The context here could be a customer in the form of an OEM vendor who gets a new hardware component or software stack to test and integrate into its solutions. From there, the resulting solution or system moves into IT or cloud organizations labs for initial testing as well as integration (or debugging). Eventually, the solution is integrated into a data infrastructure as part of an IT stack so that users of applications can consume information services.

Figure 8.1 shows on the horizontal axis various technology-relevant adoption and deployment timelines. On the vertical axis are different focus areas of adoption and deployment, starting on the bottom (low-level) with research and development, moving up to higher levels. The point of Figure 8.1 is to show different timelines for awareness, adoption, and deployment across various audiences.

Figure 8.1 is an example where the time from a researcher announcing a new breakthrough technology until mass production can be years. By that time, those at the early side of the timeline may see what they worked on in the past as dead or old and time to move on to something

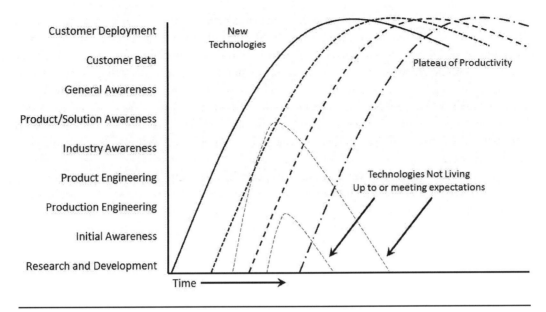

Figure 8.1   Different adoption and deployment timelines.

new. Meanwhile, others who are getting exposed to the new technology may see it as just that, something new, while others further downstream (or higher up in altitude) see as still being future technology. The industry press, media, analyst, bloggers, and other pundits tend to like to talk about new things, so keep timelines in context as well as what temporal phase of a technology, trend, or tool is being discussed.

Tip: Context is important to understand when something new is announced, particularly what level or audience it is ready as well as being relevant for. Just because something is announced at a lower level does not mean that it is ready for deployment at a higher level. Likewise, something being used, updated, enhanced, and still in use may be declared dead by those who have a focus on something new.

Another context meaning is around *customer*. For example, when a vendor of a component such as a server processor, network or I/O chip, or other device says it is shipping to customers, what is the context of customers? The customers might be original equipment manufacturers (OEM) and system builders to test in their labs, or prepare beta systems for their customers to in turn test and trial in their labs. To clarify, an OEM uses components from other manufacturers such as a processor, I/O, networking, or other components, including memory, drives as well as software and combines them into a solution.

Containers (Docker, Kubernetes, Mesos and other tools, technologies) will continue to gain popularity as data infrastructure host platforms. This includes for some environments ephemeral and persistent storage-based containers to meet different application needs. For some environments there may be a push to put everything into containers, others will align containers to the task or application needs, similar to when and where to use VM, cloud instances, PM and DPS at a cloud or managed service provider.

Automation and orchestration across different technology and data infrastructure layers will also rely on policies, workflows, and processes to be defined by templates, plays, playbooks, or other rules for implementation via automation tools. In addition, automation and orchestration across cloud, software-defined, and hybrid environments will include convergence at various levels. Convergence includes cloud (public, private, hybrid, multi-cloud), serverless, hyper-converged (HCI) and hyper-scale-out for aggregated as well as disaggregated solutions.

Tip: Start your automation focus on common recurring tasks, events, and activities that have well-defined behaviors and solutions, or processes for resolution. This may not be as exciting as taking on something more newsworthy, with big budget impact, and sophisticated. However, whenever you can find and remove complexity, even if small, on a large scale it adds up quickly, perhaps even into a large impact. Also, by automating common tasks, responses, and remediation, you can build successful tradecraft experiences to leverage for the next round of automation. This theme also applies to artificial intelligence (AI), as well as DL, ML, cognitive along with other real-time or batch analytics, and related activity.

As a general trend to support large-scale applications and amounts (volume) of data of various size (little data and big data), new techniques are needed for using new and old tools as well as technologies. Instead of simply adding faster servers, NVM (e.g., Non-Volatile Memory–based, not to be confused with NVMe access) storage such as SCM and SSD, along with 40/50/100/400 GbE networks, along with NVMeoF and Gen-Z fabrics or networks, to support growth, new techniques are needed. For example, instead of spending the time to scan files, objects, volumes, databases, and other repositories for data protection, checking for virus or malware, data classification, data footprint reduction, data integrity and consistency checks along with proactive repair, more of those functions need to be done at ingest. When data is ingested, it is tagged (i.e., metadata information added or stored), protection copies made (backup, replica, snapshot, archives), security and access control applied, data footprint reduction (DFR) applied (compress, de-dupe, SIS, thin provisioning), data integrity and checksum enabled. The result is that less time is spent later handling the processes mentioned above, enabling faster protection and management with less overhead.

8.4. Chapter and Book Summary

Key themes, buzzwords, and trends addressed have included server storage I/O tradecraft, data demand drivers, fundamental needs and uses of data infrastructures, and associated technologies.

Our journey and conversation have spanned architecture, hardware, software, services, solutions, tools, techniques, and industry trends along with associated applications, management, and deployment across different environments. This has included IoT, big data and little data, data protection, performance, software-defined, PM, VM, CI, HCI, CiB, cluster, cloud, containers, SSD, SCM, RoCE, and much more.

Depending on when you read this, some of the things discussed will be more mature and mainstream. Meanwhile, other topics, technologies, and trends may be nearing or have reached the end of their usefulness. Some new things will be emerging, while others will have joined the "Where are they now?" list, some of which may currently be being touted as the next "big" thing.

General tips, considerations, and recommendations include:

- Avoid flying blind, leverage insight, become aware to make informed decisions.
- Clouds, containers, CI, HCI, SSD, SDS, SDN, SDDC, and SDDI are in your future.
- Leverage automation with good insight, and manage the automation policies.
- Software-defined does not eliminate hardware; it shifts the location and usage.
- The best server, storage, and I/O technology depends on what your needs are.

Key themes to remember include:

- Context matters regarding data infrastructure and software-defined topics.
- Data infrastructures include servers, storage, network hardware, software, and services.
- Data infrastructures protect, preserve, secure, and serve applications and data.
- Hybrid is the home run for legacy and brownfield data centers and data infrastructures.
- NVM including SCM, Flash, SSD, and others are in your future.
- The best server I/O is the one that you do not have to do (locality of reference).
- Things below your area of focus are considered infrastructure.

We have come to that point in any journey where it is time to wrap up this particular discussion. For those of you who travel via different mediums (plane, train, boat, bus, automobile), it is time to wrap up and stow your things in relative safety as we begin preparations for arrival. Where we are about to arrive may be your final destination or endpoint for this particular journey, or perhaps simply somewhere you are making a connection or layover as part of a longer journey.

There is no such thing as a data or information recession. Society is addicted to information and its availability and reliability, people and data are living longer, and getting larger, which means increased needs as well as demands placed on data infrastructures.

A convenient way of thinking about balancing needs and wants is "You can't always get what you want, but if you try, sometimes you might find you get what you need." What this means is that you should know and understand your wants, needs, and options to address them.

Keep in mind that the fundamental role of data infrastructures is to protect, preserve, secure, serve, and enable applications programs (algorithms), data structures, and data to be transformed into and used as information. This means to design, configure, and deploy flexible, scalable, resilient software-defined (and legacy) data infrastructures that are also efficient and cost-effective. It also means enabling data infrastructures that are easy to manage, able to expand with elasticity to support growth as well as being managed and maintained with minimal disruption.

Bottom line: This is not the end, it is part of a continuing journey that might be beginning, transitioning, refreshing, or evolving. However, this particular leg, trip, or segment as part of an evolving journey about IT, data center, and data infrastructure has now landed.

Ok, 'nuff said, for now . . .

Cheers,
GS

Appendix A

Companion Websites and Where to Learn More

Table A.1 shows various companion material sites and related content for this book.

Table A.1. Companion Material for This Book

storageio.com/sddi	Companion page for this book with links to related items
storageio.com/converged	Converged topics, technologies, trends, and tools
storageio.com/events	Various industry events, webinars, and activities
storageio.com/lab	Server StorageIO Lab reports and updates
storageio.com/links	Various industry and data infrastructure link resources
storageio.com/news	Various industry news, comments, and trends perspectives
storageio.com/nvme	Various NVMe-related tools, trends, topics, and technologies
storageio.com/performance	Server, storage, I/O performance tools, and topics
storageio.com/management	Server, storage, I/O management tools and related topics
storageio.com/network	Server, storage, I/O networking topics
storageio.com/server	Server-related topics
storageio.com/protect	Data protection, including backup, HA, BC, DR, security
storageio.com/reports	Server StorageIO thought leadership and trends reports
storageio.com/softwaredefined	Software-defined topics, technologies, trends, and tools
storageio.com/store	Various items used and mentioned via Amazon.com
storageio.com/ssd	SSD-related topics, technologies, trends, and tools
storageio.com/tips	Tips, articles, and other resources

In addition to the items in Table A.1 and elsewhere in the appendix as well as chapters, Table A.2 lists my other solo books that have common themes concerning data infrastructures. Each of the books in Table A.2 has a different color for the cover that also ties in with related themes. Red, green, and blue are primary colors, also known as lambda, that are used in optical networking for local and long-distance communications (I/O networking). Some modern video equipment also introduces a fourth color, yellow, as part of an enhanced visual display. Learn more at www.storageio.com/books.

Table A.2. Books by Server StorageIO Founder Greg Schulz

Book	Title	Subtitle	ISBN 13	Published
Red	*Resilient Storage Networks*	*Designing Flexible Scalable Data Infrastructures*	978-1555583118	2004
Green	*The Green and Virtual Data Center*		978-1420086669	2009
Yellow	*Cloud and Virtual Data Storage Networking*	*Your Journey to Efficient and Effective Information Services*	978-1439851739	2011
Blue	*Software-Defined Data Infrastructure Essentials*	*Cloud, Converged, and Virtual Fundamental Server Storage I/O Tradecraft*	978-1498738156	2017
White	*Data Infrastructure Management*	*Insights and Strategies*	978-1138486423	2019

Glossary

*NIX	Linux, and UNIX
10 GbE	10 Gigabit Ethernet
24×7	24 hours a day, seven days a week
4 3 2 1	Data protection guide rule
4K	4KB sector size, 4K video resolution
512E, 512N, 4K (AF)	512-byte emulated, native, 4KB sector size
9's availability	How much availability in a given period
AaaS	Application as a Service, archive as a service
Access method	How applications and servers access resources
ACL	Access control list
Active data	Data being read or written; not idle
AD	Active directory, archive device, active data
AES	Advanced Encryption Standard
AF	Advance Format
AFA	All-Flash array or all-Flash storage system
AFR	Annual failure rate
Agent	Software for performing some tasks or function
Aggregate	Disk or RAID group, virtual or physical device
Aggregated	Consolidated resources; combined server storage
Aggregates	Collection of different aggregates or disk groups
Aggregation	Consolidating resources together
AI	Artificial intelligence
AiC	PCIe add-in card
Air gap	Physical distance between resources for protection
A la carte	Order or select items individually
Altitude	How high or low in a stack of software
ALUA	Asymmetric logical unit access
AMD	Manufacturer of processing chips
AMI	AWS EC2 machine instance
AMQP	Advanced Message Queueing Protocol
Analytics	Applications and algorithms for data processing

ANSI	American National Standards Institute
ANSI T11	Standards group for Fibre Channel protocol
Apache	Open-source data infrastructure software
API	Application Program Interface
Appliance	Hardware or software that performs some function
Application blades	Server, storage, and I/O networking blades
Application	Programs or software that performs some function
Archive	Preserve inactive data to alternative media
ARM	Advanced RISC Machine; Azure Resource Manager
ARP	Address Resolution Protocol
Array	Data structure, virtual, physical storage, enclosure
ASIC	Application-Specific Integrated Circuit
ASM	Automatic storage management
ASP	Application service provider
AR/VR	Immersive technologies, including Augmented Reality, Virtual Reality
Asynchronous	Time-delayed data transmission
ATM	Asynchronous Transfer Mode networking
Authoritative copy	Master, definitive version or copy of data
Autonomous	Self-operating or automatic operation
AWS	Amazon Web Services
AZ	Availability zone, site, data center
Azure (Microsoft)	Microsoft cloud and web services
BaaS	Backup as a service
Backing store	Where data gets written to
Ballooning	Dynamic expanding with elasticity
Bandwidth	Throughput, amount of data moved
Base 10	Decimal numbering system
Base 16	Hexadecimal numbering system
Base 2	Binary numbering system
Base 8	Octal numbering system
BBU	Battery backup unit
BC	Business continuance
BE	Back end, where storage attaches to
Benchmark	Workload, real, replay, synthetic for comparison
BER	Bit or block error rate for storage devices
BI	Business intelligence and analytics
Big data	Large volume or amount of unstructured data
Big iron	Large-form-factor, high-capacity hardware device
Binary	1 (on) or 0 (off) numbering scheme, architecture
Bind	Physical or logical connect, concatenate a resource
BIOS	Basic input/output system
Bitnami	Collection of applications and data infrastructure
Blade center	Packaging with blade servers, I/O, and networking
BLE	Bluetooth Low-Energy

Bleach	Digital secure shred (wipe clean) data so unrecoverable
Blob	Binary large object, collection binary data, object
Block	Allocation of memory or storage, sector, or page
Blockage	Congestion, or something causing a bottleneck
Block-based	Raw, cooked, SCSI, NVMe LUN volume access
Block chain	Distributed data for growing list of data blocks
BM	Bare metal or physical machine
BOM	Bill of material
Boot	Starting up and loading software into a server
Bound	Resources combined; bound disk, not a stripe
BR	Business resiliency; business recovery
Bridge	Physical, software to connect protocols, resources
Brownfield	Existing applications and environments
BTU	British thermal unit; heat from energy used
Bucket	Organization of resources, data, or data structures
Bulk	Large quantity use, or amount of resources
Bundled	All-inclusive resources or services, vs. a la carte
Burst	Surge, increase in activity or usage
Buzzword Bingo	Game played with industry buzzwords
BYOD	Bring your own device
C3	Command, control, communication
Cache hit	Data accessed, I/O resolved from cache
Cache warming	Reloading or populating cache after start-up
Capacity	Space or amount of resources, available inventory
CapEx	Capital expense
CAS	Content addressable storage
Cascade	Chain or series of events, flat linear topology
Cassandra	NoSQL database repository
Cat 5/6	Physical cable commonly used with Ethernet
CBT	Change block tracking, computer-based training
CD	Compact disc
CDM	Copy data management
CDMI	Cloud data management interface
CDN	Content distribution network
CDP	Continuous data protection
Centos	Linux operating system
Ceph	Open-source software-defined storage
CERT	Community Emergency Response Team (security)
Certificate	Security access credentials, accomplishment
CFR	U.S. Code of Federal Regulations
CHAP	Challenge Handshake Authentication Protocol
Chargeback	Billing and invoicing for information services
Checkpoint	Consistency point, snapshot, recovery point
Chunk	Allocation size used by RAID, data protection
CI	Converged infrastructure with disaggregated resources

CiB	Cluster-in-box or cloud-in-box
CIDR	Classless interdomain routing
CIFS	Common Internet File System data sharing
CIM	Common information model
CIO	Chief information officer; concurrent I/O
Cipher	Security, crypto, encryption, or locking code
CKD	Count Key Data mainframe data access protocol
CLI	Command Line Interface
Client	Physical, software, or person using resources
Cloud	Public, private, hybrid data infrastructure and service
Cloud access	Hardware, software, protocol for accessing cloud
Cloud computing	Internet or web remote-based application
Cloud instance	Instantiation of an image on a cloud resource
Cloud storage	Storage provided via a cloud service or product
Cloud-in-box	Self-contained private or hybrid cloud
Cluster	Group of resources working collectively
Clustered file system	Distributed file system across multiple servers
CM	Cloud machine, cloud virtual machine, cloud instance
CMDB	Configuration management database
CMG	Computer Measurement Group
CMS	Content management system
CNA	Converged Network Architecture
CNAME	Canonical Name record
CoAP	Constrained Application Protocol
Cognitive	Advanced analytics, including AI, ML, DL
Cold Aisles	Cool-air aisles between equipment cabinets
Cold data	Inactive data, dormant, not being used, archives
Colo	Co-location facility
Compliance	Complying with and meeting requirements
Component	Smaller piece of a larger system or application
Composable	Finer grained allocation of server compute, memory, I/O, and storage resources
Compression	Compact, reduce size of something
CompTIA	Testing and certification organization
Congestion	Busy with activity, possible bottlenecks
Connectivity	Hardware or software connecting resources
Consistency	Data that is as accurate as it is expected to be
Consistency point	Point in time (RPO) where data has consistency
Consumer	User of information services or data infrastructure
Container	Application packaging, repository, micro-service
Contiguous	Data or resources grouped close together
Controller	Hardware, software, algorithm that controls some function
Cookbook	Guide, reference on how to make something
Cooked	Formatted, organized, software-defined; not raw
Cooling ton	12,000 BTU, to cool 1 ton of air

CoreOS	Lightweight Linux derivative operating system
COTS	Commercial off-the-shelf, white box, commodity
Coverage	What is included in scope of being covered
Cpanel	Web and hosting management dashboard interface
CPU	Central processing unit
Crash consistency	Consistency protection in case of fault or crash
CRC	Cyclic redundancy check; name of a publisher
CRM	Customer relationship management
Cross technology	Solutions or tools that address multiple disciplines
CRUD	Create/Read/Update/Delete
CSP	Cloud service provider
CSV	Comma-separated variables for data interchange, Microsoft Cluster Shared Volume
Curl	Web HTTP resource access tool
Customer	User of applications or data infrastructure services
Customer adoption	What customers are doing and deploying
Customer deployment	What customers are installing and using
D2C	Disk (HDD or SSD)-to-cloud copy
D2D	Disk-to-disk snapshot, backup, copy, or replication
D2D2C	Disk-to-disk-to-cloud copy
D2D2D	Disk-to-disk-to-disk snapshot, backup, copy
D2D2T	Disk-to-disk-to-tape snapshot, backup, copy
D2T	Disk-to-tape backup, copy, archive
DAM	Digital asset manager
DAR	Durable availability reduced; lower-cost service
DARE	Data at rest encryption
DAS	Direct attached storage, internal or external
Dashboard	Management tool for monitoring, insight, awareness
Data centers	Habitat for technology, physical facility
Data-in-flight	Being moved between locations or systems
Data infrastructure	Server, storage, network resources and software
Data lake	Large repository, big pool or pond of data
Data pond	Small lake or repository of unstructured data
Data pool	Repository of structured, unstructured data
Data protection	Availability, security, BC, DR, BR, HA, resiliency
Data scientist	Somebody who studies and analyzes data
Data services	Feature functions for data access and management
Data structure	Bits and bytes organized into some defined entity
Data value	Known, unknown, no value, possible future value
Data variety	Different types of data
Data velocity	Speed at which data moves and flows
Data volume	Amount of data; a storage volume for data
Data warehouse	Large-scale repository or place for data analytics
Database	Structured means for organizing and storing data
DAX	Direct-access persistent NVM, NVDIMM, SCM

Day 1, day 2	First and second days of new install, environment
DB loss	Degradation of signal over optics or electric cable
DBA	Database administrator
DBaaS	Database as a service
DC	Direct-current electricity
DCB	Data center bridging
DCE	Data center Ethernet for converged networking
DCIE	Data center infrastructure efficiency
DCIM	Data center infrastructure management
DCPE	Data center performance efficiency
DDR/RAM	Double data rate random access memory
DDR4	Next generation of DRAM memory
De-dupe rate	How fast data is reduced (effectiveness)
De-dupe ratio	How much data is reduced (efficiency, space saving)
De-duplication	Elimination of duplicate data
De facto standard	Widely used convention, not set by a standards body
Delta	Change between points in time, such as for PIT snapshots
DEM	Digital evidence management (e.g., police body cameras)
Demand drivers	Need for application and resource consumption
De-normalize	Optimize, balance for performance and capacity
Dense	Large number of data or resources close together
Depreciate	No longer being developed, planned end of life
Desktop	Workstation or laptop computer, aka PC
Deterministic	Predictable, steady, known behavior
Developer	Creates applications for business, data infrastructures
DevOps	Development operations
DFR	Data footprint reduction (compress, de-dupe)
DHCP	Dynamic Host Configuration Protocol
Dictionary	Reference resource of known items
DIF	Data integrity features
Differential	Difference between time and state of something
DIMM	Dual Inline Memory Module
DIO	Direct I/O operations
Director	I/O and networking large-scale, resilient switch
Disaggregated	Not aggregated, server and storage separated
Disk partition	How storage is organized and allocated for use
Dispersal	Data spread across resources, site, or sites
Distance gap	Space between copies of data (for protection)
DIY	Do-it-yourself
DL	Disk library, storing backup and other data
DLA	Data loss access
DLE	Data loss event
DLM	Data life-cycle management
DLP	Data loss prevention, data leak prevention
DMA	Direct memory access

DMTF	Distributed Management Task Force
DNS	Domain Name System for internet domain names
Docker	Container micro-services and management tools
DoS	Denial-of-service attack
Downtime	Planned, scheduled, or unscheduled nonavailability
DPDK	Data Plane Development Kit low latency I/O protocol library
DPM	Data protection management; Microsoft protection software
DPS	Dedicated private server
DR	Disaster recovery
DRaaS	Disaster recovery as a service
DRAM	Dynamic Random Access Memory
Drive	A physical, logical storage device (SSD or HDD)
DRO	Data replication optimization
Dropbox	Cloud data storage sharing, consumer and EFSS
DRP	Disaster recovery planning process
Drupal	Web and content management application
DSL	Digital Subscriber Line
DTDS	Disaster-tolerant disk system
Dual-path	Two or more physical, logical paths to resource
Dual-port	Two or more ports, active or passive, to resource
Dual-socket	Two sockets for CPU processors on motherboard
Duplex	How communication exchange is handled
Durable	Copies exist to protect against data loss, damage
DWDM	Dense wave division multiplexing
DWPD	Disk writes per day (Flash endurance metric)
E2E	End-to-end
East/west	Management, system to system traffic, replication
EBCDIC	Character encoding scheme for IBM mainframe
EBS	AWS elastic block storage
EC2	AWS elastic cloud compute
ECC	Error correction code
ECKD	Extended Count Key Data
Edge	Remote data infrastructure location or device
EDI	Electronic data interchange
eDiscovery	Electronic search and data discovery
EFS	AWS elastic file service
EFSS	Enterprise File Sync Share
EH&S	Environmental health and safety
EMR	Electronic medical record
Encoding	8b/10b, 64b/66b, 128b/130b
Encryption	Encode data so it is private, secure
Endpoint	Access address of a resource or service
Energy Star	U.S. Environmental Protection Agency Energy Star program
Energy-effective	Increased productivity per energy used
Energy-efficient	Reduced energy usage

EPA	U.S. Environmental Protection Agency
Ephemeral	Temporary, nonpersistent, volatile, short-lived
EPT	Extended Page Translation memory
Erasure code	Reed-Solomon (RS) parity derivative; see also LRC
ERP	Enterprise resource planning
ESCON	Access protocol for legacy IBM mainframe
ESRP	Microsoft Exchange Solution Reviewed Program
Ethernet	Network interface
Eventual consistency	Consistency occurs sometime in the future, async
Export	Volumes, file shares, data exported or unloaded
Extents	Fragments, resource allocations, extended file
FaaS	Function as a Service, such as serverless
Fabric	Network, collection of resources or applications
Fan-in, fan-out	Many into one or few, few expand out to many
Fault domain	Domain, scope of what can fail or cause faults
Fault region	Large-scope, geographically dispersed fault area
FBA	Fixed Block Architecture on HDD and SSD
FC	Fibre Channel
FCIA	Fibre Channel Industry Association
FCIP	Fibre Channel on IP for long-distance movement
FCoE	Fibre Channel over Ethernet
FCP	Fibre Channel SCSI_Protocol
FEC	Forward error correction
Federated	Loose collection of affiliated items, management
FedRAMP	Federal Risk Authorization Management Program
FICON	Mainframe storage access protocol
FIFO	First in, first out
FIO	Benchmark tool for creating test workloads
FIPS	Federal Information Processing Standard
Firewall	Network security device or software
Firmware	Low-level software that gets loaded into hardware
FISMA	Federal Information Security Management Act
Flash	Adobe Flash software, NAND NVM SSD storage
Fog	Reference to cloud-like computing located at edge or remote location
Fog compute	Distributed resources between cloud and data source
Footprint	Physical or logical space, resource used, overhead
Formatted	Organized, software-defined; not raw or uncooked
FPGA	Field Programmable Gate Array chip
FPV	First Person View with Augmented Reality (AR) or Virtual Reality (VR)
Fragmentation	Noncontiguous (scattered) data, nonoptimized
Frame	Physical enclosure, logical data transmission unit
Frequency	How often something occurs
Front end	Where and how resources are accessed by others

FRU	Field replacement unit
FTL	Flash translation layer
FTM	Fault tolerance mode to enable resiliency
FTP	File Transfer Protocol
FTT	Failures or faults to tolerate
FUD	Fear, uncertainty, and doubt
Full-stripe write	All data in stripe written together to reduce overhead
FUSE	File system in userspace
Gap in coverage	Items not covered, skipped, missing, forgotten
Gateway	Hardware, software access to resource or services
GbE	Gigabit Ethernet
Gen-Z	Server I/O protocol that supports composable data infrastructures
Ghosted	Native file or object not in SharePoint, content database
GHz	Gigahertz frequency, a measure of speed
Github	Place with lots of open-source software and tools
Global namespace	Directory address namespace access resource
Gold copy	Master backup or data protection copy
Google	Search engine; cloud data infrastructure resources
Govcloud	Public cloud optimized for government use
Gpart	Storage partitioning tool
GPS	Global Positioning System; author of this book
GPT	GUID partition table
GPU	Graphics processing unit
Granularity	Coarse, broad focus, or fine-grained detail-centric focus
Green gap	Disconnect between messaging and IT challenges
Green IT	Efficient and effective information services
Greenfield	New applications and environment, clean sheet
Grid	Local or wide-area cluster of resources
Grooming	Logical data clean-up, reclamation, optimization
GT	Giga transfers
Guest	Guest operating system in a VM or LPAR
GUI	Graphical User Interface
GUID	Globally unique identifier
HA	High availability
Habitat	Place where technology lives, such as a data center
Hadoop	Software tool for performing big data analysis
HAMR	Heat-assisted magnetic recording
Hardened	Hardware, software, or cloud resilient to faults
Hash	Computed sum or key for lookup comparison
HBA	Host bus adapter for attaching peripherals
HCA	Host channel adapter for InfiniBand
HCI	Hyper-converged infrastructure
HCIBench	VMware test harness wrapper benchmark testing
HCL	Hardware compatibility list
HD	High-definition broadcast or video

HDD	Hard disk drive such as SAS, SATA, or USB
HDFS	Hadoop Distributed File System
HDMI	High-definition media interface
HDTV	High-definition TV
Heat map	Display of hardware heat; view of active data
Hero number	Benchmark number to show in best way
Heterogeneous	Mixed types of technologies and configurations
High-latency	Slow, long-response wait time for work to finish
Hitech	Health Information Technology Act and Standards
HOL	Head-of-line blocking
Homogenous	Same type server, storage, hypervisor, operating system
Hosting	Facility or service provider that hosts IT services
Hot aisle	Aisle between cabinets for warm air exhaust
Hot data	Data that is actively being read and or written
HPC	High-performance computing
HSM	Hierarchical storage management
HTML5	New version of HTML
HTTP	HyperText Transfer Protocol
Hub	Physical or logical place where things are shared
HVAC	Heating, ventilation, and air conditioning
HVM	Hardware virtual machine
Hybrid	Mixed mode using different technologies and techniques
Hyper-V	Microsoft virtualization infrastructure software
Hypervisor	Virtualization framework
I/O	Input–output operation, read or write
I/O rate	Number of I/O operations (IOPS) in a given time
I/O size	How big the I/O operations are
I/O type	Reads, gets, writes, puts, random or sequential
IaaS	Infrastructure as a service
IAM	Identity access and authentication management
IBA	InfiniBand Architecture
IDS	Intrusion detection software or system
IEEE	Institute of Electrical and Electronics Engineers
IETF	Internet Engineering Task Force
ILM	Information life-cycle management
Image	Photo; operating system, virtual machine, or container copy
Immutable	Persistent, not changeable
In-band	Management done in-line or in data path
Industry adoption	What industry and vendors talk about that is new
InfiniBand	High-speed, low-latency network
Information factory	Clouds, data infrastructure, and data centers that produce information
Ingest	Data being read and processed by de-dupe engine
Initiator	Something that starts or initiates I/O operation
Instance	Occurrence of an item, cloud machine, container

Intel	Large processor and chip manufacturer
Inter-	Across domains, internet, intersystem
Interface	Hardware or software for accessing a resource
Intra-	In domain, intranet, intrasystem, intracabinet
IoD	Internet of Devices
Iometer	Load generation and simulation tool
IOPS	I/O operations per second
Iostat	I/O monitoring tool
IoT	Internet of Things
IOV	I/O virtualization
IP	Internet Protocol part of TCP/IP; intellectual property
IPL	Initial program load (i.e., boot)
IPMI	Intelligent Platform Management Interface
IPsec	IP-based security and encryption
IPv4, IPv6	Internet Protocol versions 4 and 6
ISCSI	SCSI command set mapped to IP
ISL	Interswitch link
ISO	International Standards Organization; data format
ISR	Intelligence surveillance and reconnaissance
ISV	Independent software vendor
IT	Information technology
ITaaS	IT as a service
ITSM	IT service management
JBOD	Just-a-bunch-of-disks, with no RAID
JDEC	Joint Electronic Devices Engineering Council
Journal	Logical log for data consistency, a repository
JRE	Java Runtime Environment
JSON	JAVA Script Notation format
JTA	Job task analysis
Jumbo frames	Large I/O network packet, maximum transmission units (MTU)
JVM	Java Virtual Machine
K8s	Abbreviated name for Kubernetes and related services
Kerberos	Network authentication protocol
Key management	Managing encryption keys
Key value	Key that identifies a stored value in a repository
Knowledge base	Where de-dupe metadata, index, and pointers are kept
KPI	Key performance indicator
Kubernetes	Container management tools and framework
KVM	Keyboard–video monitor, kernel-based virtual machine hypervisor
Lambda	A light wave; AWS serverless/FaaS service offering; split path data analytics processing architecture
LAMP	Linux, Apache (web handler), MySQL, and PHP
LAN	Local-area network
Landscape	Collection of software for a given application
Lane	Physical, logical, virtual path for moving data

Laptop	Portable computer
Latency	Response time or elapsed time
Lazy write	Deferred, delayed, asynchronous, or eventual update
LBA	Logical block address
LBN	Logical block number
LCM	Life-cycle management
LDAP	Lightweight Directory Access Protocol
LDM	Logical disk manager
Legacy	Existing, not new, mature
Library	Collection of software, where things are stored
LIFO	Last in, first out
Lightsail	AWS Virtual Private Server (VPS)
Link	Physical, logical path for data access or address
Linux	Open-source operating system
LIS	Linux Integration Service
Little data	Not big data or database, small files
Load balance	Spread access, optimize across resources
Locality of reference	How far away data or resource is for access
Logical size	Logically represented without data reduction
Loosely coupled	Clustered, aggregated, not tightly coupled
Lossless	No data lost during compression or reduction
Lossy	Some data loss during compression or reduction
LPAR	Logical partition, or virtual machine
LRC	Local reconstruction code, variation of erasure code
LRU	Least recently used
LTFS	Linear tape file system
LTO	Linear tape open
LUN	Logical unit number addressing for storage
Lustre	High-performance, large-scale, big-data file system
LVM	Logical volume manager
LXC	Linux container service
LZ	Lempel Ziv compression
M.2 NFF	Next-generation form factor for NVMe
M2M	Machine-to-machine
MaaS	Metal as a service
MAC	Media Access Control, layer for networking
Magnetic tape	Low-cost, energy-efficient, removable media
Mainframe	IBM legacy large server; large frame-based server
MAN	Metropolitan area network
Management tools	Software to support various management needs
Mapping	Assigning access, making resources available
Marketecture	Marketing architecture
Masking	Hiding or concealing a resource from being seen
MBR	Master boot record
MD5	Hash algorithm

Mdadm	Linux software RAID and storage tools
Media	Medium where and how data stored
Medium	Magnetic, electronic media for memory or storage
Mesos	Container management tools and framework
Metadata	Data describing other data
Metrics	Measurements and results
Mezzanine	Upper level, place, or card that sits above others
MHz	Megahertz frequency, an indicator of speed
MIB	Management information block for SNMP
Micro-services	Container services
Microcode	Low-level software for programming hardware
Micro-tiering	Fine-grained tiering
Migration	Physical, logical move, convert to somewhere else
Mitigation	Prevent or reduce impact of something
MLC	Multi-level cell NAND Flash memory
MMU	Memory management unit
Motherboard	Mainboard of server, storage, network device
Mount	Physical or logical attach and make ready for use
MPIO	Multi-path I/O
MPLS	Multiprotocol labeling WAN network protocol
MQTT	MQ Telemetry Transport
MSP	Managed service provider
MTBF	Mean time between failures
MTTL	Mean time to loss
MTTR	Mean time to repair or replace or rebuild
MTU	Maximum transmission units, jumbo frame
Multi-path	More than one path or access to resource
Multi-protocol	More than one protocol supported
Multi-tenancy	Shared occupancy of a resource
MySQL	Open-source database
Name brand	Apple, Cisco, Dell, HPE, Lenovo, Samsung, or other brands
Namespace	Collection of address endpoints
NAND	Non-volatile computer memory such as Flash
Nano	Small, lightweight Windows operating system
NAS	Network attached storage NFS, SMB data sharing
NAT	Network address translation
NBD	Network block device
NDA	Non-disclosure agreement
NDCA	Non-disruptive code activation, no restart
NDCL	Non-disruptive code load, restart needed
NDMP	Network Data Management Protocol
Near-line	Non-active data that does not need fast access
Nesting	Encapsulating, wrapping item inside of something
Networked storage	Storage accessed via storage or general network
NFS	Network File System (NAS) file and data sharing

NFV	Network function virtualization
NGFF (M.2)	Next-generation form factor for NVMe and SATA
NIC	Network interface card or chip
NIST	National Institute of Standards and Technology
NLM	Network lock manager
NOCC	Network operations control center
Node	Member of a cluster or resource pool, controller
Normalize	Optimize, reduce redundant data resources
North/south	Application or server to resource access
NoSQL	Non-SQL access, database, key-value repository
NPIV	N_Port ID Virtualization for Fibre Channel
NSM	Network status monitor
NUC	Next Unit computing (e.g., Intel NUC)
NUMA	Non-uniform memory access
NVDIMM	Non-Volatile DIMM or persistent memory in DIMM form factor
NVIDIA	Maker of GPU and other compute acceleration devices
NVMeoF	NVMe over Fabric
NVM	Non-volatile memory
NVMe	NVM Express protocol
NVRAM	Non-volatile RAM
OAuth	Open authorization access and security protocol
Object access	How objects are accessed, HTTP REST, S3, Swift
Object storage	Architecture, how data are organized and managed
Object	A place, thing or entity, many different contexts
OC	Optical carrier network
OCP	Open Compute Project
ODBC	Open database connectivity
ODCA	Open Data Center Alliance
OEM	Original equipment manufacturer
OFA	Open Fabric Alliance
Off-line	Data or IT resources not on-line and ready for use
OLTP	On-line transaction processing
On-line	Data and IT resources on-line, active, ready for use
On-prem	On-site or on-premises vs. in the cloud
Opacity	No knowledge of data structure in a file or object
OpEx	Operational expense
Optical	Network or storage based on optical mediums
Orchestration	Coordination of resource access, management
Orphaned storage	Lost, misplaced, forgotten storage space or virtual machine
OS	Operating system, VM guest, instance, image
OSD	Object storage device
OSI	Open system interconnection
OU	Organizational unit
Outage	Resources are not available for use or to do work
Out-of-band	Management done outside of data path

OVA	Open Virtualization Alliance
Oversubscription	Too many users have access at the same time
OVF	Open Virtualization Format
P/E	Program/erase, how NAND Flash is written
P2V	Physical-to-virtual migration or conversion
PaaS	Platform as a service
PACE	Performance, availability, capacity, economics
Packaging	Physical, logical how item is wrapped or enclosed
Para-virtualization	Optimized virtualization with custom software
Parity	Extra memory or storage for data protection
Partial file read/write	Portion of a file or object accessed instead of all
Partial stripe write	Some data written, resulting in extra overhead
Partitions	Resource organization and allocation or isolation
Pass-through	Transparent access, raw, no management
PBBA	Purpose-built backup appliance
PC	Personal computer, program counter, public cloud
PCI	Payment card industry; Peripheral Computer Interconnect
PCIe	Peripheral Computer Interconnect Express
PCM	Phase-change memory
PDU	Power distribution unit
Perfmon	Windows performance monitoring tool
Persistent	Data is stateful, non-volatile
Personality	How resources abstracted, act, and function
Phys	Physical connector
Physical volume	A single or group of storage devices
PIT	Point in time
PKZIP	Popular data compression tool
Pl	Probability of loss
Platform 1, 2, 2.5, 3	Platform generations: 1, central mainframe; 2, client server, the web; 2.5, hybrid between 2 and 3; 3, open software-defined and cloud, containers, converged along with IoT/IoD
Plug-in	Software module for additional functionality
PM	Physical machine, physical server or computer
PMD	Poll Mode Driver
PMDB	Performance management database
PMEM	Persistent Memory such as SCM, 3D XPoint, Everspin MRAM, and others
pNFS	Parallel NFS (NAS) high-performance file access
POC	Proof of concept, prototype, trial test, learning
Pool	Collection of resources or repositories
Port	Physical, logical point of interface attachment
POSIX	Portable Operating System Interface Standard
POST	Power-on self-test
PowerShell	A command-line interface
Protocol	Defined process for how something is done

Protocol droop	Performance degradation due to protocol impact
Provisioning	Allocating, assigning resources or service for use
Proxy	Function representing someone or something else
PST	Microsoft Exchange email personal storage file
PUE	Power usage effectiveness measurement
Puppet	Data infrastructure resource configuration tool
PV	Para-virtual
PXE	Preboot execution environment for network boot
QA	Quality assurance
Qcow	Virtual disk format used by QEMU hypervisors
QLC	Quad Layer Cell Nand Flash SSD storage memory
QoS	Quality of service
QPI	Quick Path Interface used by Intel CPUs
QSFP	Quad small form-factor plug
Qtree	Similar to a subfolder, with additional functionality
Quad Core	Processor chip with four core CPUs
Queue depth	Items, things, I/O, work waiting in queue or line
Rack scale	Scaling by rack or cabinet basis vs. single device
RADIUS	Remote Authentication Dial-In User Service
RAID	Redundant array of independent disks
RAIN	Redundant array of independent nodes
RAM	Random-access memory
RAS	Reliability, availability, serviceability
Raw storage	Storage not formatted with a file system or RAID
RBER	Recoverable bit error rate
RDM	Raw device mapped storage
RDMA	Remote direct memory access
Reduced redundancy	Lower level and cost of durability, AWS S3 RR
Reduction ratio	Ratio of how much data is reduced by
Reference architecture	Example of how to use a technology
Refs	Microsoft Resilient File System
Region	Geographical location, resource location
Re-inflate	Expand, un-compress, restore data to original size; re-expand de-duped data during restore
Reliability	How available a resource or service is
Remediation	Fix, update, repair, bring into compliance
Remote mirroring	Replicating data to a remote location
Reparse point	Object, item in file system to extend its capabilities
Replication	Mirror, make a copy of data elsewhere
Repository	Place for storing information and data
Response time	How fast work gets done, latency
REST	HTTP-based access
Retention	How long data is retained or saved before discard
RF	Radio frequency
RFID	Radio-frequency ID tag and reader

RFP	Request for proposal
RHDD	Removal HDD
RISC	Reduced instruction set computing
RJ45	Connector on Cat 5 and Cat 6 Ethernet cables
RMAN	Oracle database backup and data protection tool
ROBO	Remote office/branch office
RoCE	RDMA over Converged Ethernet
ROHS, RoHS	Restriction of hazardous substances
ROI	Return on investment
Role	What someone, or software, does or is assigned
Root	Base, foundation software, resource organization
Rotation	Migrating usage across different resources
Router	Networking or storage device for routing
RPC	Remote Procedure Call
RPM	Revolutions per minute; RPM Package Manager
RPO	Recovery-point objective
RR	Reduced redundancy, lower-cost storage service
RSA	Crypto, encryption keys utilities; also a company
Rsync	Tool for synchronizing data across resources
RTO	Recovery-time objective
RTOS	Real-Time Operating System
Rufus	Tool for making bootable ISO images
RUT	Rule-of-thumb
S2D	Microsoft Windows Server Storage Spaces Direct
S3	AWS Simple Storage Service; object protocol
S3fs	Plug-in to access AWS S3 buckets from Linux
SaaS	Software as a service; storage as a service
SAMBA	Data access protocol, SMB, Microsoft file share
SAN	Storage area network block storage access
SAP HANA	In-memory database and big data analytics
SAR	System analysis and reporting tool
SAS	Serial attached SCSI; statistical analysis software; shared access signature; server attached storage
SATA	Serial ATA I/O interface and type of disk drive
SCADA	Supervisory Control and Data Acquisition
Scale-out	Expand horizontally across multiple resources
Scheduled downtime	Planned downtime for maintenance
SCM	Storage class memory
Scope	Limits, breadth, boundaries, what is covered or included
Scratch, workspace	Temporary work area for various functions
SCSI	Small Computer Storage Interconnect
SCSI_FCP	SCSI command set for Fibre Channel, aka FCP
SD card	Small Flash SSD for laptops, tablets, cameras
SDDC	Software-defined data center
SDDI	Software-defined data infrastructure

SDK	Software development kit
SDM	Software-defined marketing; software-defined management
SDN	Software-defined network
SDS	Software-defined storage
Sector	Page, block, allocation unit for storing data
SED	Self-encrypting device, such as a SSD, HDD
Semistructured	More organization than unstructured
Serdes	Serializers and de-serializers
Server	Physical, virtual, logical, cloud resource
Serverless	Containers, FaaS, microservices resource abstraction
Server SAN	Shared storage management
Service catalog	List of service offerings
Service port	Physical or logical network management port
SFF	Small-form-factor disk drive, server
SFP	Small-form-factor optical transceiver
SHA	Secure Hash Algorithm
Shard	Chunk or pieces of some data, file, object
SharePoint	Microsoft software for managing documents
Shares	Portion or allocation of resources, data, file shares
SHEC	Shingled erasure codes
Shelfware	Software that is bought but not used
Shell	Physical enclosure or case; software interface
Show-back	Report of resource usage and consumption
Shredding	Physically breaking up a resource, secure digital erase
Shrink-wrapped	Software you buy in a box with shrink wrapping
SIOC	Storage I/O control
SIS	Single-instance storage
Size on disk	Actual space on disk vs. logical size
SLA	Service-level agreement
SLC	Single-level cell NAND Flash
SLO	Service-level objective
SLOB	Silly Little Oracle Benchmark
SMART	Self-monitoring analysis reporting technology
SMB	Small/medium Business; server message block
SMB3	Microsoft data access protocol
SME	Small/medium enterprise; subject-matter expert
SMR	Singled magnetic recording
Snapshot	A picture or image of the data as of a point in time
SNIA	Storage Networking Industry Association
SNMP	Simple Network Management Protocol
SNT	Shiny new thing
SOA	Service-oriented architecture
SOHO	Small office/home office
SONET/SDH	Synchronous optical networking/synchronous
SP	Service provider

Sparse	Blanks, white spaces, allocated but not used
SPC	Storage Performance Council benchmark
SPEC	Performance benchmark
Specmanship	Promoting, competing on speeds and features
SPOF	Single point of failure
SQL	Structured Query Language
SRA	System or storage resource analysis
SRM	Storage/system/server resource management
SRM	Site recovery manager
SRP	SCSI RDMA protocol
SSD	Solid-state device or solid-state drive
SSE	Server-side encryption
SSH	Protocol and tools to access resources CLI
SSHD	Solid-state hybrid device
SSL	Secure Socket Layer
SSO	Single sign-on
Stack	Layers of software and hardware resources
Stale cache	Data in cache that is no longer current and valid
Stamps	Collection of server, storage, network resources
Standalone	Single system, server, storage system, appliance
Stand-up	Setup, configure, install, make available for use
Stateful	Consistent and persistent
Stateless	Non-consistent, non-persistent
Static data	Data that is not being changed, but is read
STI	System test initiator; self-timed interface
Storage system	Hardware and software that provide storage resources
STP	Spanning Tree Protocol
Stripe	Spread data evenly across storage resources
Stripe size	Width of devices across which data is spread
Strong consistency	Synchronous, guaranteed data integrity of updates
Structured data	Data stored in databases, well-defined repositories
Sunset	Retire, phase out, depreciate a technology
SUT	System/solution under test or being tested
SUV	System/solution under validation or verification
Swift	OpenStack storage; object access protocol
Synchronous	Real-time data movement, strong consistency
Tape	Magnetic tape, off-line bulk storage medium
Tar	*nix data protection and backup utility
Target	Destination or location where stored
TBW	TB written per day, metric for Flash durability
TCP/IP	Transmission Control Protocol/Internet Protocol
TDM	Time division multiplex for communications
Telemetry	Log and event activity data from various sources
Template	A pattern, format to define resource into item
Temporal	Temporary, non-persistent, volatile, short-lived

Tenancy	Isolation, separation, shared resources
Tensorflow	An AI, ML, DL software library
Test harness	Connector cable, software wrapper for testing
Thick-provision	Space fully allocated, not thin provisioned
Thin provisioning	Virtually allocates, overbooks physical resources
Threat risk	Things that can happen or cause damage
Throughput	Bandwidth; data moved, or data flow rate
Tiering	Moving between tiers
Tiers	Different types and categories of resources
Time gap	Delta or difference in time to facilitate recovery
Time to first byte	Delay from start of I/O until first byte is available
Tin-wrapped	Software packaged with hardware as an appliance
TLC	Triple-level cell
Toolbox	Physical or logical place for data infrastructure tools
Toolchain	Collection of different development tools
TOR	Top of rack
TPM	Trusted platform module for securing resources
TPS	Transactions per second
Tradecraft	Experience, skills of a craft, trade, or profession
Transaction integrity	Ensure write order consistency of transactions, events
Transceiver	Electrical or optical connector for I/O cables
Trim	SATA command for NAND Flash garbage clean-up
Trunking	Aggregating network activity on shared resource
Trust relationship	Secure access, where known trusted partners exist
Turnkey	No assembly required, install, start using
U or RU	Rack unit, 1 U = 1 RU = 1.75 in.
U.2	NVMe SFF 8639 interface used on some 2.5-in. SSD
UBER	Unrecoverable bit error rate
Ubuntu	Linux operating systems support
UDP	User Datagram Protocol, aka TCP/UDP
UEFI	Unified Extensible Firmware Interface
UI	User interface, such as GUI, command line, shell
ULP	Upper-level protocol that runs on top of a network
UNC	Universal Name Convention
Unghosted	File or object abstracted, in a content repository
UNMAP	SCSI command similar to Trim for NAND Flash
Unscheduled	Unplanned downtime for emergency work
Unstructured	Data such as files stored outside of databases
UPS	Uninterrupted power system
URE	Unrecoverable read error
URI	Uniform resource identifier
URL	Uniform resource locator
USB	Universal Serial Bus
V2P	Virtual-to-physical migration or conversion
V2V	Virtual-to-virtual migration or conversion

VAIO	VMware API for IO filtering
VAR	Value-added reseller
Vault	Physical or logical place to store things
Vdbench	Benchmarking and workload generation tool
VDC	Virtual data center
VDI	Virtual desktop infrastructure
Vendor adoption	New things to talk about to get customers to buy
VHDX	Virtual hard disk used by Microsoft platforms
Virtual disk	Software-defined storage located in various places
Virtualization	Tools to abstract emulate and aggregate resources
VLAN	Virtual local-area network
VM	Virtual memory; virtual machine; video monitor; volume manager
VMDK	VMware virtual disk
VMFS	VMware file system
Volume	Physical, logical, virtual, or cloud storage device
Volume manager	Software that aggregates and abstracts storage
VPC	Virtual private cloud
VPN	Virtual private network
VPS	Virtual private server
VSA	Virtual storage array, virtual storage appliance
VSAN	Virtual SAN
VSI	Virtual server infrastructure
VSphere/ESXi	VMware hypervisor
VT	Virtual technology; video terminal; virtual tape
VTL	Virtual tape library
VTS	Virtual tape system
VVOL	VMware virtual volume
VXLAN	Virtual extensible LAN
WAN	Wide-area network
Warm data	Data that has some read or write activity
WDM	Wave division multiplex
White box	Commodity, commercial off-the-shelf, no-name brand
Wi-Fi	Wireless networking for relatively short distances
Windows	Microsoft operating system
Wirth, Niklaus	Coiner of phrase "Programs = algorithms + data structures"
WordPress	Popular blog and content management software
Workflow	Process, flow steps to accomplish task or work
Workload	Activity from applications using resources
Workstation	Desktop PC or laptop computer
WORM	Write once/read many
Write amplification	Extra write overhead resulting from single write
Write grouping	Optimization, group I/Os, reduce amplification
Write-back	Writes are buffered and eventually written
WTC	Write through cache (writes are cached for reads)
WWN,	World Wide Name

WWNN	World Wide Node Name
WWPN	Worldwide port name for addressing
X86	Popular hardware instruction set architecture
Xen	Open-source–based virtualization infrastructure
Xfs, zfs	*NIX filesystems
XML	Extensible Markup Language
YCSB	Yahoo Cloud Serving Benchmark
YUM	RPM package manager installer for some Linux systems

Index